T0374564

Bird Legs

Cheryl Sinz

WestBow Press books may be ordered through booksellers or by contacting:

WestBow Press
A Division of Thomas Nelson & Zondervan
1663 Liberty Drive
Bloomington, IN 47403
www.westbowpress.com
1 (866) 928-1240

ISBN: 978-1-4908-3090-2 (sc)
ISBN: 978-1-4908-3089-6 (e)

Library of Congress Control Number: 2014905470

Printed in the United States of America.

WestBow Press rev. date: 11/05/2014

Dedication

To Mom and Dad, with abiding gratitude for raising me in the Word and exemplifying Christian perseverance.

Cheryl with parents, Clysta and Ronald, 1948
Humphrey's Studio

Foreword

Testing times come to all of us. For most of us these unwelcome, unexpected, and unavoidable encounters with life's tests come and go. For Mrs. Sinz, however, the testing time began at birth and continued unabated with agonizing physical and emotional consequences for twenty years.

In *Bird Legs*, Mrs. Sinz invites us to step into her experiences and to discover, as she illustrates again and again, the Lord Jesus Christ standing with her and her family in the crucible of these years. Reading *Bird Legs* assures us of His presence in our testing times.

William S. Phillips
President Emeritus
Yellowstone Baptist College

Acknowledgment

With deep appreciation to my husband, John, for his loving support, steadfast encouragement, and editorial expertise.

In some cases, names may have been changed to protect the privacy of the individuals.

Chapter One

To Ronald, my daddy, I was undoubtedly the most beautiful newborn on the face of the earth. I wasn't blotchy-red and wrinkly all over the way most babies are, I had no obvious unsightly birthmarks to mar my cherubic countenance, and most particularly, I had unusually large, expressive brown eyes. My "peekers" were just the kind of peekers country and western songs were written about--to my Dad's way of thinking.

Immediately after Dad handed his picture-perfect daughter to my broadly-beaming Mommy, she was quick to thank Jesus for the fact that I appeared to be the epitome of radiant health. Without hesitation, she proceeded to count my ten teensy toesies and teensier tiny fingers to be certain all twenty digits were accounted for. When she had finished, my mommy was convinced that her eight-plus pound bundle of joy had successfully passed her inspection with flying colors.

"Ol' Doc Pedigo says with her outstandin' good looks and health, our little Cheryl is apt to be a movie star or at least a calendar girl some day, Clysta!" my father touted.

How happy Dad's words must have made Mom. How Mother must have glowed. Their baby was beautiful! Their baby was normal! God was good!

Since our family had no known inherited maladies on either side, my parents both believed that the Good Lord had been gracious to them and that my entrance into the world had been accompanied by pulchritude, probable good health and likely success. The two of them couldn't have been more thrilled with my blessed event or more unaware of the bizarre physical anomaly that would gradually reveal itself in the years to come . . . for I *seemed* to start out just perfectly.

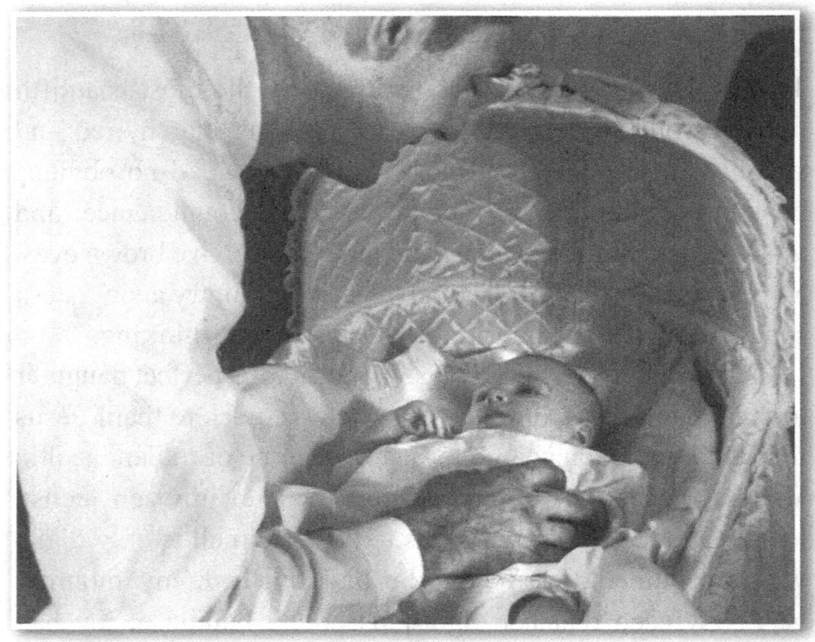

Ronald and baby Cheryl, 1944
Humphrey's Studio

As I grew from infancy into childhood, my uncle, Roger Humphrey, a professional photographer, insisted on keeping a photographic record of my development. For Christmas in 1947, Uncle "Skip" made greeting cards of me sporting a cute little blue velvet holiday outfit, hands neatly tucked away inside a fluffy-white furry muff. Color photography was not yet the norm, so Aunt Pauline tinted my image until I literally seemed to spring to life!

Merry Cheryl on Christmas card, 1949
Humphrey's Studio

Of course, Mom and Dad were delighted to show off Roger's charming picture of their little darling. In fact, Dad was so inspired by my uncle's shutter-bug creativity that he, too, was soon motivated to jump onto the photography bandwagon. Consequently, between my uncle and my father, my parents ended up with accurate evidence of the progressive disease that was about to shape my future--both physically and emotionally.

The following year, my parents and I left our country home in Meigs County, Ohio, and moved to Ohio University territory in Athens. My father rented a comfortable house for the three of us on Pearl Street, just across the block from the university's Music Hall.

Perhaps to help me adjust to my new surroundings, my father coaxed me to concentrate on the music students "within eyeshot" of our dwelling. Dad told me that studying music at O.U. might be lots of fun for me, too, when I was older, and he promised he'd get the money to send me to college "somewhere down the road," if I wanted. I had no idea how limited my father's income was as a mechanic, but his enthusiasm definitely disguised any monetary lack that might have clouded his prediction.

"Why, with that other uncle like you've got," he'd go on, "someday you might even turn out to be one of them fancy concert pianists like I hear on television, you know--like Liberace, maybe! Your Uncle Frank coulda been one of them concert fellers, too, Cheryl. Yep, Frank's one really talented guy. He's somethin' else!"

I never realized it back then, but my father had no idea how close he came to forecasting my future. I *did* understand that my father wanted the very best for me and would do whatever it took to help make me the star that Dr. Pedigo had predicted. If playing the piano like my "Unkie Pank," as I fondly called him, was my ticket to a bright tomorrow, Dad was definitely in favor of it . . . so I paid close attention to the students at the Music Hall, and I secretly dreamt of the day when I, too, might be one of them.

Chapter Two

As I grew older, Sunday became the high point of every week. My parents and I always went to church together every Sunday without fail--Dad saw to that! Dad said it was his "fatherly duty" and "Christian obligation" to see to it that we all heard the Word and obeyed the Word to the best of our abilities, no matter what extenuating circumstances got in the way. After all, any distractions were proof that Satan really existed and was up to his disruptive tricks! If we overslept, so be it--we went to church unkempt. If we had the sniffles, so be it—we went to church toting clean, white hankies tucked inside our Bibles. RAIN OR SHINE—SO BE IT! WE WENT TO CHURCH! Honestly, I think if my mother or I had contracted leprosy, my father would still have made us attend church, and he continually buffered occasional resistance from either of us by stating, "When you get back home, your reward for keepin' the Sabbath holy will be readin' the Sunday paper! The comics will be somethin' for you to look forward to if praisin' Jesus isn't satisfyin' enough!"

Sometimes I just wanted to haul off and kick my Dad in the shins . . . but I had sense enough to keep such sinful notions to myself.

The thing was, my father used such a soft-spoken tone of voice when "laying down the law" that he never came across as being the slightest bit tyrannical. Curiously enough, I noted, whenever we returned home from church, my Dad--without fail--was always the first one to make a mad dash to read *Dagwood and Blondie*.

Mom advocated attending church just as much as my father and taught Sunday school to children in kindergarten through third grade. Mom appeared to feel truly gratified whenever she taught her students in the Wesleyan Methodist Church and would often let me help her prepare her lessons. To illustrate, she always used a large easel draped in white flannel. Together we'd cut out pictures of Bible characters and appropriate scenes to adhere to the material, then we'd move the cutouts wherever we wanted till they helped illustrate her stories and make her lessons more realistic. My mother had a real artistic flair about her and seemed to know precisely where to place those cutouts so they would emphasize her lessons perfectly. She put her heart into preparing her classes.

Once, during Sunday School class, while Mom had to leave the room for a couple of minutes, this real showoff from the Children's Home rearranged her carefully positioned pictures of Noah's ark and the flood so they made no sense whatsoever. Snotty-nosed Timothy turned the ark upside down on the easel and stacked all the animal pairs on top of the each other like one tall totem pole! He moved the deep blue sea where the firmament should have been then placed the sky underneath Noah's big sailing vessel.

I was so angry!

When Mother returned, Timothy quickly scampered back to his seat as her class simply roared with laughter!

I pointed to Timothy and shouted, "He did it, Mom! He did it!"

Mom just smiled.

"Now Timmy," she said calmly, "that wasn't very nice of you to ruin the pretty picture I made of Noah's ark, was it?"

"N-no, Ma'am, I . . . I guess it wasn't."

"Well, why did you do it, then, Timmy?"

There came a contrite, almost inaudible "Donno," which I expected.

I could see Timothy was very uncomfortable as his eyes started to redden and he lowered his head in shame.

Boy, I hoped he was really going to get it from my Mom!

Instead, Mother strode quietly over to Timmy, knelt down on the floor beside him, put her right hand tenderly on his tiny left shoulder and asked, "Do you know what I think, Timmy?"

Timmy tried to pull away, but Mom gently held her position and resumed her gentle train of reasoning.

"I think you did it because you don't really know Jesus. I think maybe we should all pray for you and ask God to forgive you for what you just did."

It was a sight I shall never forget--seeing all my little Sunday school classmates' hands simultaneously clenched tightly in prayer around the table, heads bowed, eyes *mostly* shut--while my mother prayed aloud for Timmy:

"Dear Heavenly Father, please look down on this, Your blessed child, Timmy, and forgive him for his actions. Help him know that You love him just as much as You love the rest of the children here who have come to worship this day, and let Timmy see that You are truly his friend. Thank You, Lord Jesus, thank You. Amen."

A single tear trickled down Timmy's face, and I think he let Jesus into his heart that morning.

Attending church was not the only place my parents and I praised God. Norma and Everett, my grandparents on mother's side, had a nifty little gas station about fifty miles northeast of Athens in a small town called Caldwell. They also managed a little farm there with a couple of horses, a flock of Plymouth Rocks, and two or three milk cows.

Whenever we'd drive to visit them we'd sing hymns in Dad's cherished Chevy sedan, trying our level best to harmonize our voices, and man alive--did we ever raise the roof!

My very favorite hymn was "When We All Get to Heaven," and I could really belt out the melody. The best part by far to me was the chorus: "When we all get to hebben, what a day of rejoicin' that will be! When we all see Jesus, we'll sing and shout the bictowee!"

For some reason, Grandma Norma always seemed to find humor in my singing that hymn, although I never managed to figure out why. Every time I'd get to the chorus, she'd laugh uncontrollably, then reward me with a shiny new nickel! Off I'd hurry to buy some sugary orange-marshmallow "peanuts" at Grandpa's grocery store. Yummy! If I really sang especially loud, she'd even let me have a treat from her special milk glass candy dish--the one that was shaped in the spittin' image of a prized Plymouth Rock! That's what *truly* motivated me to sing at the top of my lungs, 'cause I could hardly wait to taste those delicious confections she kept in her chicken-dish. Sometimes there'd be jelly beans, sometimes chocolate drops, sometimes peppermint patties--but scarfing down that candy was goal enough for me to bust my vocal chords!

To tell the truth, I always thought Grandma Norma had a sadistic nature about her, though, when it came to raising poultry. I declare, she had pet names for every single chicken and rooster in their barnyard, and she *usually* treated them like royalty. Whenever we or other company were visiting her, however, she'd turn from a regular Dr. Jeckel-type into a nasty ol' Mr. Hyde!

"Everett!" she'd order. "Betty Lou's been in an awful slump for two whole weeks, now. She's just not a-layin' right. I think she'd make fine stock for some tasty dumplins tonight!"

That was the only cue my grandpa ever needed to hear, and shortly thereafter, the executioner in Everett would carry out Norma's requested decapitation posthaste.

On such occasions, I'd feign a tummy ache and renege on dinner . . . but I'd sneak a little piece of candy from Grandma's glass chicken for our return trip to Athens.

Chapter Three

About the time I turned five, my parents announced that we were going to move to a different location in Athens, and Dad rented a decent apartment for us on a busy street called Columbia Avenue. I knew I would miss the melodic strains of piano music I'd grown accustomed to hearing from Ohio University, but my father said he was sure I would adjust. Besides, he added, his good-natured mother, Amy, would be close by, and he just *knew* she and I would really have a good time when we got to know each other well.

Dad was so right! As it turned out, Grandmother Amy seemed to be the sitter-of-choice in her part of town. Unusually short in stature compared to the rest of my relatives, Amy looked just like another little playmate to me, for when we were standing side by side she was only about two inches taller. Most importantly, she had a real knack for meeting me at my age level like she apparently did with the other children for whom she babysat. In fact, Amy was just downright fun!

My grandmother taught me how to play board games like monopoly and checkers when she sat with me, but the happiest times we had together usually involved playing a card game called "Go Fish." "Go Fish" didn't involve much strategy, and I soon got to the place where I could actually beat Amy about seventy-five percent of the time. Whenever it was her turn to draw a card from the pool of cards in front of us, if she picked the card she wanted she'd jump straight up like a little chipmunk and enthusiastically yell, "I GOT IT! I GOT IT!" at the top of her lungs! Her behavior always had a rather intimidating effect on me as her competitor, but it made me try all the harder to beat my exuberant grandmother whenever we engaged in "battle."

Of course, "Go Fish" was mostly a game of chance plus a smidgeon of skill, and I suspected Amy often played her cards carelessly so I could win. Looking back, I wonder if Amy's losing was an intentional way of trying to instill some measure of confidence in me.

Nevertheless, I wouldn't have dampened Amy's spirits for all the world. My grandfather, Earl, Amy said, was most generally "sick upstairs in bed" when my parents took me to stay with her, and more than once Mother hinted that Amy would be left alone before much time passed.

Mother's remark meant very little to me at my tender age, yet Mom was correct in her assessment of my grandfather's health. Sure enough, Earl passed away long before I was halfway through grade school, and after his death, Amy seemed to cherish me all the more.

Sometimes when I stayed with Grandmother Amy, the two of us would relax on her front porch and swing in her white-painted, slatted porch swing--she, occupied with knitting--I, content reading storybooks such as *Poly Anna* and *Fairy Tales* by the Brothers Grimm. Whenever I came across a word I couldn't pronounce, Amy was always eager to help me. The fact that she had been a school teacher in her younger years was obvious.

My grandmother's porch was flanked by two fragrant blue spruce trees that towered above her house, and sparrows and little song birds would often dash in and out of the branches with incessant twittering and tweeting.

"Grandmother," I once asked her, ". . . why do you think God made birds, anyway?"

Amy analyzed my query very little before she eagerly offered one obvious possibility. "Maybe, just maybe, Cheryl, He created birds to inspire people to fly!" That was Amy--always showing me possibilities, always stimulating my imagination, always making me more curious.

Although I was an only child, I did have another relative to play with besides Amy--my first cousin, Fred, who was just two years older than I. Grandma Norma and Grandpa Everett led me to believe that Fred had the potential to be a little bully, and Grandpa, especially, would sometimes take me aside and warn me to be careful when Fred was around.

"You better watch out for that Freddy, little Cheryl," he'd advise. "Sometimes boys can be pretty rough, you know, and they aren't always nice to itsy-bitsy girls like yourself. You just be mindful, now!"

Grandpa was so mistaken. Fred was completely kind to me and we always had a good time whenever we played together. Fred was truly a good-looking lad with locks of black, curly hair framing his cheerful face, plus an infectious laugh that could charm his mother, Robbin, into almost any no-no. It took me years before I could tell that my cousin was somewhat manipulative, but by then it had become plain to see how successfully he had learned to control his mother. Somehow, I respected his control as he seemed to know exactly how to get most anything he wanted. I just wasn't quite certain how Christian he was by being so conniving! After all, wasn't one of the Ten Commandments "Honor your father and mother"?

Fred's father, Ferdinand, a decidedly attractive Marine, had died during World War II and was the most handsome man

I'd ever seen in my life. Fred and Robbin kept a large framed picture of Ferdinand on the coffee table in their living room--his father in full military regalia--and WOW, was he ever something to behold!

Anyway, whenever I'd go visit my cousin, we'd spend time out in his backyard playing hide-and-seek or war games. Once in a while we'd dash up to his attic where he kept fascinating old encyclopedias and musty, stained military uniforms. Sometimes, Fred would show me how to handle real machetes and weapons that his father had used during the war, but he was extra careful not to injure me. We got along just beautifully, so long as I never dared call him "Ferdy," or the positively unthinkable "Ferdy-Turdy," as some children did in public school.

"Oh, I can *handle* that nickname, Cheryl," he'd proclaim, "I just don't like the awful way it *sounds*! My name is Fred--just Fred, *period*--and don't you ever dare forget it!"

I suspect my mother would have had a heart attack had she known I was playing with potentially dangerous military "toys," but I could sense Mom was worried enough about me the way it was without her learning any details about my whereabouts.

You see, by the time I was eight years old, no matter what tasty morsel I put into my mouth I'd almost always lose my appetite immediately and flat-out stop eating. Mom would spend endless hours in the kitchen fixing nourishing food and child-pleasing entrees for me, only to be discouraged by my protests of "NO, NO, Mother--I just can't eat another bite," or "I'm really, really sorry, Mom. Please put my food in the fridge and I'll try it again tomorrow!"

Sometimes, Mom would become artistically inspired and *design* food for me, hoping, in vain, that the blueberry pancake she shaped exactly like Brer Rabbit would taste extra-special to Brer Fox (me, of course) or that the Humpty-Dumpty cake with the licorice suspenders would be just too, too cute to resist! (Humpty-Dumpty had a great fall into the garbage can when Mother wasn't looking.)

My playmates were growing *up* and filling *out*. Me? I was soaring upwards but caving *in.* Whereas my little girlfriends were becoming soft and curvy, I was becoming boney and angular--and by the third grade I was starting to look much different than other pals my age.

Clysta and Cheryl, 1953
Humphrey's Studio

To add to the situation, I frequently ran high fevers for days at a time--my temperature often reaching 104 to 105 degrees per episode. Mother made me stay in bed and miss school during those numerous periods, and Dr. Woodworth, my doctor of record, made house calls time after time whenever she phoned him.

It wasn't so bad, though, being homebound, 'cause Mom and I would watch television together or play tic-tac-toe or sing songs when I was up to it. We'd also toss bread crumbs out our apartment window onto the adjoining roof below, and colorful birds would flock there, amusing us. In their own unique way, I suppose, those birds became my avian friends, and I never tired of watching them.

I learned to make the most of my unexplainable malady when I was growing up, while--try as he might--Dr. Woodworth never had one plausible explanation for my mysterious high fevers; I grew weaker and weaker, scrawnier and scrawnier, skinnier and skinnier, until the cap sleeves on my dainty dresses encircled my upper arms like stiff, over-sized cowls.

I looked positively tubercular.

To my recollection, Dr. Woodworth always appeared reluctant to give me a "shot" or draw blood from my boney little fingertips, though I knew he felt he had no choice whenever I was ill. Sometimes, I think he feared the needle he used might puncture my finger and dart out the opposite side! I'd try my very best not to cry or scream, but often just the thought of another prick would start me sobbing quite uncontrollably.

Dr. Woodworth also had me take periodic basal metabolism tests to make certain my thyroid was functioning normally, but "Yes," he assured my parents, ". . . her master gland is doing its job splendidly."

In essence, repeated doctor visits and laboratory work always came to the same conclusion: nothing at all was wrong with me except a little anemia, and iron pills should fix that situation!

Yet, no amount of iron, vitamins, or mineral supplements ever helped me to gain one ounce of weight or supplied me with one iota's worth of energy.

As a last resort, Dr. Woodworth suggested my mother call in another physician just in case he might see me in a different light.

"I'm going to be one-hundred percent honest with you, Clysta," he told her. "I think it's time we sent Cheryl to a specialist, perhaps one out of state. I'm truly at a loss to know what's going on with her. I've been trying to figure out why her weight's not keeping up with her height for years now, and . . . and frankly, Cheryl's case is totally baffling."

Mother was leery of what Dr. Woodworth was going to suggest.

"There's a fine pediatrician in Parkersburg, West Virginia, across the Ohio River, who might have a different perspective on your daughter," he said. "He's a specialist, actually, who is really good with children Cheryl's age."

Dr. Woodworth sounded adamant and very serious.

"Well, then, who is he, doctor?" Mom asked.

"His name is Dr. Blumfeld."

"Dr. Blumfeld . . . Dr. Blumfeld . . . *Dr. Blumfeld*? Isn't he an internist?"

"Yes, he is, Clysta, and he's a very experienced one. It wouldn't hurt to see what he has to say. You and Ronald might want to talk this over."

Mother was quick to respond with the very reply I expected. "In our house, we serve the Lord, doctor. We don't need the help of any internist if we have the help of Jesus.

"No. No internist, Dr. Woodworth. Absolutely NOT! We'll just continue to pray for our little girl . . . harder!"

Chapter Four

In addition to being blessed with doting grandparents who were always there at my parents' summoning, "Unkie Pank" seemed unusually interested in my welfare and happiness. Frank, in fact, was one of the few people in my family who could brighten my days when I was feeling less than chipper.

A somewhat portly man, Franklin Maerker had a downright jovial personality and reminded me, curiously, of Santa Claus. He frequently cracked jokes and laughed uproariously when he came to visit us, finding a source of levity in most everything and everyone around him. Usually whistling or singing, Frank managed to see sunshine on the gloomiest of days and could almost always keep my more serious-minded father in a respectable mood. He lived in a beautiful house on Peach Ridge Road--nestled among redbud and dogwood trees--and was married to a charming woman, Sybil, my mother's sister.

Frank also conducted a small choir at our Wesleyan Methodist church, and most intriguingly, at least to me, my uncle could play the piano and organ "like nobody's business" (to borrow one of my father's favorite expressions). Not only did my uncle own a beautiful Knabe grand piano and a Hammond organ, but he could actually "read" music instead of laboriously plunking out melodies on his instruments by ear.

Uncle Frank conducting the Wesleyan Methodist Choir, 1954
Ronald Kimes, Photographer

That's how Grandma Norma played. Grandma would "tickle the ivories" just about any old way, and despite random mistakes a hymn tune of questionable accuracy would eventually surface. Sometimes, I noted, it might take way, way more than one attempt to for her to coax out such a melody, and the mistakes that ensued were enough to make my head spin! No matter. Grandma could play the piano . . . and I *couldn't.*

It was just a matter of time before my uncle posed the following question to me: "Would you like to take piano lessons, Cheryl? Do you think that'd be fun? Do you? Then you could play like your grandmother and me!"

Inwardly, I jumped at the notion. Outwardly, I thought it best if I didn't respond with too much elation.

"Well, maybe," I finally answered, "but . . . but how much would I have to practice, anyway?"

My uncle became more solemn.

"If you took piano lessons, you wouldn't want to waste your parents' money, now, would you, Cheryl? And you wouldn't want to disappoint your teacher . . . whoever she might be."

"Yes . . . yes, but . . . how much practicing?" I repeated.

"That'd be up to your teacher, but I'd say about half an hour a day would do it. Would that be so terrible?"

My response must have been what my uncle wanted to hear, 'cause before I knew it, a large, imposing upright materialized in our living room. The awesome instrument was made of red oak and had gnarly, decorative wooden scrolls on it, fifty-two keys of pure African ivory, thirty-six more of ebony, and a sounding board that nearly reached the ceiling.

I was overjoyed!

Shortly thereafter, my father drove me to a delightful piano teacher about five miles away from home, and this sweet-natured lady, Mrs. Peterson, taught me the fundamentals of playing the piano.

As it turned out, practicing the piano was no issue. Playing the piano was just plain cinchy, and I progressed twice as fast as all the other students in my teacher's piano class. I simply loved the piano!

For my first piano recital, after only two years of study, I was placed last in order of difficulty out of twenty students. While all the other little pianists were playing pieces like "Off We Go" and "Birthday Boogie," I played a rendition of Bizet's famous "Oh, Lamb of God" about five levels above the other pieces.

My parents attended the recital and had never been so proud!

And the clapping? Oh, you should have heard the applause! It was actually embarrassing to get so much attention, while the other little pianists received so little by comparison.

Following the recital, there was avid congregating around the refreshment table--everyone pawing all over me, congratulating me--some older people I'd never met before nearly shaking my hands off!

"How'd you memorize all those notes, Cheryl?" they asked, and--

"Boy, you must practice night and day!" and--

"How can anyone so tiny make such a big sound?" and--

"Gee whiz. Look at how *skinny* she is! Gosh! There's nothing to her!"

That last comment just plain hurt my feelings . . . but I didn't cry.

I felt horribly self-conscious, yet at the same time I realized I could do something special that few others my age could do. Besides, classical music sounded spectacular to me, and I never wanted to stop playing!

As it so happened, there came a crisis at my church one Sunday, when our regular pianist was absent, apparently with a virus.

Our song leader was alarmed. Who could play the opening "Praise and Worship" warm-up in place of Millie? Wouldn't someone step forward to help? Didn't anybody present feel like giving his best to the Master?

I slowly slid downward in my chair, hoping, in vain, that my musical abilities would remain unnoticed. It was Timothy, doggone his hide--Timothy from my mother's Sunday school class--who, to my consternation, had the unmitigated nerve to pop up out of his seat, rudely point directly to me, and brazenly proclaim, "CHERYL CAN REALLY PLAY GOOD! SHE SHOULD PLAY THE PIANO TODAY. SHE CAN DO IT! CHERYL SHOULD PLAY!"

Before I knew it, spontaneous clapping erupted and I found myself inching towards a strange piano I'd never before played--an old, old behemoth of an upright, pathetically out of tune, half the keys chipped--a piano in desperate need of attention.

Yet, this was an opportunity to serve the Lord.

Hesitantly . . . I sat down on the piano bench.

Our song director was delighted!

"Well, Cheryl . . . I've heard all about you! I understand you're quite the little pianist!" she announced.

I squirmed.

"What would you like to pick for us to sing, Cheryl?"

No! That's not the way this routine is supposed to go! She thinks I'm not capable of playing all the songs in the hymnbook! Brother. She thinks some of these simple tunes are actually too hard for me to play!

Again, I squirmed.

Again, I was asked the same question:

"Cheryl, what can you play for us this morning?"

"Ma'am," (honestly, I wasn't trying to be smug) ". . . shouldn't *you* pick out songs for us to sing and tell *me* what to play? I believe I can play *all* of them!"

I guess my being in the third grade qualified me for the snickering that followed, but our song director could immediately see that I was not to be treated like a person of my chronological age.

Besides, I *was* certain I could play every single song at sight with no difficulty.

Was I supposed to hide my light under a bushel?

At last, our director cautiously chose "The B-I-B-L-E, Yes, That's The Book For Me," then one tune followed another . . . after another . . . after another . . . till it was way past time for our worship session to be over!

"Well," our director quietly uttered, while pulling incessantly on the belt around her waist.

Gee whiz. Here she goes again.

"Cheryl, you certainly have been blessed with talent. God has been good to you. Would you care to play for us again next week? That'd be just wonderful! Do you think you might be willing to help us out here a little more, my dear?"

Applause, applause, applause!

"Of course!" I muttered.

Was there any other answer?

From then on, in my own small way, I started serving Jesus, my Lord . . . and I believe my contributions were appreciated in Sunday school.

Chapter Five

Thanksgiving, 1953.

I wrote a poem for my parents, and the minister at church liked it well enough to put it in the morning bulletin. I titled it "I Am Thankful," and it read like this:

For a mother and father whom my love I give,
For a wonderful home in which I can live,
For the church of my choice,
For a bird's mellow voice--
Thank you, Lord!

For my relatives who give me love,
For the trees that tower up above,
For the things I share,
For the clothes I wear--
Thank you, Lord!

Dad said I didn't quite rival Henry Wadsworth Longfellow *yet*, but Mom said it was a wonderful Thanksgiving poem and she was proud of me.

As it so happened, on that same Sunday a male college quartet from Indianapolis, Indiana, had been invited to perform gospel music at our adult service. I could hardly wait to hear them! All of us Sunday schoolers were virtually on fire with enthusiasm. Several of us dressed in special new holiday church clothes, and many children resorted to an inordinate amount of pushing and shoving to find seats way up front.

The church was decorated almost as lavishly as it would have been for Christmas, with pretty pumpkins, sprigs of bittersweet, golden mums, and colorful autumn leaves surrounding the pulpit. The general mood of the congregation was that of eager anticipation, much as it had been for us little folks on the lower level.

Grandma Norma had made a new orange satin dress for me, and I couldn't wait to wear it! It was trimmed in black lace and had puffy sleeves--an attempt to make my wispy arms appear larger than they actually were. God love her, she even bought me a new pair of black patent shoes to complement my homemade dress. Grandma told me I'd really be "all twigged up" that morning in church.

Grandma had especially large feet, which she laughingly referred to as "gunboats," and we both had difficulty finding shoes anywhere that would come close to fitting either of us properly. She always chuckled about the length of her footsies and told me she wore size twelve, but thirteens felt so good that she bought fourteens!

My feet were long like Grandma's but were also especially thin to boot. In order to keep shoes on, I had to wear two sizes smaller than I measured, which painfully bunched up my big toes and overlapped the remaining toes beside them. In addition, shoe salesmen felt obligated to place thick cork insoles inside my shoes to make them fit even *more* snugly. Often, my shoes would come off regardless, but they were gobs of fun to slide around in when their new soles were nice and slick.

Uncle Frank, this particular Thanksgiving, was displaying unusually fancy footwork on the organ pedals. The congregation always enjoyed his musical renditions, and someitmes he would invite me to play duets with him in the service as well. For this special Sunday, he included me in an appropriate Thanksgiving duet well-known by most churchgoers as "We Gather Together." In my uncle's arrangement of this hymn tune, he and I were to trade the melody back and forth--first Frank on organ, then me on piano--and we hoped to set a festive tone for the pastor's message.

As was customary when we performed together, Frank would begin the service with an organ prelude. I'd wait in the front pew, biding my time until I could dash up to the piano when he beckoned me. Usually, he would motion for me to come up after the pastor's opening remarks while the congregation was in prayer. In that way, I could move to the piano rather discreetly and not attract too much attention to myself.

The order of the service was a bit confusing this Sunday, however, for the Indiana quartet, seated directly behind me, was apparently scheduled to sing *before* I was supposed to play.

This, I found out the hard way!

As all heads were bowed, I *thought* my uncle nodded for me to rise. Immediately, I made tracks towards my post. Halfway there, however, Frank, *very* fervently, with rapid swinging of his right arm and a panicky, pained expression on his face, pointed vigorously back to the pew from where I had just risen.

What was I to do? Did I misunderstand his gesture? Might he have meant, instead, for the quartet to get up and present their special music next--instead of me? I was just plain stuck! By this time, many of my little peers in the front pew were glaring at me--some snickering with hands cupped over their silly faces--all just dying to see what I was going to do before the pastor's fateful 'amen.'

Oops! Suddenly, the college quartet started toward the stage. It was, not surprisingly, Timothy, who first rather loudly called out, "Come back, Cheryl! Cheryl, come back here!"

I quickened my pace to my seat.

A host of other little voices blurted out "Come back, Cheryl, come back NOW!"

"Hurry up, Cheryl!" cried Myron.

"Faster, faster!" yelled Linda.

I might have made it back to my seat before the congregation lifted their heads, except for the embarrassing fall I suffered as I slid around the end of the imposing wooden pew near my destination.

Blasted new shoes! Blasted ol' Grandmother!

Suddenly, there I was, face down, crumpled up just steps from my seat, knobby legs sticking out in opposite directions, brand new Thanksgiving dress crinkled halfway up my boney torso like cellophane on a candy stick!

Powerful hands reached down and grabbed me around my waist.

Was it Frank?

No! The organ was still playing.

Was it one of my Sunday school peers?

Of course not! Most of them were laughing unashamedly at me by this time--not even *trying* to contain themselves.

Was it . . . yes . . . yes . . . it *was* one of the Indiana college quartet members!

"It's alright, little one," he whispered in my ear. "Everybody takes a tumble now and then. I'm right here to help you. Come on, now, and stand up with me! We can do it together--for Jesus!"

Gently, very gently, our guest helped me to my feet and pointed to the pew where I belonged. Then, just as quickly, my Good Samaritan took his place with the other members of his vocal group, waiting for their turn to perform.

"Cheryl's got a boyfriend . . . Cheryl's got a boyfriend . . ." one of the Sunday schoolers beside me chanted in a stage whisper.

It was so hard not to hit him--I really wanted to--but, of course, Christians don't behave that way . . . so I sat on my hands.

Before I knew it, that Indiana quartet really let go and had our church a-hoppin'!

I never expected the jazzy type of songs they were singing--and truthfully, I couldn't believe what they were getting away with! Most of the tunes our church congregation was used to singing were starchy, old-fashioned hymns--but this college quartet? BOY, did they ever change the pace!

All of a sudden--although I'm not sure what they were singing at the time--our usually staid congregation began to clap in rhythm! It put me in mind of driving to Caldwell to see my Grandparents years earlier. The music I was hearing was very similar to what we sang together as we drove to the farm back then, and the beat was just as catchy--but now, they were doing it in church!

I'm sorry, Grandmother. It's not your fault I fell down. You gave me these new black shoes with a loving heart . . . and I asked the Lord to forgive me for blaming my Grandmother for my embarrassing unsightly tumble.

"Now, for our last number," (the same young college student who had helped me off the floor was speaking) ". . . we'd like to do an old Southern spiritual that's kind of our trademark back in Indiana. We hope you'll enjoy it!"

I gave the college quartet my undivided attention.

"It's called 'Dry Bones,'" the spokesman continued, "and if you feel like clappin' for the Lord, just let the Spirit lead you!"

No one could have adequately prepared me for the additional humiliation I was about to endure. Had any excuse existed for me to exit the sanctuary, I would have taken it . . . but there I sat, veritably plastered in my seat, front and center, in full view of everyone in the church as the words and music rang out:

Ezekiel saw dem--dry bones,
Ezekiel saw dem--dry bones,
Ezekiel saw dem--dry bones,
Now hear de word of de Lawd.

It repeated:

Ezekiel saw dem--dry bones,
Ezekiel saw dem--dry bones,
Ezekiel saw dem--dry bones,
Now hear de word of de Lawd.

I felt an little elbow jab my side.

"Hey, Cheryl! Get up there! They're singin' your song!"

I wanted to die.

I heard another confirmation:

"Hey, BONES! Are you listenin'?" Now, *that* was Timothy!

Yet another voice chimed in with "Aww, go on, Bones! Get up there and dance!"

At that point, the quartet started a slow minstrel-like walk, gradually increasing their musical pace on stage, first reaching their hands up high, then low, then high again . . . while belting out the words:

Dem bones, dem bones gonna--walk around,
Dem bones, dem bones gonna--walk around,
Dem bones, dem bones gonna--walk around,
Now hear de word of de Lawd!

But, they weren't finished! Nope--they had to melodically "connect" the bones, from toe bone to foot bone, to ankle bone, to leg bone, to knee bone . . . all the way up to the head bone . . . then "disconnect" the bones back down, descending all the way to the toe bone.

I thought they'd never shut up about it!

Frank glared at me in an insistent sort of way. It must have been about time for us to play our duet, I supposed.

I didn't care.

I tried desperately to think of a Bible verse that would help me hold my head up high.

I couldn't think of a single one!

The quartet returned to their seats.

I didn't budge.

Again, I caught my uncle's eyes, this time even more penetrating than before!

Today is Thanksgiving. I must make myself get up for Jesus. I must get my mind off little me. Isn't there some Bible verse I've learned that would help?

I stuck like glue to my pew.

What if I fell again? I couldn't bear to hear any more laughter!

Mother had always taught our Sunday school class that committing verses to memory from the Good Book would insure they'd be on tap when we needed them. I needed one right then!

Help me Jesus. Help me right now, I prayed silently. *Give me the courage to do whatever you need me to do!*

Finally, Psalm 121 flashed into my head:

I lift up my eyes unto the mountains--
where does my help come from?
My help comes from the LORD,
the Maker of heaven and earth.

He will not let your foot slip--
he who watches over you will not slumber;
indeed, he who watches over Israel
will neither slumber nor sleep.

How much clearer could His message be? God would *not* let me slip again! I *could* do this! I *could* play our duet for my Lord!

I walked with assurance up to the piano, and my uncle and I gave his duet our best.

The church was utterly silent.

Yes, yes, yes! They liked our music! Thank you, Jesus! Thank you, Lord!

I believe Frank and I did justice to our music that morning, and I know why; Jesus truly blessed us as we played together.

After the service, Uncle Frank gave me one of his customary bear hugs.

"Know what I'm thankful for today, Cheryl?" he asked. "I'm thankful that I've got a sweet little talented niece who will make music with me. Thanks for helping me out today! Let's do it again, soon, okay?"

When the pastor had concluded his Thanksgiving sermon that Sunday, he told us all to be thankful for something that day.

I glanced down at my Thanksgiving bulletin:

"For the relatives that give me love--"

And I was thankful.

Chapter Six

Soon after I entered the sixth grade, our music teacher at Central asked me if I would like to accompany our school chorus. Doing so, he said, would free him from the burden of having to play the piano at the same time he needed to conduct.

Without hesitation, I agreed.

I was more than eager to assist Mr. Kessler on the piano, and before long he decided that with my assistance, he could easily develop a spectacular chorus to represent Central grade school.

Mr. Kessler's chorus met in the cold, damp basement of our antiquated school building three days a week. The same room where we rehearsed also served as the meeting place for art classes, and the aroma of moldy modeling clay permeated the atmosphere. What a distraction for the irritating so-called "singers" who persistently annoyed Mr. Kessler and me!

"Oh, phew!" they'd call out. "Smells like dead rats in here today! Gosh, I'm gonna puke! How gross! Lemme outta here!"

Sometimes, I fully expected Mr. Kessler to throttle the boys in music class (and I secretly wished he would)--but he never did. They were, for all intents and purposes, extremely disrespectful and always ridiculed him whenever his back was turned. They chewed gum, talked loudly, shot gigantic paper wads to and fro, and generally speaking--in my opinion--all belonged in detention after school if not in *jail.* Mr. Kessler, however, seemed to be able to overlook most of the pranks those little heathens pulled. Why? I'll never know. Maybe, I wondered, it was because boys' voices were so desperately needed that he was happy to take any Tom, Dick, or Harry remotely capable of singing the lower range.

At any rate, Mr. Kessler's heart was in the right place, so I supported his efforts and did all I could to help the youngsters learn their individual parts, rehearsing their melodies over and over on the piano with them till the simple tunes finally sank in.

By the end of the school year, Mr. Kessler's chorus seemed capable enough to present a little operetta by Gilbert and Sullivan, and I, alone, was responsible for accompanying them in our spring concert--in front of the *whole* school.

Most parents eagerly attended the event, plus several relatives in my family; Mom and Dad, Frank and Sybil, Norma and Everett, Robbin and Fred, and Grandmother Amy.

Happily, the operetta was a complete success!

Amy seemed particularly overjoyed with my accompanying skills, and after the musical she insisted on treating me and my parents to ice cream as a reward--a little family celebration in my honor.

Immediately, we hurried off to Broughton's!

I ordered a hot fudge sundae and listened respectfully while Amy went on and on about what a grand job I'd done for Mr. Kessler and his sixth graders.

Grandmothers. They're all alike, I mused. *If you perform anything halfway decently, they think you're a saint!*

"My piano music really wasn't that hard to play, Grandmother!" I said. "I'm just happy Mr. Kessler was able to pull that group of hoodlums together in time for the big event!"

Dad, as usual, had very little to add to the conversation, but noted that I wasn't gulping down my sundae as he'd apparently anticipated.

"You know, Cheryl," he said softly, staring at my mountain of ice cream and chocolate as it merged into mush, ". . . if you'd eat just a tad more, you might be able to gain a pound or two and be a much stronger pianist. By the way, I think I heard a couple sour notes outa you tonight, didn't I?"

My father's remark cut me to the quick! Was he saying I hadn't done a good enough job for Mr. Kessler?

Mother reached over and clenched Dad's wrist tightly, chided him sternly under her breath, then added that *she* certainly hadn't heard any wrong notes!

Amy winked at me understandingly to deflect my attention.

"Eat your ice cream, child," she said. "You did just fine!"

And for the first time in my youth, I raised my voice at my father:

"Actually, Dad," I piped up, "I don't recall making mistake number *one*! Maybe if I had a better instrument to practice on, I would be able to deliver a better performance! Did you ever think of *that*?"

My father glared at me for several seconds while I continued to ignore my dessert and stared right smack back at him!

"Well, I'll just make you a deal, daughter," he added forcefully. "You know that snappy piece your Uncle Frank plays every now and then . . . what is it . . . 'Napoleon's. . . 'Napoleon's. . . oh, what is it, now--OH, YES, THAT'S IT--'Napoleon's Last Charge'! Whenever you can master that piece, I'll buy you a brand spankin' new spinet piano. So--how 'bout it? Is it a deal?"

Mother adequately expressed her opinion of Dad's offer under the table as she forcefully brought her right foot down atop his left one.

Dad winced momentarily.

"Napoleon's Last Charge"--a real warhorse of a piece! My uncle had played it to death for as long as I could remember, and for some incredible reason my father seemed to think it represented the pinnacle of pianistic proficiency. It was okay for a piece of program music, I suppose, and I guess it probably had a few redeeming measures to remember . . . but was it worth my time and energy to learn?

"You think you've got a pretty safe bet, don't you, Dad?" I countered.

Dad struggled for rebuttal.

"Can't quite do it, huh?" he grinned.

Had the remotest possibility existed that I could have gotten away with flinging my sundae at my father, I would have. How dare he degrade me like this on my special night!

"I . . . I suppose I might give your proposed deal some thought," I replied, looking down with as much indifference as I could muster.

But I'll talk to Uncle Frank in the meantime to get his take on the situation. Frank will be honest with me. Frank will know if that questionable piece of so-called music is within my grasp.

I can count on Uncle Frank. . . .

The next morning, I had my mother take me out to Frank and Sybil's while she did some shopping. That day, despite nippy, unseasonably chilly weather, my aunt and uncle were on their patio in lightweight jackets enjoying daybreak. The aroma of sizzling bacon and eggs merged delicately with the swirling fog that filled the Hocking Valley beyond. Mother said she'd be back to pick me up around lunchtime and bade goodbye.

I felt surprisingly hungry!

"THERE'S MY STAR!" Frank shouted upon seeing me, arms open wide, as he hurried to deliver a quick hug.

Quicker than a wink, I withdrew.

Frank became serious.

"Boy, Cheryl, we surely showed everybody we were a class act yesterday, didn't we? Sorry Sybie and I had to rush off afterwards, but we really are proud of you! Here ya go, gorgeous--have some pork and eggs! Want some pancakes on the side, too?"

A nod of my head indicated to Uncle Frank that hot, syrupy pancakes would be very much in order.

"How many can you put away, Cheryl?" he continued. "I've got a buttermilk mix here that just screams 'delicious' and I'll make you as many as you want!"

I could see, most clearly, how my well-meaning uncle was trying to encourage me to stuff myself at the time, and I felt quite certain that I could eat a stack of at least ten!

On the other hand, maybe two or three hotcakes would fill the bill, so I pointed my spindly index finger up to the sky.

"How 'bout just one big one, Uncle?" I replied.

"Only one, Hon? Orrrrrr, how 'bout you try a short stack and just see how many you can dispose of? Ol' Brucey will be happy to clean up any leftovers if Sybie'll let him! Say--where *is* that lumbering ol' pooch, anyway? Here Brucey!" Frank shouted enthusiastically. "Come here, boy!"

A high-spirited brawny boxer, Brucey was probably as emotionally close to Sybil as any human child of her own could have been. Sybil had been told by Brucey's breeder years earlier that her dog was an actual descendant of the very boxer Humphrey Bogart himself had once owned, so to Sybil that fact made Brucey extra special, and she treated him like royalty. The two of them were practically inseparable.

"What? Give a pancake to my sweet li'l Brucey? Are you teasing me, dear?" I plainly overheard, as at once Sybil and her dashing dog appeared on the patio to join in the morning ballyhoo.

"Now, Franklin," Sybil chided, "you know how bad sugar is for dogs, don't you, darling?"

I thought of the many times Sybil had given her Brucey lollipops--HUGE lollipops. Her inconsistency made absolutely no sense at all to me, but it was obvious how much she adored her canine of assumed notoriety.

Frank continued. "You know what, Sybie Dearest? If you say 'no pancakes,' that's exactly the way it'll be! I'll gladly eat any extras myself if our little Cheryl can't handle them!"

"Then you'll surely ruin your macho physique, dearest!" Sybil replied as she arched her right eyebrow in a way that would have made Jezebel jealous!

Suddenly, without provocation, Auntie's monster-sized dog did an about-face and sprang in my direction like a crazed puma! Knocking me to the ground with his oversized paws, Brucey effortlessly pinned me down on the cold cement, while thick strands of drool streamed onto my quivering chin.

Help! I was at this mutt's mercy!

"CHERYL! CHERYL!" Frank yelled in alarm. "CHERYL! ARE YOU OKAY? OUR BIG OL' BRUCEY ISN'T HURTING YOU THERE, IS HE?"

I attempted to pick myself up before Uncle came to my rescue, but I couldn't budge!

"OH, NO! OF. . . OF COURSE NOT!" I choked out. "I . . . I NEVER felt better. Brucey is just having fun with me! I'll be fine, Uncle Frank! REALLY, I will . . . REALLY!"

Sybil ran over to pull her devil-dog off me and assess any possible damage to my person. Brucey jerked away and bolted pell-mell to the front door. Frank followed.

"I'm SO, SO very sorry about our Brucey, Cheryl!" Sybil said. "You look like you'll recover, though, honey pie. Are you okay? Are you sure you're okay, now?"

Sybil gingerly smoothed out my dress as she tried to help me struggle to my feet and I tried to ignore the fact that both my elbows were scraped and bleeding slightly.

I managed to whisper "S-say, Aunt Sybil . . . my . . . my Dad was wondering if Frank thought I might be able to play 'Napoleon's Last Charge,' you know . . . he questioned if it would be too hard for me o-or not. What do you think? Dad said he'd even buy me a new piano if I could master it!"

"Well, *I* certainly think you could do it, sweetie! Why don't you just dash inside and try it out on our piano?"

So . . . I was just magically supposed to restore myself and dart off to the music room?

I made an attempt. I went nowhere fast!

Sybil was gracious. "You *do* look a little scuffed up there, Cheryl. Just toddle inside when you feel like it! We'll put Brucey away into the basement. Okay, Hon? Okay?"

I must have lay perfectly still for at least five more minutes. It was Uncle Frank who ultimately returned and had the words I needed to hear to urge me inside.

He stood over me like the towering giant from *Jack and the Beanstalk.*

"Did I overhear your telling my Sybie that your father might be thinking about buying you a new piano, Cheryl?"

"Why, yes . . . yes he *did* suggest that, Uncle."

Frank helped me to my feet, grinning from ear to ear all the while, with a typical twinkle in his eyes and a whistle on his lips.

"'Napoleon's Last Charge'?" he repeated between his whistling stanzas.

"Well?" I queried.

"Well what, Cheryl?"

"Do you think it might be way too difficult for me to play or--"

"Too difficult for my pretty little show-stealer? Heavens NO, though I hardly think it'd be appropriate to play in a Sunday church service!" he chuckled. "Let's go take a look at it, Cheryl!"

Once inside, my uncle located the sheet music that I hoped would have "new piano" written all over it. He handed it to me as though it was his prized possession and told me to peruse the first three pages. I'd never seen such a mass of notes in all my life!

Frank could see I looked somewhat panicky.

"Now, now, Cheryl," he said, laughing. "You need to see learning this piece as a challenge. 'Napoleon' is simply an example of a piece that uses what's called a stride bass--that's all. Sure, it jumps all over the place like crazy, but success in playing it is all in your initial approach. If you isolate the bass line and work it up very, very, slowly, why I'll bet you could master the whole shebang over this weekend!"

Was he serious? Did my uncle really have that much confidence in my musical abilities?

Without a second thought, Frank yanked "Napoleon" from my tiny fingers and waved it back and forth, high above his towering frame. I jumped desperately to reach it but unhappily, of course, could not.

Before long, I was chasing my uncle from room to room, both of us enjoying the chase--my uncle, no doubt, using amateur psychology in his attempts to inspire me.

"OH!" he said. "You *really* want to play 'Napoleon' now, don't you?"

"Okay, okay!" I replied, growing increasingly out of breath. "Are you going to give me a chance, Uncle Frank, or aren't you?"

"Well . . . what are you waiting for then, Cheryl?" he concluded, as he firmly planted "Napoleon" on his grand piano's music rack.

"Go on, now, Darlin'. Give it your best shot--just remember to do it slowly!"

I never ate any pancakes that morning. In fact, I don't recall eating any food at all that day. I just remember taking my place at Frank's beautiful mahogany grand and playing for three hours straight till my fingers felt like they were going to drop off. And I learned one of the most important practice techniques of my life that morning--to curb my enthusiasm and take my time when learning any new composition.

Uncle Frank obviously knew what he was talking about.

By noon, when mother came to pick me up, she had to practically pry me off the piano bench! I had all the notes of "Napoleon's Last Charge" totally, completely, one-hundred percent down . . . by heart!

Mother was impressed.

"Well, what do you think, Mom? Do you think Dad'll buy me a new piano, now? Do you think he'll actually do it?"

Mother was totally speechless as she hustled me out the of the house to drive home.

I glanced back over my shoulder.

Uncle Frank had a few choice words to tell me as I departed, and he shouted them at the top of his lungs as my mother and I neared our car: “I KNEW YOU COULD DO IT, CHERYL! I JUST KNEW IT!”

Chapter Seven

It was with pride and enthusiasm that my parents took me to a local piano dealership the very next day. I could hardly wait to try out all the pianos the nice salesman had to show me, and my father was at the height of his paternal glory as I demonstrated I could easily handle "Napoleon's Last Charge."

"It shows where he met his Waterloo, you know," Dad told the salesman.

"Oh, I'll just bet it does," the salesman concurred, ". . . and your daughter certainly plays it with gusto!"

He turned to me while scratching his head.

"Just how old are you, anyway, little one?" he asked as the two of us made eye contact.

"I'm eleven, sir," I replied.

"ELEVEN? You're only ELEVEN? Well! I swear, you play that piano like you were a senior in high school!"

My mother was quick to indicate they'd buy a piano whether he flattered me or not--so long as I truly liked the instrument myself.

"You don't have to butter up our daughter," she quipped. "We know very well how capable our little Cheryl is. If she finds a piano she wants, we'll buy it outright for her today. You can count on that!"

I went from piano to piano to piano, playing till I finally settled on a beautiful mahogany spinet--a Jesse French--and my father wrote out a check on the spot.

Was that possible? Could my father really afford such a cash layout? My uncle was a business executive--but Dad? Dad was a blue collar auto mechanic.

On the way home, I told Mom and Dad how much I appreciated my new piano.

"I think you're just about the greatest parents in the whole wide world! I'll make you proud of me some day. You'll be glad you did this!"

"Just enjoy it, Cheryl," Dad said. "So long as you'll practice, that's all the thanks we need!"

"Oh, I promise I'll practice, Dad! I promise!"

And practice, I did. I discovered, in fact, that an absolute plethora of piano music was available easily rivaling "Napoleon's" novelty, and the more music literature I came across, the more I wanted to learn!

Didn't Uncle Frank know about these other piano works?

I saved my allowances for all the "longhair" piano records I could get my hands on and talked my mother into taking me to numerous recitals at Ohio University. I read everything I could find about the lives of famous composers, as well, and finally discovered who had written all those exciting piano pieces I'd heard from the Music Hall years earlier!

I'll bet I could play most of those piano works myself like my father had suggested on Pearl Street . . . if I really tried . . . with the help of Jesus. . . .

In a few months, Mrs. Peterson knew I was reaching way beyond her. She told Mom she'd hate to lose me but said she'd heard about a more advanced piano teacher in Athens not too from where we lived--if I wanted to consider studying with her. Mrs. Peterson felt she could talk this other teacher into taking me, if I was interested.

"Might you be willing to switch to a different instructor? *Would* you care to audition for her?" Mom questioned.

Of course, I said "YES!"

In the fall of 1956, the year I entered junior high, I toted "Napoleon" and a couple of my other favorite piano pieces to a middle-aged piano teacher by the name of Elizabeth Phelps, and I hoped I would make a reasonably good impression.

Mrs. Phelps lived in an old two-story white house on Second Street, easily within walking distance from our own house on Columbia Avenue. She greeted Mother and me at the door wearing a very conservative gray dress, artsy-craftsy wooden earrings (which looked homemade to me), and long, unkempt graying hair in disturbing disarray.

Wasn't she expecting us?

Mom and I were totally taken aback. We had anticipated someone much, much more elegant in appearance--perhaps like Elizabeth Barrett Browning.

"Oh, do come in, ladies!" Mrs. Phelps flung the door open with the fervor of Loretta Young. "I was just practicing my part for an ensemble that's meeting here later today," she continued, ". . . but that can wait. You must be Cheryl, my dear, and you're her mother, Mrs. Kimes?"

Mrs. Phelps courteously extended her gnarly hands and knobby fingers to tightly grip my hesitant, quivering hands.

"My, oh my, you're so cold, Cheryl! You're not nervous, are you?"

"Just a bit," I admitted. "I'll probably feel lots better after you've heard me play something, though." I said.

"Then, please take a seat at the piano, my dear. Mrs. Kimes, you may make yourself comfortable in the living room while I hear what your daughter brought to perform for me."

Again, for what felt like the four-hundredth time, I put "Napoleon" through his paces. Mrs. Phelps was duly impressed--I could really tell--and she also had me sight-read bits and parts of several other pieces to confirm her opinion of my talent.

Excitedly, she called mother back to her studio.

"I would be simply ecstatic if you allowed your talented daughter to study with me, Mrs. Kimes. I guarantee I'll expect a great deal more out of her than her previous teachers did, but I believe I can challenge her and I'd love the opportunity to try!"

Mother was close to crying, for some silly reason.

"It's alright, Mom," I consoled. "Playing the piano is really important to me and I want to learn harder pieces than I've been playing . . . if you'll let me."

Mother sniffed back a couple of tears and embraced Mrs. Phelps momentarily.

"Cheryl's always been much frailer than other young people her age, as you can plainly see. I honestly don't know if she can handle seventh grade plus a more demanding piano teacher at the same time. This . . . this change might be way too much for her."

Mrs. Phelps shrugged her shoulders and looked somewhat perplexed. "Anybody can see your daughter's on the thin side, Mrs. Kimes, but she's not *ill,* is she?

I felt as if I were being scrutinized under a magnifying glass.

"Gosh, Mom, give me a break, here! What's the worst Mrs. Phelps can do to me, anyway?" I blurted.

Mother was clearly at a loss for words, but Mrs. Phelps apparently felt it necessary to explain her teaching strategy further if she was going to win Mother's approval.

"It's alright, Mrs. Kimes. I understand your concern. Let me tell you what I would change if you let me take your daughter. First, I'd give her much different pieces to play than 'Napoleon's Last Charge.' She's capable of far more difficult music, and there are hundreds of works from the annals of music history that would motivate her to advance."

Mrs. Phelps glanced at me in an understanding way.

"You wouldn't care if we tried some new kinds of music, would you, Cheryl?"

Boy! This teacher really understood me!

"Secondly," she went on, "I'd get her involved in a few contests and musical events around town so she could see what other stellar people her age are doing. I'm a member of a group of local teachers who get together several times a year and we have large recitals--not only for pianists, but for violinists, brass and woodwind players, singers--you get the picture. Our recitals are very inspirational for people of your daughter's caliber."

Mother looked like she was going to come completely unhinged!

Again, Mrs. Phelps tried to be reassuring. "Really, Mrs. Kimes, I think I can help your daughter grow as a musician, and I just can't see why you should hesitate to let me teach her. I could take her on a trial basis if you like, I suppose, you know--have her here with me for six months or so and see how she likes it. If I gave her more than she could handle, you could always let me know and I would certainly lighten up."

I thought about all the Bible verses my Mom had taught in her Sunday school classes, hoping I could recall one to help her then, as she had helped me and my other classmates years before. Sure enough, there it was--right on the tip of my tongue!

"Mom," I interjected, "don't you remember Jesus taught us Christians that we can do anything we think we can do? The Bible says, 'Everything is possible for one who believes (Mark 9:23),' if I remember right. Well . . . I truly believe I can play whatever this nice teacher gives me to play and I'd really like to try, at least. I just don't see how studying with her could hurt! Won't you please give me a chance?"

Mother drove me home in silence, and I wondered if I'd made any impact whatsoever on her with my pleading. She was so noncommittal.

Perhaps I should have considered what effect changing teachers would have had on my father, but it never crossed my mind that he might find a reason to object--and he *did.* As soon as I told my father about my audition when he returned from work that afternoon, Dad expressed his negativism:

"If Mrs. Phelps is so all-fired better than your present teacher," Dad said, ". . . isn't she gonna charge a lot more for teachin' you? I mean, I'm all for givin' you a chance to improve yourself, daughter, but what about the fact that you need braces on those crooked teeth of yours, too? Did you ever think of that? Money doesn't grow on trees, you know! There's got to be a limit to your requests somewhere down the line, Cheryl."

My heart sank. My father was correct of course, I truly *did* need braces. Not only did I have buck teeth, but they were crooked as well, and I had a gigantic space between my two front teeth, too. I had more or less learned to cope with my appearance, but Dad's attitude really brought me down.

I sighed deeply.

"You really know how to take the song out of a songbird, Dad," I told him. "If you can't afford braces for me, I can sacrifice my smile. Music is way more important to me than my snaggley teeth, anyway. I can just forego braces for now, Dad. It's . . . it's okay. I'll be just fine."

I don't know how I did it, but I managed to stifle a bawl. I was totally heart-broken that I wasn't going to at least be given a chance to make a small part of my appearance look more acceptable, and I could see that my mother was practically livid.

Yet, Mom bit her tongue and said nothing.

Dad was head of the house.

At least my father told me I could transfer to Mrs. Phelps.

I would be content with his parcel of generosity.

Chapter Eight

September in Ohio was truly spectacular. Sugar maples dotted the hillsides with brilliant bursts of chartreuse and crimson while aging dandelions bade farewell with their final fading flourishes of golden delight. Autumn was so, so beautiful!

Mother and I always took advantage of the fall season by gathering dried milk weeds, taking their fluffy white seed parachutes out, then spraying the empty pods with golden paint. After the paint dried, we'd place inch-long plastic babies that represented the infant Jesus inside the gilded basinet-pods. Finally, we'd carefully glue tiny rectangular pieces of white satin over the babies like swaddling clothes and create adorable little Christmas favors for Mom's enthusiastic Sunday school class. At the end of teaching, after her closing prayer, Mom would let each of her students break off a basinet from her "Jesus Tree," and the children could hardly wait to receive their annual Yuletide gifts.

My mother wasn't improving on Nature, of course--she was merely making the most of what had been left behind when summer was over. Besides, as Dad pointed out, the weeds we harvested were a gift from God and "didn't cost one red cent!"

One of our favorite places to look for fall foliage was deep in the woods where Uncle Frank and Aunt Sybil lived. Birds of all description were plentiful there, and once in a while I'd even spy an excitable downy woodpecker!

On one particular autumn excursion, my mother and I found a veritable goldmine of dried milkweeds as we were having a delightful afternoon together. As I bent over to snap off a milkweed stalk, Mom asked me a not-so-subtle question which I would have preferred to ignore: "Why haven't you been practicing much recently?"

"You noticed, huh?" I answered.

"Well . . . yes, it's been pretty obvious, though I thought we had a deal, Cheryl. I thought your father and I were going to provide you with a new piano, and you were going to take lessons from Mrs. Phelps for about six months without a lot of fuss. Wasn't that your promise?"

"Sure . . . sure . . . I remember," I replied casually.

The seasonal aroma of leaf mold filled the air as two squirrels danced merrily in the dried maple leaves about ten feet away. Why did this ambiance have to change?

I turned away. Mom, however, seemed bent on badgering me.

"Is . . . is it your teeth-problem, Cheryl? Are you upset over your teeth being so crooked? Is that what's wrong? Well? Are you sad over the way your teeth. . . ."

"What do you think, Mom? If your smile was marred by a mess like I've got inside my mouth, wouldn't you be concerned at least . . . or . . . or mildly discouraged?"

Mother nodded her head and pulled out a tuft of milkweed seeds, blowing them forcefully away with a deep breath of despair. "Well, I thought that was it, Hon. I thought so. You know, Cheryl, I've been thinking about you and your pearly whites," she continued. "I just sit around all day wondering what to do with myself, and there's absolutely no reason I couldn't get a decent job somewhere for a little extra spending money--maybe even enough to pay for your braces myself. Wouldn't you really like to get your teeth all straightened?"

"Are you serious, Mom? Would you actually do that for me?"

"You've truly got a lovely face, Cheryl--except for those uneven teeth of yours. If you ever want to see an orthodontist, this is the time to do it. You're just the right age for it now, from what I've been told."

Mom paused. "So . . . what do you think of the idea?"

"Don't you think Dad would protest?"

"Not necessarily. You and I could just check into it. We could drive over to Parkersburg tomorrow when your father will be at work and try on some new winter clothes together. We could also just see if the orthodontist feels you'd be a good candidate for correction. It'd be a potentially fun time, Cheryl, wouldn't it?"

I didn't quite know how to react. I had all but given up the idea of having braces. Besides--wouldn't my father be beside himself with anger if he found out we were going to see an orthodontist without telling him first?

"You mean . . . you wouldn't tell Dad about it, Mother?"

"No, not right away until we get some actual facts. It'd be our little secret for the time being, Cheryl."

"You promise, Mom?"

"Absolutely!"

How incredible was this idea, anyway! My mother was willing to sacrifice her free time for me and get a job for extra income and . . . and I was elated!

"OH, YES, MOTHER! YES, YES, YES!" I said as I gave her a quick hug.

So, my mother and I agreed to take a little trip together on the q.t. the next day without informing my father. Leaving, so it turned out, proved to be super simple because of Dad's reliable nature.

You see, my father always went to work at the crack of dawn. I suppose that was truly a good thing about Dad--he was perpetually punctual. He'd make sure his car was full of gas the night before, then he'd line up his underclothes, shoes, and freshly-pressed work clothes on the chair right next to his bed--that way, he could jerk them on the next morning, immediately upon arising. Finally, at 7:00, without wasting a second of his valuable time, he'd fly out the door just like Dagwood Bumstead.

Way to go, Dad!

I never ever knew him to be late--not even *once*!

Mom and I decided to hit two major department stores on our little adventure, Broida's and Dill's, and shop for about three hours before I went to the orthodontist. If we left our house by 8:00 in the morning, we could easily be looking at dresses by 9:30, grab a sandwich somewhere by 12:30, see the orthodontist around 1:30, and still have more than enough time to be back home by, say, 4:00--a good hour before Dad bounded through the door at 5:00. All Mom had to do was make my orthodontist's appointment.

Cinchy!

I felt positively guilty--at first.

Mom, on the other hand, assured me that "We're not doing anything wrong, Cheryl, we're just taking a little deviation from our everyday routine to enjoy some well-deserved time between the two of us. I'll make it up to your father in the future."

So, I cheerfully agreed. Incredibly enough, Mom found out Dr. Rudolph had a cancellation just when we wanted to be in his vicinity, so I inwardly wondered if the Lord had our trip in mind from the very beginning.

The first leg of our excursion went well. We actually arrived at the parking lot outside Dill's about one-half hour ahead of schedule, and the two of us ravaged the dress department racks in record time! Mom found a cute little pink blouse she thought she could well afford, though I, of course, found nothing that would fit properly. Mother, to compensate, bless her heart, bought a colorful silk scarf for me with beautiful orange and maroon fall leaves on it--a loving attempt to boost my spirits.

"Don't fret, Cheryl," she encouraged. "I'm sure you'll find a thing or two you'll fall madly in love with when we get to Broida's!"

In only five minutes, we'd hustled ourselves down the street and were standing at the entrance to one of the most progressive dress stores in West Virginia.

"Oh, look, Mom! They're having some sort of a style show here or something! Can we watch for awhile?"

Broida's. Many wealthy people from Athens shopped there for the finest and most contemporary attire in the area, and their stylish hats were legendary. A regal runway had been erected on this particular day, with purple velvet draped around the bottom of a large platform and chairs arranged to accommodate at least one hundred patrons or so. In fact, standing room only remained for Mom and me as we pressed towards the back where models were to exit their dressing rooms.

"How exciting, Cheryl," Mom whispered, ". . . and there's free demitasse here for us to enjoy and delicious-looking little mints. Have one with me!"

I bit into a mint and immediately spit most of it into a nearby trash can.

"Aren't they good, Cheryl?"

Not to me. . . .

I eyed the models as they started to make tracks right beside me onto the runway.

One model brushed by me so closely that the sleeve of her garment gently grazed my inquisitive face.

"Hurry up and change, girlie!" she scolded. "You're on next!"

"Who? You mean me?"

Oh, my gosh! Did she think I was one of them?

A forceful foreign hand grabbed my elbow and pulled me into a gigantic changing room.

"Here ya go, sweets! Put this on and HUSTLE, GIRL!!! You're on right after Candace!"

Oh, brother. This is really nuts!

"Let me go!" I raged. "I just came here to *watch*!"

I yanked my arm away from my would-be kidnapper and angled myself into a corner where I felt secure.

All at once, some matronly saleslady grabbed my elbow and started to deliver the lecture of her life:

"Now, you look here, sister!" she scowled. "I haven't got all day! I'm not paying you to just stand around, ya know! Now get into your garment and take your . . . your . . . HEY! WHO THE HECK ARE YOU, ANYWAY?"

"That's what I've been trying to EXPLAIN, lady! I just came by to *watch* your style show! I've never *seen* one before! Lord knows, I don't want to *be* in one!"

Apologies exuded.

"Oh, Miss, I am so, so, very sorry. I . . . I thought you were one of us! You're so tall and slim, and . . . and I just thought you were one of our imports from Charleston or somewhere! Can you ever forgive me?"

I was speechless. Did she actually think I looked like a model--or was I dreaming?

Mother, having temporarily lost sight of me, frantically poked her head into the changing room.

"What exactly is going on here, Madam?" questioned Mom.

Again, more apologies!

"Well, you, I can tell, you must be the proud mother of this graceful young woman," the saleswoman went on.

"Please, please forgive my honest mistake, ma'am. I tell you, your daughter looks just like the models we feature here at Broida's. I made a . . . a logical mistake, that's all!"

Go on, Mom! I thought. *Milk this for all it's worth!*

"Well . . . well . . . *next* time, you . . . y-you just better be more careful, lady!" Mom reprimanded.

Go get her, Mom!

"I mean," Mom continued, ". . . this certainly was an embarrassing situation for my daughter, as you can plainly see, and I think you should compensate her in some way. Get my point? You really *did* upset her! Can you not see how distraught she is?"

I looked solemnly down at the floor.

I feigned rejection.

I wiped my eyes.

"You stay right here, now--both of you! I'll be right back," the clerk announced. "You two lovely ladies both just stay put!"

Mom cupped her right hand and placed it diagonally across her mouth.

"Did you *ever* in *all* your life, Cheryl? Did you *ever* think you could pass for a model? Maybe this is your calling! Maybe this is a sign you should actually be a model some day! What do you think, Cheryl? Do you think this could be a sign from above?"

I was startled by a flurry of activity around my mother and me as the two most gorgeous hats I had ever seen were delivered and planted firmly upon our respective heads.

"There! There, now! Don't you two girls look just positively elegant? Please accept these hats as a gesture of Broida's sincere apologies," the saleslady insisted. "I hope these flattering hats will compensate for any unintentional displeasure we have caused either of you!"

With that, Mom and I strutted back out the front doors, heads held high!

I thought the two of us would never stop laughing when we hit the pavement! We walked and giggled, proudly showing off our beautiful new hats while attracting an uncommon share of attention.

"Please accept these hats as a gesture of our sincere apologies!" Mom said as she bowed to me in polite Oriental fashion, stopping her gait momentarily to mimic the saleslady.

"I do hope this will compensate for any displeasure we've unintentionally caused you, madam," I added, bowing in turn to Mom in an effort to continue the farce!

My mother finally gained her composure after about ten minutes to pose an unrelated question.

"Say, Cheryl. Would you like to grab a soft drink while we mull over our recent good fortune?"

We stopped at a sidewalk café and Mom ordered a fizzing diet cola.

I gulped down half a glassful of ice water.

"Away we go, daughter!" Mother encouraged. "Dr. Rudolph is just around the block. I surely hope you'll like your orthodontist, Cheryl. His receptionist sounded really pleasant over the phone to me!"

"How do you know he's actually going to be my orthodontist, Mom?"

"Well, there aren't too many orthodontal choices in these parts. Dr. Rudolph is not only supposed to be the *best* in the area, he's also one of the *few.* If you're going to follow through and get your teeth straightened, he's the one who'll do it!"

Mother seemed unusually excited.

"So, Mom . . . do you really expect to get a job at any time in the near future?"

Mom savored each delicious slurp of soda as a warm glow spread across her face.

"Didn't you hear the phone ring around 7:45 this morning--right before we left in the car?" Mom replied.

"I guess I didn't pay much attention, Mom. Who was it, anyway?"

"You'll never believe this, Cheryl, but I actually had a call from a banker asking me to come in tomorrow for an interview. How 'bout that!"

Mother was practically rejoicing!

"I don't understand. Did you send an application to a bank? I don' t remember your going to a bank or even calling one."

"Well, that's because . . . I never did!"

"Then, how come they--"

"I'll never know how they heard about me, Cheryl, but I have a good feeling about this interview. You know what it says in Matthew 17:20, don't you?"

Was there a Christian alive who didn't know this Bible verse?

"Oh, sure, Mother! It says, '. . . if you have faith as small as a mustard seed . . . nothing will be impossible for you.'"

"Yes! I just *knew* you'd remember that verse!" Mom said. "Well, I never doubted that God would help me find a job--I just think it's incredible that He chose to do it as soon as He did!"

"But you don't know that you've landed it, yet. Aren't you being a little bit premature?"

"Just you wait and see, Cheryl! Look at how this day's gone already. The Good Father not only gave us a safe trip to our destination, He also gave us a fantastic time together plus two phenomenal hats!"

"You don't actually believe He had something to do with our getting these awesome hats, do you?"

"Of course! James 1:17 proclaims that 'Every good and perfect gift is from above. . . .' I think He not only *gave* us these presents," Mom continued, "I believe He also got a great deal of satisfaction from doing it!"

That was my sainted mother for you. She knew and believed the Bible inside out. "You mean, as in '. . . your Father has been pleased to give you the kingdom (Luke 12:32),' don't you, Mom?"

"Oh, yes . . . I *do* believe that."

"So do I, Mother . . . so do I."

And the two of us proceeded, arm in arm, to Dr. Rudolph's.

Chapter Nine

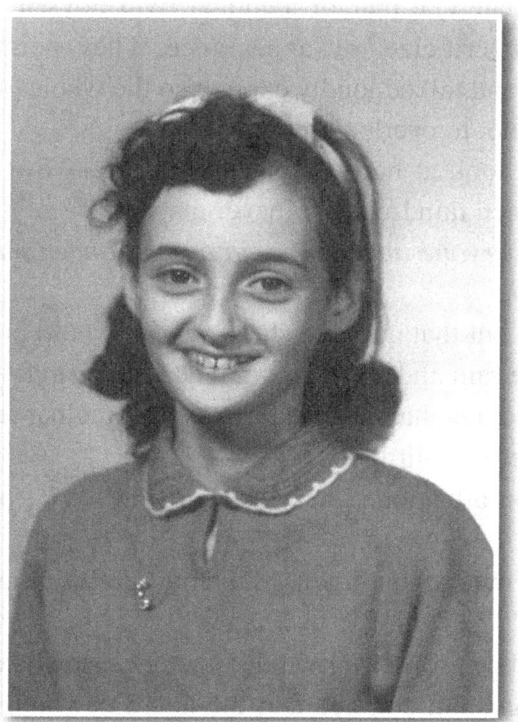

Time for braces! 1955
School Photo

It was quite unnerving to see so many children running to and fro at Dr. Rudolph's, and their noise was unbearable. It was more than noise, to be exact--it was one annoying, incredible, loud, perpetual *din.*

Mom checked me in with the receptionist and tried to find a secluded spot where we might find some semblance of quietness. Such a place didn't exist, so we sat on the window ledge instead.

I picked up a copy of a Dr. Seuss favorite I'd never read before and tried to act engrossed.

Immediately, a pair of identical twin boys made it their business to criticize my appearance. They pointed at me, snickered, and talked loudly enough so the whole office would be certain not to overlook my presence.

"Gosh, look at how skinny that one is! Wow! She could walk between raindrops and never get wet!"

Now everyone noticed me, in case I'd been miraculously overlooked.

"Yeah, but that ugly hat she's wearin' would prob'ly catch most of the rain and she'd drown when the brim let go!"

Waves of laughter gushed forth as their mother reached over to shake her rude little munchkins.

"Pay no attention, Cheryl," Mom said, ". . . but take off your hat."

"I like my hat just fine, Mom, and I prefer to leave it right where it is!"

The office grew surprisingly quieter as slowly, one by one, the waiting room emptied and the hoard of youngsters made their way to see Dr. Rudolph.

I watched the clock and tried to think of an excuse to leave.

"Do you know we've been here way over an hour already, Mother?"

"Settle down, Cheryl. The doctor will see you soon enough," Mom answered.

"Soon enough for you, maybe, but I'm thinking I've lived with these teeth for thirteen years the way they are and I can roll merrily along for at least another thirteen just fine."

My mother shifted positions and moved closer to me.

"Do you think I can't see or hear what's happening here this minute? Do you think I'm not aware of the unkindness directed at you?" she said in a whisper.

I bit my lip.

"Why don't you just go over there and slap those two kids silly, then, Mom?"

"And exactly how would that help *you* cope with the situation, Cheryl?"

The fact was, I'd never really figured out what to do when I was poked fun at. Over and over, for as long as I could remember, I'd said to myself "Sticks and stones may break my bones, but names can never hurt me," but that simply wasn't true. I loathed being the brunt of ridicule and longed to look like any average, normal, young person for just a day or two. What would that feel like, I wondered. What would it feel like to be able to amble down the street, *any* street, *anywhere*, or sit in a public place like I was today and not be viewed as a circus spectacle in a sideshow?

"God has the capacity to empower you, Cheryl. Don't you know that, yet?" Mother said.

"Got a Bible verse to back up that statement, Mom? Well, have you?"

Mom's attempt to reply was broken by an blood-curdling shriek from the orthodontist's chair.

"It sure sounds like *that* kid's havin' a real blast, Mom!" I said.

"I never said getting braces would be without discomfort, Cheryl. I never once said that! What I said was that we could check this situation out, that's all. And . . . and I don't appreciate your attitude. You're starting to act a bit impudent to me. Do you know that?"

Silence loomed between the two of us for about five minutes.

"You never answered my question, Mom." I repeated again, trying to underplay my apprehension.

"Where's a Bible verse now, when I need it, Mother?"

"I can't think of any specific verse right off, Cheryl, but I *can* suggest an outlook. It's an outlook we have to develop as Christians to overcome any problems we may encounter in life, even pain, perhaps--like that young fellow's experiencing in the other room right now. We have to make ourselves emotionally and spiritually tough, and our God is able to give us the strength we need to withstand all derisive circumstances."

"How would *you* know what it feels like to be laughed at, Mom? How could *you* possibly know what it's like to be scorned?"

"You mean like Jesus was repeatedly scorned . . . on the cross?"

I had to grin. "Well, I'm sure neither one of us was ever treated half as badly as Jesus our Lord was!"

"Maybe not, Cheryl, but I've certainly had my share of persecution, and I'll bet my emotional pain was far more horrific than the physical pain you hear in the other room!"

Was my mother kidding me? What was she talking about, for heaven's sake? "Come on, Mom. Why would you ever have to deal with being put down?"

I had always admired my mother. She looked great no matter what she wore and could fit into any dress she wanted to buy without having umpteen alterations on it. She had lovely facial features, beautiful hazel eyes, and the most gorgeous auburn hair I'd ever seen in my life.

"Oh, Cheryl. Just look at me. Did you ever really look at this head of hair I have? Did you ever honestly notice how red it is?"

"What are you talking about? What's wrong with your hair, anyway?"

"Isn't it obvious, Cheryl? All my life, I've longed for brown hair, or black hair, or blond hair, or blue hair--anything but this ridiculous red hair. Don't you think I've not been teased to death for the hair I was born with?"

"I . . . I guess I never gave it any thought. To me, your hair's just perfect the way it is—and it's a gift from God!"

"Well, it may be God's gift, but I never wanted it. I wanted to look just like all the other girls in school. I didn't want to be unique. I wanted to fit in. Get the picture?"

"But your hair is truly incredible, Mom!"

"Not to me, it isn't! And in school, you'd be surprised how I always got teased . . . every single day I went to class."

"Kids made fun of you just because your hair was red?"

"Oh my, yes! The boys even made up poems about me, like 'Redhead, gingerbread, five cents a cabbage head!'"

"That rhyme doesn't even make sense, Mom!"

"Of course, it doesn't, Cheryl, but it *hurt* me deeply just the same--like being called 'carrot top.' That was another one of my loathsome nicknames, 'carrot top.' Over a period of years, I came to the point of really feeling I must have been ugly."

"You? Ugly? I can't imagine your feeling that way about yourself!"

A call from the dental assistant, Maryanne, interrupted the conversation I was having with my mother.

"Cheryl, ahhh . . . Cheryl Kimes? Dr. Rudolph will see you now."

Finally, I thought. *It's about time!*

I inched myself into Dr. Rudolph's chair and gritted my teeth hard as his assistant flung a bib around my neck and anchored it with a lightweight chain.

"You just sit tight and relax, Cheryl," she instructed. "This will not hurt you--at all!"

Dr. Rudolph approached me with the broad smile of the fabled Cheshire cat from *Alice in Wonderland.*

"First thing you'll have to do, young lady, is open up wide," he said forcefully. "I can't see your teeth unless you open wide, can I?"

Of course not! That was the whole idea. Now, here was an intelligent man!

"That's it," he went on, "wider . . . *wi-i-i-i-der. . .*" then there followed a series of grunts, sighs, snorts and other miscellaneous mouth sounds emanating from my noisy orthodontist--designed, I was sure, to annoy the very life out of me.

"Maryanne, help me measure here, please," he ordered, and tooth by tooth, Dr. Rudolph and his assistant recorded enough data to formulate the predictable outcome of the day's visit for my mother to hear: "Your daughter needs braces."

How astute.

My mother took the news standing up.

"Fine," she concurred. "I thought so. This is exactly what I expected!"

No mention was made about my experiencing possible agony during the procedure, no discussion about my choking or gagging or spitting up blood, and no suggestions whatsoever about the inescapable financing. I had a "serious malocclusion," and that was a bad, bad thing to Dr. Rudolph.

My mother agreed.

"How long would Cheryl have to wear braces, doctor?" she probed.

"One year, probably, maybe two. . . ." he replied. "But when I get done with this little gal, I guarantee she won't look like the same bobby-soxer! I'll close up that big ol' space between her two front teeth so she won't resemble a jack-o-lantern," Dr. Rudolph quickly turned to me and winked, ". . . and I'll align her other teeth correctly so she can chew her food the way she should. The entire shape of her face will change dramatically. You'll be pleasantly surprised."

So, what was so wrong with resembling a jack-o-lantern, anyway? Shouldn't a patient have the right to decide if she wanted to look like a Halloween pumpkin or not?

Mother apparently felt she had heard all she needed from Dr. Rudolph.

"I'll get back to you, doctor," she said, and she hustled me out to the parking lot.

"Why all the big rush, Mother?" I asked as we fled the scene.

"I just want to get home before your father gets off work--that's all."

"But . . . but *I* had questions that I needed to ask, Mom. What about *my* questions? Don't they matter? Don't my feelings count at all?"

"Of course, they do, Cheryl--but I refuse to let you go through junior high with cosmetic problems that can be easily remedied. If you don't get braces now, you'll regret it for the rest of your life. I won't let that happen to any daughter of mine. No! This is one thing I can help you fix!"

I glanced down the hall from Dr. Rudolph's on the way to the car. His office was one in a large complex of many other medical specialties and I spotted a sign that said Internal Medicine.

"Oh, look, Mom! This is the same medical building where Dr. Blumfeld works. He's that specialist Dr. Woodworth recommended for me, isn't he?"

Mother stopped dead in her tracks.

"Well, well, Cheryl. I had no idea," she said.

Mother stood as motionless as a pillar of salt and stared at Dr. Blumfeld's door. After about a minute, we resumed our pace and continued our dash out of the building. We almost *ran* once we hit the sidewalk then flew even faster to our car.

Whew! My Mom. That woman winded me!

It seemed like a long, long ride back to Athens.

I tried my best to make conversation.

"It was neat that we got these new hats today, wasn't it, Mom? Shopping sure was fun!" I said.

"Yes, it certainly was."

Silence.

"Broida's is a really great store. Dill's is nice, too," I added.

More silence.

Mom seemed like she was terribly deep in thought and for some reason acted almost sullen.

"Anything wrong, Mom?"

"Oh, no . . . no, Cheryl. I've truthfully just been wondering exactly how we'd work it all out--your braces and everything."

"Are you worried about it?"

Still more silence.

Mother had this *problem*, sometimes. She, like her sister, Sybil, tended to clam up whenever they had significant issues to deal with. My father and Uncle Frank laughingly referred to their behavior as being in "one of those moods," and they'd coax and humor their wives with baby talk until I thought I'd spew.

"Now, Clissie, Clissie, what's da matter with li'l Clissie? Dat ol' puddytat got your tongue, again?" Dad would ask Mom.

Yet all of Dad's questioning never helped matters at all. He'd just have to wait it out with Mom--sometimes for hours at a time--and after Mom finally got her act together again, she'd be conversant.

What a waste of time.

It was the same story with Sybil, except Sybil's pouting would oftentimes last for several days until even *she* couldn't remember what the initial issue was!

Me? Whenever I had a dilemma, I just wanted to confront it right away, resolve it as fast as possible, and get on with life!

I tried to make Mother verbalize what was going through her head.

"Mom, I just don't get it. We had a great day today, didn't we? I guess getting braces should be a real consideration of mine."

"I'm sure it should."

"I suppose I'd probably look a lot better after the procedure, too."

Silence.

"Well, then, what in the world is wrong? Have I upset you in some way or said something that displeased you?"

No response.

In fact, during the remaining forty-five minutes it took to drive back to Athens . . . Mother never said another solitary word.

Chapter Ten

Mother waited until after dinner was over to tell my father about our clandestine trip to Parkersburg. At first, as we had expected, Dad seemed somewhat upset, though hardly as antagonistic as Mom and I had feared.

"I never, *ever* would have tried to stand in the way of our daughter getting braces, Clysta," he said. "I just don't understand why you didn't tell me about this trip in the first place. I'da given you my blessin' to leave today!"

Mother shrugged.

"I . . . I thought you'd question how you'd ever be able to afford everything for Cheryl, that's all," Mom replied.

My father, though seemingly hurt to some degree, delved for more details.

"And so . . . so how much did Dr. Rudolph think the whole deal would cost, anyway?"

"We never got into it that far," Mom replied.

"You *didn't,* Clis? Now, I really don't get it. Didn't Dr. Rudolph think she needed his services?"

"Well . . . yes. No question about it."

"Then, what . . . what exactly was the problem? Are you holdin' something back from me, woman? I have a right to know what happened to our little girl, you know. She's my daughter, too, isn't she?"

Mother paced back and forth on the living room carpet, pausing now and then to run her fingers up and down the wooden casements of our tall picture windows. I headed for my bedroom as my parents continued to talk.

"What would you say if I told you I had an opportunity to get a job to help out, Ron?"

"Why . . . why I'd say if it was necessary to put braces on Cheryl's teeth . . . I reckon I'd *appreciate* your workin'. How else could I feel?"

"What would you say if I told you Dr. Blumfeld's office was just down the hall from Dr. Rudolph's. How would you look at that, Ronald?"

Dad was puzzled.

"Don't tell me you had a meetin' to see Dr. Blumfeld with Cheryl as well?"

"No, no, Ronald--I certainly *didn't*. It just happened that Dr. Blumfeld's office was right there, close to Dr. Rudolph's, and I just thought that was peculiar . . . *very* peculiar . . . almost providential."

I partially closed the door to my bedroom, leaving a tiny crack in it so I could overhear what was about to transpire.

There was another brief pause.

"Okay, then," asked Dad, ". . . why was it so strange that two doctors would share the same building, Clis?"

Mom struggled for words.

"It was just . . . just a weird coincidence, I thought . . . too much of a coincidence to actually *be* a coincidence, really . . . the fact that we just happened to have an orthodontist who just happened to be directly down the hall from *the* internist Cheryl needs to see as well for her bigger problem--her malnourishment disorder."

Dad was suddenly, most definitely, *alarmed.*

"Disorder? DISORDER?" he repeated. "Who in the world ever once hinted our little daughter's got a bloomin' disorder, Clis? Tell me! Did *any* doctor ever, *ever* suggest she's got an actual, factual disorder? Where in the tarnation did you ever come up with a crazy idea like that, woman? You're goin' way off the deep end here!"

Mom was talking faster and becoming more emotional. I could hear it in her voice as she continued.

"Don't you see, Ron? D-don't you understand what's going on here?"

Now it was my father who was without comment.

"Look, Ron," Mother said. "No doctor ever speculated that our daughter had any major physical problem he could accurately diagnose, but she *is* forty pounds underweight! I know you think Cheryl's just built like you by nature--that she's underweight 'cause she inherited a tendency to be thinner than most people--but *you* don't have trouble eating like Cheryl does. You never leave the table feeling half-starved like our little Cheryl! I . . . I think there's more going on with her than meets the eye!"

I knew silence from my father meant one of two things: Either he didn't agree with what my mother was trying to say, or he was worried about whether he could handle any additional financial obligations he might have to face in my behalf.

That was it!

"A-and just how do you propose I go about payin' for Cheryl's braces plus a visit to this specialist . . . this . . . this incredible Dr. Blumfeld?"

Mother loved my father dearly, and she always knew how she had to handle Dad when she needed to make a point; the Bible was Dad's rock.

It's about time for another Bible verse, I thought . . . and I was right! In order to make certain my father would see Mother's point clearly for himself, Mother reached into the end table by our sofa where we kept our trusty family Bible, and together she and Dad read James 1:2-4:

"Consider it pure joy, my brothers and sisters, whenever you face trials of many kinds, because you know that the testing of your faith produces perseverance. Let perseverance finish its work so that you may be mature and complete, not lacking anything."

My father seemed enlightened.

"Oh. You think the Good Lord's telling us to sit tight and hang onto our faith 'cause He intends to heal our little girl sometime . . . from some lurking hidden problem, don't you, Clis?"

"Yes I do, Ron, and I believe that Jesus will provide the money we need to pay for her medical bills if it turns out she needs some kind of treatment that's real expensive!"

"You . . . you think it wasn't no happenstance that Dr. Rudolph and Dr. Blumfeld were together in the same building."

"Well, what do *you* think, Ronald? Doesn't it look to you like we were directed to Dr. Rudolph for more than the obvious reason?"

My Dad father was dumbfounded. My parents turned out the lights and called it a day.

I was concerned. It was hard enough to grapple with the notion of having ugly braces put on my teeth--I was trying hard to accept the idea, but I truly didn't want to endure the fitting. If I had to concurrently face some mysterious "disorder" on top of getting braces, wouldn't it all be way, way too much to handle?

I jumped under the bedcovers with my clothes still on, pulled the sheets up tightly around my neck, and prayed sincerely with all my might:

Dear Jesus, thank you for the wonderful time I had with my mother in Parkersburg today. Thank you for a good visit with Dr. Rudolph and a safe trip home, again. Thank you for two loving parents who care deeply about me and want me to be happy . . . and . . . Jesus, please, please guide Mom and Dad to figure out how to get me all fixed up! Thank you, Jesus. Amen.

Sleep came easily. I knew Jesus would look after me and give my parents the wisdom they needed to make my life better. I knew, beyond a shadow of a doubt, that Jesus would provide the three of us with His wisdom when it was time. I didn't know *how* He'd work everything all out, but I knew He *would.*

Hoo-a-hoo-hoo-hoo!

I awakened with a start.

Again, I heard it.

Hoo-a-hoo-hoo-hoo!

Was that an owl? Was that an owl outside my bedroom window--or was I dreaming?

I continued to listen.

Over and over, he hooted, *hoo-a-hoo . . . hoo-a-hoo . . .* though try as I might, I simply couldn't see him.

Wait. I heard talking in the background. Was that Mother?

I gently opened my door and put my ear as close to the opening as I could.

Yes, yes, it *was* Mom, at two o'clock in the morning of all things! On the phone? At this hour?

How in the world was a person supposed to get any shut-eye around here, anyway?

"Oh, you should have seen her, Sybil. Honestly, all the kids in the office were snickering at her, putting her down, making horrible comments about her--and she just sat there and took it without crying, without shedding a tear. She just stayed glued to her seat and bit her tongue!"

I could hear mother blowing her nose and sniffling repeatedly.

"Those awful kids just kept going on and on, Sybil, about how skinny she was and how silly she looked in her beautiful new hat. It just broke my heart, Sybil. I felt so very sorry for her."

Although I couldn't begin to hear what Mom's sister was saying on the other end of the line, I *could* hear the dismay in my mother's voice.

"I . . . I just don't know what to do next, Sybil, but I really hate to put Cheryl through more examinations with another doctor. It's hard to tell what all he'd want to do to her--or am I wrong? Should I take her to see Dr. Blumfeld, too? Do you think I should make her go to an internist or not? Do you think she could take it, Sybil? How much more can our little Cheryl take, anyway--more blood tests and more procedures and God-knows-what?"

The owl was quiet. It was as though he had awakened me on purpose so I could hear what my worried mother was saying.

"No . . . no, Sybil. I have no way of knowing exactly what might be wrong with Cheryl," Mom went on, ". . . but Dr. Woodworth has basically given up on trying to help her. He's done all he knows how to do.

"Yes, of course, I know I have to be strong for our daughter. Yes, I *do* believe our Lord will look after her. Oh, I don't know . . . I'm just . . . I-I'm just . . . *troubled*."

I recalled many times I had listened to my great-grandfather, Charlie Beckley, strum his favorite hymns on his autoharp while singing at the top of his feeble old lungs. The old man's favorite hymn was no doubt "What a Friend We Have in Jesus," but once he got inspired he could play and sing a dozen or more inspirational hymns at the drop of a hat.

Just then, while Mom was talking to Sybil, I remembered another old hymn that Charlie was fond of called "Does Jesus Care?" I started to whistle it, walking slowing towards mother so she would hear it, too.

She looked up at me in surprise.

"Cheryl? Whatever are you doing up at this time of the night? Did I awaken you?"

"It's okay, Mom. Why don't you just hang up the phone now, and let Sybil sleep? There's nothing you and I can't handle with the help of Jesus! Isn't that what you've been trying to teach all your kiddies in Sunday school?"

A morose look spread over Mother's face as she said good-bye to Sybil and hung up the receiver.

"I'm . . . I'm sorry, Cheryl. Sometimes I just can't figure everything out--even with your father and the Lord to help. Sometimes, I need more input, that's all. Sybil is more than just a sister--Sybil is my best friend."

I went over to Mom and gave her a big hug. She latched onto me tightly.

"Cheryl, this is a big decision to make, isn't it?"

"What is? Whether or not I should see Dr. Blumfeld?"

"Yes, honey. I just felt Sybil might be able to give me more insight, that's all. She's had lots of experience with physicians herself, you know."

"Well then, what advice did she have to give you, Mom? What did she think I should do?"

"Sybil never hesitated. Sybil said if you were *her* daughter, she'd definitely take you to a specialist--to as many specialists as she could find--until she found *the* physician who could make you one-hundred percent well!"

Mom and I sat down together on the sofa and just held hands, quietly.

"What do you think about her advice, Mom?"

I heard the owl off in the distance, once again reminding me to listen.

Mother heard the owl, too.

"Did you hear that, Cheryl?"

"Yes . . . he woke me up a while ago, Mom. It was like that ol' bird wanted me to pay attention to what you were saying."

"Do . . . do think he was a sign from God, Cheryl?"

"Maybe, Mom. Actually . . . I do! I think God used him to awaken me so I could help you!"

"Help *me*? I'm not the one who needs help, Cheryl--*you* are!"

"But, Mom! I am totally willing to see Dr. Blumfeld! I really *want* to see Dr. Blumfeld, in fact, in order to make me normal! I just don't understand, Mom. Why do you hesitate to let me go?"

"I don't know, Cheryl. I . . . I just hate to see you--"

"Then I have to conclude that you don't practice what you teach your little tots in Sunday school."

"What are you saying, Cheryl? More than any other thing in life, I want you to be healed!"

"Well, then . . . did you happen to hear what I was whistling a while ago, Mom?"

"'Does Jesus Care'?"

"Yes, the song great-grandpa used to enjoy singing years ago."

"I know it well," she said. "The chorus goes, 'Oh yes, He cares, I know He cares, His heart is touched with my grief.'"

"'When the days are weary, the long nights dreary, I know my Jesus cares.'" I finished.

"I really believe there's truth in those words, Cheryl. I really do believe there is."

"Then, mother, if Jesus is your friend, and He cares about you and your little Sunday schoolers--isn't He surely just as much my friend, too? I believe that Jesus loves me and is going to heal me, Mom! I just think you're temporarily having a hard time completely trusting Him yourself!"

Mom and I stood up together. Suddenly, she seemed to relax.

"It's been a long night, Cheryl. Let's go back to bed. I'll call Dr. Woodworth in the morning and talk to him about an appointment with Dr. Blumfeld for you. I promise I'll take care of it. I promise. . . ."

So, it was decided.

I prayed that the Lord would look after Mother and continue to give her resolve.

Tomorrow would be a move in the right direction.

Tomorrow would open another door.

Chapter Eleven

The next morning after her interview at the bank, Mom called Dr. Woodworth and requested he send my records to Dr. Blumfeld. Dr. Woodworth was "ecstatic," Mom said, that I was willing to see the internist he had recommended.

"Exactly what does 'ecstatic' mean, Mom?" I questioned.

"Oh, ecstatic means really, *really* happy, Cheryl, like I feel since I secured that job at the bank two hours ago!"

"What? What did you just say, Mother?"

Mom started to laugh.

"Oh, I think you heard me correctly, Cheryl! I start to work at the Hocking Valley Bank next week as a teller, and my boss says there'll be plenty of opportunity for me to advance after a few months! Isn't Jesus just wonderful?"

I was truly overjoyed for my mother but also had some personal concerns of my own.

"Well, when you call Dr. Blumfeld, make sure you don't rush my appointment. You know, I'm supposed to play a piano solo in the National Federation of Music Clubs Contest in two weeks, plus I've got to practice for the school chorus, too, and--"

Mom interrupted me.

"Aren't you overdoing things a little? Aren't you tackling too much at the same time with all your classes and such?"

"Overdoing it? I'm not overdoing anything, Mom! I'm keeping my grades up, aren't I?"

"Yes, you are, Cheryl, and I'm proud of you for that."

Good! Mom had no complaints with me.

"Frankly, Mom, I don't see all that much difference between the sixth grade and the seventh grade, anyway. The school work isn't that much harder to me--there's just a little more of it to do, that's all."

Of course, physical education was a different story. In the sixth grade, our classes had recess outside where I could pretty much do my own thing by myself. But in the seventh grade, we had more group activities, and we usually had team sports inside the gymnasium. For me, that togetherness was much worse! We had to play soccer, baseball, and other ridiculous games together, and I detested every single activity. Often, Mother would write "hair-brained excuses" for me (as my father liked to refer to them) to make certain I didn't overexert myself. She insisted on doing so because my heart would frequently beat so fast upon exercising that she couldn't begin to count the beats!

Naturally, I was always grateful when I got to sit out physical education, for it wasn't as though I was good at any sport--that was a laugh! I was predictably the last person to be chosen for any team, and I very much resembled a stork whenever I had to don my little white gym shorts. To try to make my spindly legs appear bigger, Mother bought shorts for me that had stylish little cuffs on them. Personally, I thought those cuffs called *more* attention to my legs and further accentuated my bird-like appearance, but I never mentioned that fact to Mom lest I hurt her feelings.

Anyway, I was scheduled to play in the Federation Music Contest on Saturday--the very next day after gym class was over--so having gym out of the way would be a relief in itself.

That way, I could just concentrate on my piano piece for the competition.

"Dr. Blumfeld can see you three weeks from Friday, Cheryl. Will that be a good time for you to go?" Mom asked after she made the appointment for me.

Fantastic! That's one time I will have a legitimate excuse to stay out of gym!

"Sure, Mom. That'll be just fine!" I said.

Playing in the Federation Contest, on the other hand, would certainly prove to be a worthwhile experience for me, and I was really looking forward to competing pianistically. Mrs. Phelps had chosen a fantastic piano solo for me to perform by Edward MacDowell called "Hungarian," and I felt certain I would earn a superior rating--a "one" as we student-competitors liked to call it. Plenty of other musicians I knew were playing in the same contest, too, but nobody could touch me! Without question, "Hungarian" was far more difficult to play than anything else my peers were attempting, and I just knew I would do a "bang-up-job" (to echo my father's sentiments).

Two weeks seemed to fly. I felt more than ready to play in the music contest, and the day before, our physical education teacher assured us we were all going to be in for a real treat; we were all going to get to take turns jumping on a genuine, honest-to-goodness regulation-sized trampoline!

"Can you believe it, Cheryl?" my friend, Lauretta, exclaimed.

"Wow!" she continued. "This isn't a little kid's trampoline . . . this is one of those huge, awesome, neato trampolines that athletes actually use! Won't it be fun, Cheryl?"

Right. It'd be fun for Lauretta, for sure--she totally excelled in sports.

Cheryl (far left) with costumed schoolmates
Lauretta Glasgo, Sheila Michaels, Barb Phillips,
Pam Whaley, and Toni McGrath, circa 1956
School Photo

Lauretta was my very best friend at the time. How I admired her! We had grown up on the same street together, roller skated and ridden our shiny bikes together, gone to movies together, gotten into mischief together and, well . . . she was just the greatest girlfriend *anywhere* to have around when I needed one.

I suppose we probably looked like "Mutt and Jeff" to most people, though. Whereas I was way too skinny, Lauretta could have made two of me! She wasn't fat--not at all--she was just more muscular and more . . . more *robust.* Lauretta was way cool.

It was understandable that Lauretta was extremely excited to get to try out the new trampoline on that fateful Friday when gym class started, and we both hurried into the locker room to get our shorts and tops on like the rest of the gym class.

About twenty-five of us girls participated in total, and our phys ed teacher, Miss Cline, sometimes had her hands full maintaining order. For some reason--which I never understood--all the girls actually thought it was fun to run around in the gymnasium as fast as gazelles. They loved to climb ropes and fool around on the uneven bars and . . . they were all loony in my book!

After dressing, we had to stand in line, in order, while Miss Cline checked us off in her attendance book and introduced us to the monstrous trampoline at hand. "Now this, class, is not a toy to play around on. A trampoline can be fun for sure, but it can also be very, very dangerous!"

What? Dangerous?

Seriously, you could have heard a pin drop.

"If any of you, I mean if *ANY* of you create the slightest amount of disturbance or do anything remotely out of turn, I will mark you down for an "F" today and send you straight to the principal's office. Do I make myself perfectly clear?"

Miss Cline looked directly at Lauretta and me . . . but mostly, at *me*. I was quite certain she didn't like me--*why,* I'll never know. Maybe she could sense how uncomfortable I felt participating in her stupid class, or maybe she thought merely *looking* at me caused painful eye strain, but Miss Cline, I strongly suspected, didn't like me.

Our teacher directed us closer to the trampoline.

"Now, class," she continued, "I want you all to spread out and encircle the trampoline's perimeter. I want you to put an equal amount of space between yourself and the person standing next to you so there won't be any unequal gaps in sight."

Now, this was easy.

Oops!

She jerked me by the arm!

"*NO*, Cheryl! You stand over here beside me on my right, and Lauretta, you stand over here on my left."

You've got to be kidding me! She's separating the two of us so she can keep her evil eyes on us at all times! What's her problem, anyway?

Miss Cline loosened her tight grip on my arm and continued to lecture:

"The trampoline is made of a special kind of elastic canvas that's practically impervious to tearing, and it's stretched tightly by the springs around the edge. You can exert the slightest amount of energy on it and get it to respond. Before you know it--even if you jump very slowly--you can start going really high.

"May I have a volunteer?"

Nearly half the class enthusiastically thrust their hands into the air.

Not me!

"Okay . . . Pamela! Pam, back up to the trampoline and hoist yourself on really carefully," said Miss Cline.

Pamela was one of those sweet, carefree, easy-going types. In addition to being a good student, she was always friendly to be around and made a favorable impression on all her peers. She also seemed to enjoy health class--which was a totally perplexing concept to me--the other subject that Miss Cline taught in addition to gym.

I was hardly surprised, therefore, when Miss Cline honored Pam with the privilege of being our official trampoline-tester. I was quite certain Miss Cline would never have chosen me had I offered.

Pam was pleased to accept Miss Cline's nomination and giggled as her gaggle of friends cheered her on. She effortlessly and enthusiastically eased herself onto the trampoline and moved as gracefully as a slinky cheetah about to make a predictable killing.

Success! She was on target!

How simple.

"Okay, now, Pam. Stand up carefully and slowly walk out to the center of the canvas, that's it . . . very slowly . . . now just stand still."

Pam stood motionless as the drill instructor had dictated. She looked quite like a Greek statue at that point--her long, golden hair gently cascading down her back, her body posed as artistically as if she'd be carved out of a block of marble.

Miss Cline momentarily caught her breath, then heaved a great sigh. "Alright. Now, Pam, very, *very* carefully, start to jump and keep your eyes here, right *here*--right on me. You've got to keep a focal point or you'll lose track of where you are on the canvas."

What a simple request!

Then, Pam began to jump and jump and jump in dainty, wee increments, all the time staring at the force between Lauretta and me . . . all the time smiling as happily as if she were Winnie the Pooh tasting honey.

"Good girl, Pam! VERY good!" Miss Cline commended.

Miss Cline was obviously pleased.

The rest of us all stood respectfully in our places, hands interlocked . . . palms sweating . . . eagerly anticipating the flights of our lives!

Then, it was Toni's turn.

Oh, it looked so easy!

In fact, Toni was so good at jumping that Miss Cline cheerfully advanced her to the next level of difficulty--kneeling on the way down, straightening her legs out on the bounce back up--back and forth, back and forth, and Miss Cline said Toni was a "real natural."

I was getting rather excited.

I could do this!

Next, it was Lauretta's turn. "Go, Lauretta, go!" the class shouted.

I couldn't believe my eyes. It was as if Lauretta had been born on a trampoline! It looked perfectly natural when she jumped--her body hardly moved, it seemed, only her feet propelled her up masterfully--and the height she achieved was astounding!

I grew suddenly intimidated. I figured the more you weighed, the higher you'd go.

Oh, brother! Maybe this'd be impossible for me, after all!

Unavoidably, it was my turn next. Miss Cline momentarily looked at her watch, wrinkled her mouth ever so slightly, then turned in my direction.

"Okay, now, Cheryl, I think we have time for one more to jump today. Are you ready?"

Oh, don't worry, Miss Cline! There's no need to check your watch! I'm gonna hop on and hop off this thing quicker than you can say Jack Robinson!

I took my place in the center of the mat.

I stood still.

I focused on Lauretta.

I started to ascend.

"Over *here*, Cheryl--look over here at ME!" commanded Miss Cline.

I looked at Miss Cline.

Miss Cline looked apprehensive.

I ascended higher, but I made certain I didn't take my eyes off my instructor.

If Lauretta can do this, so can I! I told myself.

I went higher!

"Enough, Cheryl!" Miss Cline shouted.

"That's enough, I said, Cheryl!"

But I was just getting warmed up!

Something came over me I'd never felt before. Something inside my very being rebelled and I just decided I should keep soaring. The way I looked at it, the trampoline was all mine and nobody present could stop me!

Miss Cline yelled at the top of her voice: "CHERYL, CHERYL, COME DOWN HERE THIS VERY MINUTE! DO YOU HEAR ME? STOP THAT JUMPING AND COME RIGHT DOWN THIS INSTANT!"

Suddenly, I couldn't hear a single word Miss Cline was saying. I just kept right on staring at my powerless gym teacher while soaring higher and higher like a rocket ship!

Miss Cline looked rather sickly.

"CHERYL! GET DOWN, CHERYL!" she yelled.

"WHAT? WHAT ARE YOU SAYING?" I yelled back. "I CAN'T HEAR YOU, MISS CLINE!"

The class roared with delight!

"I SAID, I CAN'T HEAR YOU MISS CLINE! SPEAK UP! SPEAK UP!"

And then, the most surprising thing occurred. The entire class--Miss Cline excluded, of course--all began to shout together in rhythm as I jumped. Every single time I'd descend and hit the canvas, they'd all chant, "BOING" in unison, then "BOING" with every successive jump!

Soon, a whole series of resounding "BOING . . . BOING . . . BOINGS" was ringing throughout the gymnasium till Miss Cline turned positively red in the face!

BOY, was she ever furious.

Uh-oh . . . I was in a heap of trouble!

I would have continued to jump (the "boings" sounded even better to me than applause), except for the fact that my heart rate was accelerating right along with the new heights I was achieving! This might be overdoing it. My body was telling me to stop.

The party was over.

Amid squeals of "DON'T STOP, CHERYL! DON'T STOP NOW!" I fell to sitting position and hurriedly scooted off the trampoline as fast as I--

Wait! Wait! Something was wrong! I WASN'T MOVING!!!

"WHERE'D SHE GO?" I heard Lauretta say.

"WHERE'S CHERYL?" another girl echoed.

"CHERYL? CHERYL?" rang out from other nearby voices.

If I hadn't been raised in a Christian environment, I'd have been tempted to utter phrases that would have made demons blush, for I was somehow anchored, swimming in mid-air--dangling helplessly *underneath* the trampoline on one of its insidious springs--caught precariously by the right cuff of my beautiful little white shorts, on that cute little cuff that had made such a fashion statement to my sainted Mother--that cuff that had made me stand out even further in gym class like a sore thumb.

How incredibly embarrassing. How perfectly awful.

Looking down at me, unable to contain her laughter, stood my "favorite" teacher.

"HELP ME, MISS CLINE! PLEASE HELP ME!" I begged. "I'M STUCK, MISS CLINE! GET ME DOWN, MISS CLINE! GET ME DOWN, NOW!"

By the time Miss Cline figured out how to unfasten me from the spring, most of the class had squatted on the floor to ogle me under the trampoline.

"She looks just like a granddaddy longlegs hangin' from his web!" I heard someone say.

"Whoa! Talk about lookin' spidery!" said another.

I was mortified.

As if I hadn't been humiliated enough, Miss Cline seized the opportunity to yank me by the hand and march me down to the principal's office. The *principal's* office, no less!

"I tell you, Mr. Lackey," she declared, "Cheryl just wouldn't pay any attention to me. I kept telling her and telling her to stop jumping and she wouldn't even acknowledge that I existed! I swear, she could have gotten herself killed!"

"Is this true, young lady?" grilled Mr. Lackey.

Obviously, it was impossible for me to deny my terrible crime of disobedience, and it was impossible for me to avoid my anticipated punishment.

So, for the next month, every single day after school, I was forced to stay over in detention and wait for my father to pick me up an hour after classes ended.

I would probably have been the laughing stock of the entire junior high except for the fact that the following day I was slated to play in the National Federation of Music Club's prestigious music contest.

I will get a superior rating.

I'll show that Sergeant Cline a thing or two. . . .

Chapter Twelve

I'd never been inside the Music Hall of Ohio University before, but the music contest was to be held exactly where my father used to tease me about attending some day. I was simply elated! Conveniently enough, Grandmother and Grandfather Rosser had recently moved from Caldwell to Athens, and they resided directly down the street from where I was scheduled to perform my contest piece, "Hungarian," by Edward MacDowell.

Mother wondered if I cared if she sat in on my performance. Actually, I thought her presence might make me feel calmer, so without hesitation I encouraged Mom to attend. She parked in her parents' driveway, then joined me about fifteen minutes before I was supposed to perform.

Mrs. Phelps, as well, decided she wanted to hear me, and I was truly delighted to see her when she entered the lobby all confident and cheery-looking.

"Cheryl, you will do just beautifully," Mrs. Phelps reassured me. She took my hands in hers, squeezed them tightly, and seemed to know exactly what to say to help pacify me.

"B-but what if I should forget?"

"Why would you forget, Cheryl? You've played your piece perfectly hundreds of times, so there's no reason you should worry about having a memory lapse. Just relax and let the notes roll off your fingers. This will be a good experience for you. You will do fine!"

As I looked around me at the entrants who were waiting to perform, I noted that many of them were pacing to and fro--some very solemn, some rather glum--all deep in thought. On the doors of several studios where adjudicators were to rate us young musicians, sheets were posted to indicate our respective names, our scheduled times, our levels, and ultimately . . . our ratings.

Guarding each doorway was a student attendant, dutifully calling whomever was up next, and most importantly, recording the ratings of those who had just finished playing. Every time a door opened, it was fascinating to see the looks on the faces of those who had just finished presenting their particular pieces. You could easily tell by their expressions whether or not they had played acceptably, and it was more than obvious when they knew they had done poorly.

I casually strode to a door to check the ratings. Gosh! The judges would be rating me before long!

Uh-oh!

I called Mrs. Phelps over to view the twenty ratings that had been previously posted in my designated performance room.

"JUST LOOK! These judges are *really* strict! There's only been one 'superior' rating so far. That's just terrible! Most of the pianists are earning 'twos' and 'threes.' One person even rated a 'four!'"

Mrs. Phelps was unmoved. "That means your judges expect a lot, Cheryl, but it doesn't mean they're impossible to please. The important thing is that the judges are being consistent with themselves. Besides, it's not important what your rating turns out to be, is it? The important thing here is that you learn something valuable from the experience!"

The door opened and musician number twenty-one rushed out, sobbing from the very depths of her being.

What a bad omen!

Mrs. Phelps just shook her head.

"Pay no attention to her, Cheryl. There's no way to know what happened in there. Just focus on your own piece and remember what I told you. Your job is just to play 'Hungarian' the way Edward MacDowell wrote it. You'll just sparkle!"

I closed my eyes tightly and thought about MacDowell. I knew very little about him, really, only that Mrs. Phelps was somehow enamored with his compositions. She and MacDowell had apparently both grown up in the New England area, although the composer had been born several years earlier than she. Mrs. Phelps thought his works were outstanding.

"Trust me on this Cheryl," she reiterated. "Just play the way I've taught you!"

"Number twenty-two!" the attendant announced.

Oh, no--that was me!

I took a deep breath and closed both eyes.

Dear Jesus, I prayed silently. *Help me get through my MacDowell acceptably, Lord. Please be with me, Father. . .* and I entered the studio.

A panel of three adjudicators was seated behind a long, narrow table, and they kept writing . . . and writing . . . and writing . . . about the pianist who had just performed.

What could possibly have required so much criticism?

I stood by the piano and waited to be acknowledged.

Their writing continued.

I thought about the incident in gym class the previous day. *What a fool I'd made of myself! How totally inept and utterly stupid I must have appeared.*

Still . . . the writing continued.

Probably no one since the invention of the trampoline had ever pulled such a boner as I . . . trying to slide off too quickly . . . getting stuck on that daggone spring . . . dangling around like an ugly spider--

"Miss Kimes . . . MISS KIMES! We are ready for you to play your piece. Are you ready to begin, Miss Kimes?" the first judge said.

I practically jumped onto the piano bench and started to play my MacDowell.

"HOLD ON, MISS KIMES! HOLD ON!"

I was already halfway through the first page, for heaven's sake! Did they want me to play or didn't they?

The same judge rapped her pencil repeatedly on the table.

I stopped playing.

"WELL, *THANK YOU*, Miss Kimes. We would like you to play a scale first--and do you think you might tell us what key 'Hungarian' is in?"

Key? Key? Key? What key did Mrs. Phelps say it was in, anyway?

"MISS KIMES, I asked you if you knew what key your piece is in."

"Well, I . . . I think it's probably in the key of A."

"You don't know *for certain*, Miss Kimes?"

I struggled for an answer.

"I . . . I believe my teacher said it was in A . . . A minor."

I looked frantically for Mrs. Phelps, but she wasn't there--neither was Mom!

"Yes, that's . . . that's it . . . A minor," I reaffirmed.

The room was incredibly quiet.

Again, I waited . . . for a few more seconds.

"May I play my piece now, Ma'am?" I asked.

The second stern-looking judge gave me a decidedly stern *look*: "Do you *not* play scales, Miss Kimes?" she asked.

OH, how I hated scales! They were a perfect waste of energy to me, and no teacher had ever insisted I pay any particular amount of attention to them. How should I answer her?

"Well . . . once in a while I *do* play a scale or two, Ma'am. Do you think they're all that important?"

A collective gasp arose from the panel!

No verbal answer returned to me.

None was needed.

"What can you tell us about Edward MacDowell, Miss Kimes. Have you ever studied his compositions before learning this piece?"

Now, this *was a question I could answer!*

"MacDowell was an American from the New England area, I was told, Ma'am." I saw a very slim trace of a feeble smile from this particular judge.

"May I play now, Ma'am?" I asked once more.

Silence was apparently just as golden as Grandmother Amy had once told me--but I felt I simply couldn't wait any longer--so I went back to the beginning and restarted my MacDowell.

"MISS KIMES!"

Oh, brother. What was it now?

"*We* will tell you when to resume, young lady! Yes, Miss Kimes, yes, your piece is in the key of A minor, and yes, Miss Kimes, scales are extreeeeeeeeeemly important!"

Well, at least I got an answer!

I should have kept my mouth shut, but I just had to know:

"Why?"

"Why *what,* Miss Kimes?"

"Why are scales all that important?"

"Important? *IMPORTANT,* you ask?"

Did my adjudicator need a hearing aid?

"Yes, Ma'am. I always thought scales were kind of like delaying the inevitable. I mean to *me*, at least, I always just thought scales were a way to put off practicing the piano and my teacher never made me play them very much so--"

The third adjudicator cleared his throat profusely, then rested his elbows on the table where he was seated, supporting his head in his cupped hands.

Since his eyes were closed, I thought he might have been praying.

"Just play your piece, now, Miss Kimes," said the first adjudicator.

Oh, really?

"Miss Kimes, please play your MacDowell," she stated.

So I did. I was certain I played it just the way Mrs. Phelps had taught me, too! I didn't miss a single note, I didn't have any memory slips, I played it super-fast, and I felt confident I would rate a "one"--a superior!

I dashed out the door and gently chastised my mother and Mrs. Phelps who had finally arrived. "Where *were* you two, anyway? I thought you were going to be in there to support me! BOY OH BOY, did I ever miss the two of you!"

Mrs. Phelps and Mom smiled in unison.

"They wouldn't let us go in with you, Cheryl," Mrs. Phelps said. "They said some judges preferred not to have any outsiders. I'm sorry, Cheryl."

"But, how did it go for you, Cheryl?" Mother asked.

"It went well, Mom, *very* well . . . when they finally let me play, that is!"

"Whatever do you mean, Cheryl?"

"Oh . . . they just kept asking me all kinds of silly questions about scales and MacDowell and--"

"Oh, look, Cheryl," Mom interrupted. "Your rating's posted already! That's a good sign isn't it, Mrs. Phelps?"

I would have loved to check my rating myself, but Mrs. Phelps beat me to it. She looked positively downtrodden when she returned.

"You got an 'excellent,' Cheryl, a score of 'two,' but . . . but that's really wonderful!" She was obviously trying to let me down easy.

Only an 'excellent'?

What a disappointment.

How could that possibly be?

"There's nothing wrong with an 'excellent,' dear," Mrs. Phelps continued. "We'll just have to wait until we get comments back next week and then go from there. I told you at the outset that the comments were the important thing--*not* the ratings."

Mom put her arms around me.

"I *know* you played well no matter what the judges said. I just *know* you did, Cheryl!"

"And judging from the other ratings I saw," Mrs. Phelps added, ". . . you must have had some really critical judges. We'll know a lot more in a few days."

I had never been so disappointed in my whole, entire life put together.

What in the world didn't the judges like about my playing? Hadn't I done my piece just the way Mrs. Phelps had taught me? If I was such an incredibly spectacular pianist, why didn't I rate a 'superior'? It just didn't make any sense . . . at all.

Mom and I walked back down the hill to my grandparents' house.

"Oh, yes, she played beautifully . . . oh, no . . . she didn't get a 'superior'. . . well, we don't know exactly what went wrong . . . but Mrs. Phelps. . . ." related Mother to her parents.

My grandparents were very understanding. Grandpa was certain there was a logical explanation for my "less than perfect" rating, and he said the Lord loved me anyway--maybe even more than He did before I got an "excellent"!

"How do you figure that, Grandpa?" I asked.

"Well, because . . . because Jesus loves us all no matter what our shortcomings are. He doesn't ever expect any of us to be perfect like He is--He loves us just the same, no matter who we are, no matter how we fail."

"But I *didn't* fail today, Grandpa! Honest! I tell you, I played my piece just exactly the way I was taught to play it! I did it as well as I could have and my teacher was very happy for me!"

"AND SO WAS I, DAD!" said Mom. "Mrs. Phelps and I weren't allowed to go in with Cheryl, but from all we heard in the hallway, she was one of the best performers there!"

My grandparents had a solution to brighten my spirits: ice cream!

No matter how I protested, my loving grandparents insisted, like Grandmother Amy often did, that a dish of ice cream would make everything all better.

Which would I prefer--vanilla or chocolate? Mint or butter-brickle? They carried on endlessly. Why was *any* discussion necessary?

They'd persist on feeding me, though, until I gave in.

"Oh, whatever," I ultimately responded.

"Don't be rude, Cheryl!" Mom said.

"No . . . really . . . whatever . . . whatever you want me to eat is fine, Grandma," I mumbled.

So for the next half hour, I listened to my mother try to defend my performance and my grandparents try to justify my rating.

Two tablespoons of vanilla ice cream were more than adequate. Eating didn't change my circumstances.

Then came the long ride home.

Then came the task of telling my father the bad news.

Then came the phone call to Uncle Frank.

And nothing--absolutely *nothing* anybody said to me--could make me feel any better about myself.

But I didn' t cry.

Chapter Thirteen

The following morning when my parents took me to church, many parishioners greeted me warmly, congratulated me enthusiastically, and pushed for every last detail of my pianistic "victory."

"How very proud we are of you, Cheryl!" Rose and Gilbert told me.

"Congratulations, Cheryl! I knew you were really good--and this surely proves it!" Juanita added.

Neva, way in her seventies, put "her two cents in," as Dad called it, with a heartfelt wink, a tear, and a fervent "PRAISE THE LORD, Cheryl! You are truly a blessing to our congregation!"

I hardly expected such a reception. Had I received a "superior" rating, my well-meaning church friends couldn't have been any happier for me than they obviously already were.

Goldie, Neva's only daughter and a close friend of Mother's, was absolutely exuberant when she saw me. "You must be very pleased with the results of your performance yesterday, my dear. The Lord has given you so, so much talent and we are all overjoyed with your success! Don't *ever* stop playing in His Name, Cheryl. He loves you so much!"

I was taken aback. How had word of my musical venture reached the church so quickly?

Uncle Frank was busying himself at the organ and sounded particularly joyful playing "Shall We Gather At The River." As soon as he saw me enter the sanctuary, however, he stopped dead in the middle of a musical passage and ran over to greet me with a hug. I was embarrassed, but I suppose I should have expected his exuberant reaction.

"Here you go, star!" Uncle Frank said as he released his grip on me and thrust the Sunday bulletin into my empty hands. "I've got to get back to the organ, but you be sure to take a look at what Goldie had to say about you and the Music Federation. Goldie really painted a glowing picture of you, Cheryl, and you certainly deserve every word she said!"

So that was it! Goldie was in charge of printing the bulletin and she took the opportunity to magnify my accomplishments to the hilt. According to Goldie, "Cheryl Kimes earned an 'excellent' rating in her first Federation competition and performed an incredibly difficult piano composition for one so young."

Her article went on to tell how "dedicated" I was to serving the Lord and to giving my talents to Him, and she also added that our church was "indeed blessed" to have me as one of their young members.

I was confused. Didn't Goldie understand that an "excellent" wasn't as good as a "superior"?

Mother took me aside and gave me some Christian advice. "Cheryl, these people are all kindly reaching out to you. Don't bring *them* down by putting *yourself* down! I know you're not happy with your contest rating, but our congregation is genuinely proud of you. Just be courteous to those who shake your hand and thank the Lord that they truly care about you. You are very lucky to get such a loving response!"

Mom was right, I suppose. It *was* my first contest. Maybe the next time I entered a competition I'd have a better understanding of what was expected of me.

Our pastor assumed his position at the pulpit and called attention to the weekly announcements as he usually did. Additionally, he emphasized that one of the youngest members of our congregation had just earned a high rating in her first musical competition.

I couldn't believe him!

Several people seated behind me leaned forward to pat me on my back, and others gave me enthusiastic nods from a couple of pews nearby.

I was thankful that I had so many friends in church, but I still felt badly that I hadn't received the best rating possible.

Following church services, my parents whisked me off to Grandma and Grandpa's for a celebratory dinner. Unfortunately, they mostly wanted to mull over the previous day's events.

Grandpa Rosser was so sweet. "I'll bet when you get your scores back tomorrow you'll find there's been a great big mistake, Cheryl. I've heard you tickle them ivories many a time, and sure as shootin' you shoulda got better than an 'excellent.'"

Grandpa was heavily into sacred music. He didn't know one thing about classical music, but he thought I was the best pianist in the State of Ohio.

"You know, Everett," Grandma added, "those judges Cheryl had mighta been plum overwhelmed after hearin' so many students before her, don't ya think? It'd be awful hard to be fair-minded if you'da heard twenty kids in a row before she took the bench, wouldn't it?"

Nice try, Grandma.

"Or . . . it coulda been they had a different notion of how her piece ought to have been played or--" she went on and on and on.

I felt like screaming at the top of my lungs!

"Now, LOOK you two, IT'S OKAY!" I said. "Any number of things can go wrong when you're in a contest like I was. It's a chance you take! The important thing is what the judges have to say on the rating sheets I'll receive at school tomorrow. It'll be fine. JUST GET OFF IT!"

Having spoken loudly enough, maybe they'd bury the subject and leave me alone, for heaven's sake!

My family, however, still seemed to want to hash and rehash my experience repeatedly. I could hardly wait to return home.

About three o'clock in the afternoon, I got a surprise call from Cousin Fred.

"Well, H-I-I-I-I there, Cous'! I hear congrats are in order, kiddo! A little birdie told me you really wowed everybody yesterday at Ohio University!"

Fred had an unmistakable chuckle that just *bubbled* from the very core of his being when he was excited. I could hear it in his voice that Sunday.

"I didn't get a 'superior' though, Fred. That's what I wanted . . . a 'superior.'"

"So, what's the big deal? Isn't an 'excellent' the next best thing?"

Didn't anybody understand how I felt?

"I really tried to play my level best, Fred. I thought I'd done all I'd been taught so I thought I deserved a better rating than I got."

"Sounds like it really *kills* you to be second place, kiddo!" Fred said.

"Do you blame me, Cousin?"

"Hummm. Doesn't seem like you have a real healthy attitude, sweets. Nobody can always be first, can they? I mean . . . seriously, now. You learn from your mistakes and you try harder the next time around, that's all. When you end up doing better 'cause you didn't give up, then *that's* a real big achievement! That way of thinking always works for me, at least!"

"Well, I'll find out more tomorrow, Fred," I replied as nicely as I could. "Thanks for calling, anyway."

I thought tomorrow would never come. When it did, I was even more nervous than I had been when I'd played my piece for the panel of judges. Our school chorus director gave me my rating sheet when I got to chorus and extended her hand in a congratulatory gesture.

I declined to shake.

"I see you had Miss Zarlotti for one of your judges, Cheryl. She's one of the stiffest adjudicators in the area, you know!"

Come on, now. Was she placating my feelings?

"Honestly, Cheryl. You should be happy that she was as complementary as she was! She said the bulk of your performance was 'fine' in her evaluation--she just thought you should have been a little more expressive in the slower parts."

I hurriedly glanced through my rating sheets. Musicians were judged in several different areas; choice of music, accuracy of notes, technique, dynamics, style, memorization, and overall presentation. If one's general performance was acceptable but not superb, overall presentation could be marked down for a multitude of reasons.

Yet, none of the judges marked me down for my presentation. What *was* wrong, then?

I read Miss Zarlotti's remarks in detail. She wrote that my playing "lacked warmth and expression." The second judge wrote, "You need to put more of your heart into the slower parts. You have much potential but you play like a robot." The third judge *really* angered me: "You haven't *lived* long enough to play with feeling. I hope to hear you again in five years or so."

All in all, I came away from reading my comment sheets feeling no wiser than before I had entered the stupid competition! I had performed precisely in the manner in which I had been taught, so I thought my low ratings were completely ungrounded.

To make matters worse, the *Athens Messenger* ran an article in the paper about the competition the following day.

Oh, goody. Now EVERYBODY would get to read all about me!

The *Messenger* said, there were *". . . one-hundred fifteen entries from the Jr. Music Clubs of Athens, Columbus, Coshocton, Delaware, Lancaster, Marion and Westerville."* Then the article went on to list the six students from Athens who had earned "unanimous ratings" plus gold pins.

"Unanimous," no less! It was apparently possible to have scored even better than just a plain ol' "superior"!

But not I.

Next, the *Messenger* listed the three musicians who had earned a "superior." Lastly, the *Messenger* listed the five of us who had received ratings of "excellent."

There I was--on the bottom of the pile.

Aunt Robbin called me at home that same night: "I read about you in the morning paper today, Cheryl, while I was enjoying my hot cup of java! I'm so happy you played so well in such a stiff competition. You must feel really encouraged!"

Was my aunt toying with me?

"You really like to play, don't you, Cheryl?"

"I suppose so."

"Well, I never played any instrument myself before," Robbin related. "I can't even sing on key, they tell me!"

So what?

"Oh . . . oh, really?" I said.

"That's what I've been told . . . repeatedly!" she laughed.

When Robbin laughed out loud, she sounded just like Fred! It was as if she held back all her inner merriment as long as she could, then when she released it, she nearly exploded with gaiety!

I saw nothing remotely humorous to discuss.

Still, she continued to go on and on. "So . . . I guess you've been playing the piano for about eight years or so, now, right?"

Play along, Cheryl, play along--

"Yes, probably so . . . I . . . I think I started in the first grade."

"First grade, huh? How come you wanted to take lessons, anyway?"

"I just wanted to."

The ball's in your court, now, Auntie.

"But, you could have played the clarinet or violin or--"

That was enough!

"Look. I really *do* love to play the piano and since my parents were nice enough to buy me one, I couldn't very well just let it sit there and collect dust, could I?"

"Well, Cheryl, all that effort seems to have paid off big-time!"

"Even though I only rated an 'excellent?'"

"Of course! Who knows why you didn't get a higher rating! Everyone who has ever heard you play thinks you're just incredible. Maybe the judges were just having a bad day!

I'm just curious, though--what do you do when you're not in school, or practicing?"

"Well, sometimes my friend, Lauretta, and I go to movies or roller skate or do stuff like that--you know--girl stuff."

Robbin understood, but she kept on badgering me.

"Yes, girl stuff is wonderful. There's nothing better than having a good friend, is there, Cheryl?"

I didn't respond to my auntie's rambling, and I think she finally got the hint. After a long, awkward interlude of silence she concluded, "Anyway, Cheryl, I'm just truly happy for your pianistic success and wanted to add my kudos!"

"Thanks, Robbin. I'm glad you called. Good-bye." I said hurriedly as I hung up on her.

I wasn't trying to be disrespectful or unkind to my aunt in any way, but I just didn't think any of my well-meaning relatives or friends understood my utter disappointment.

A hymn that I had always enjoyed singing in church began to meander through my thoughts. Its text was important to me, and I honestly tried to live its message. The hymn was called "Give Of Your Best To The Master," and the words included ". . . give of the strength of your youth . . . throw your soul's fresh glowing ardor, into the battle of truth. Jesus has set the example, dauntless was He, young and brave; give Him your ardent devotion, give Him the best that you have."

Had I given my best? *Was* Jesus satisfied with my less-than-perfect rating, or could I not have represented myself far better in His sight?

Chapter Fourteen

My return trip to Parkersburg was inevitable, and Mother said I should capitalize on the fact that we had a sunshiny day to make the drive.

We had a pleasant ride, despite the fact that I was apprehensive; wouldn't I be even homelier in braces?

When we reached Dr. Rudolph's office, I was eager to get the initial procedure started. Once seated in the orthodontist's chair, I had to bite into a form of some sort so Dr. Rudolph could make a plaster cast of my upper and lower teeth. So long as I cooperated and sat perfectly still, the rigmarole of being fitted for braces hardly seemed half as uncomfortable as I'd feared, and I was eager to depart.

What a relief!

"Will my visit with Dr. Blumfeld be this easy, Mom?" I asked.

"I hope so, Cheryl. I certainly hope so."

Mother seemed to exhibit a pretty high degree of anxiety when we checked into Dr. Blumfeld's. "I wish I didn't have to put you through this, Cheryl," she said.

"Put me through what, Mom? I just want to get this visit over with and so I can go back home and practice!"

Mom and I sat close beside each other in Dr. Blumfeld's office, and we only had to wait half-an-hour before my name was called.

"The doctor will see you now, Cheryl" sounded liked music to my ears! Dr. Blumfeld shook Mom's and my hands ever so graciously and introduced himself as cordially as Emily Post would have dictated.

"I am so happy to meet you both," he stated. "I've been going over your records for several days now, Cheryl, and right off I would say that Dr. Woodworth has done a most thorough job in evaluating you.

"Mrs. Kimes, might I offer you a cup of coffee?"

Mother declined.

"Nurse!" he summoned. "Would you get this young lady into a suitable gown and prepare her for a brief examination?"

The nurse took me to an adjoining room where I had to completely undress, then she helped me into a dreadful looking gown which opened in the back. I was totally embarrassed as I climbed onto a large, cold, metal examination table.

I wanted to go home--*badly*.

"Cheryl," my nurse said in a calm voice, "Dr. Blumfeld sees dozens of naked behinds like yours every week. Try to relax and trust him here. He's used to his job. Your sitter looks just as good as everybody else's!"

Dr. Blumfeld looked focused, but pleasant, when he entered the room.

"Okay, now, Cheryl. I promise I won't do anything to hurt you. I'm just going to press gently on your abdomen and see if I notice anything irregular."

He began to poke and prod, and I felt slightly nauseated.

"Does this make you feel uncomfortable, Cheryl?" he asked.

"N-not very--I just feel a tad sick to my stomach, sir."

"That's normal," he assured me. "Just be sure to tell me if it hurts anywhere while I'm jabbing at you."

Dr. Blumfeld was gentle and in control. At no time did I feel the slightest bit of actual pain.

"I understand you're quite a musician!" he said.

Poke . . . poke . . . poke. . . .

Now where in the world had he ever heard that?

I flinched as he repeated his statement. Then he asked, "Do you not play the piano, Cheryl?"

"Sometimes I do, sir."

Dr. Blumfeld certainly seemed to be inquisitive.

"Chopin?" he went on. "Do you like Chopin's piano works, Cheryl?"

"I . . . I don't know, sir."

Poke . . . poke . . . poke. . . .

Dr. Blumfeld stopped pushing on my abdomen momentarily and glared at me in disbelief. "Haven't you ever played any works by Frederick Chopin, Cheryl?"

"I . . . I guess I've never been exposed to his music before. What's so special about Chopin?"

Dr. Blumfeld told me to roll over.

I cooperated.

"Chopin composed a very personal, sensitive style of piano music, that's all," he answered. "My two sons studied piano before they left for college, and they both enjoyed his compositions very much. So did I."

I heard the sound of squeaking latex as my doctor reached for a tube of lubricant and prepared me for the unexpected. "I'll need to do a rectal exam on you, too, Cheryl. I promise it will be over in just a second or two."

Now *this* part of Dr. Blumfeld's examination was something I could have done without! As he'd explained, thankfully, my exam was over shortly, and he commended me for being a "brave little trooper"!

I got dressed quickly and the nurse directed me back to Dr. Blumfeld's office where Mother was waiting. The good doctor joined us almost immediately.

"Well, I certainly don't see or feel anything out of the ordinary on your daughter, Mrs. Kimes," he said. "That's a good sign, but she should really have a couple more comprehensive tests."

Mother listened to Dr. Blumfeld as though my life depended on each and every word he uttered.

"Did Dr. Woodworth ever suggest she have an Upper and Lower GI Series, ma'am?"

"Why, why no--I'm afraid I don't even know what those tests *are*, doctor," said Mom.

Dr. Blumfeld made eye contact with me again: "Cheryl, if I understand correctly . . . you have an appetite but are not able to eat very much at one sitting. You say you feel full after a very small amount of food. Is that right?"

"Yes. That's exactly right. I like the *taste* of food but I seem to fill up as soon as I begin to eat."

"I see, Cheryl. I'm sure you're telling me the way you truly feel. There could be something not quite right inside your stomach or intestines, and barium X-rays would be good diagnostic tools to use. They would let me see your gastrointestinal tract clearly."

So that's what "GI" stood for.

"W-would they hurt?" I asked.

"No, not at all. You just drink some chalky white fluid called barium and we watch it as it courses through your esophagus, stomach, and upper intestines."

"What about her lower intestinal tract, doctor?" Mom asked.

"For that, we put the barium in the *other* end!" Dr. Blumfeld said, smiling.

"That certainly doesn't sound very pleasant, doctor."

"Well, it's not what one would choose to do on a Sunday afternoon, but in case Cheryl has an obstruction or other abnormality, it should be remedied before it advances."

"*Obstruction*, doctor? Are you saying you think our daughter might have an *obstruction* in her abdomen?"

"Mrs. Kimes, all I'm saying is that the possibility for abnormality exists--or she could have some other type of eating disorder. Obviously, ma'am, *something* is keeping Cheryl from enjoying food the way most people do. If I could locate any physical problem by giving her barium X-rays, I might be able to turn her life around."

Dr. Blumfeld looked directly at me.

"What do you have to say in the matter, Cheryl?"

I've got to be perfectly honest here. I've been praying for years and years that the Lord would direct my parents and me to someone, somewhere, who would help me find a way to gain a few pounds. Might this specialist be a Godsend?

"Well . . . I . . . I think if X-rays could pinpoint my problem, I think I should be trusting enough to have them. I should be willing to go through whatever tests you think I should take, sir."

Dr. Blumfeld looked pleased.

"Thank you, Cheryl. I was hoping you'd feel that way," and he turned back to face Mom.

"Well, then, Mrs. Kimes, since your daughter obviously trusts me, may I schedule the X-rays she needs?"

"No, wait, Dr. Blumfeld," I interrupted. "I . . . I think you misunderstood me. What I was trying to say was that I trusted

Jesus in this matter, not *you,* sir! But I'm sure you'd do the best you could with Him guiding you!"

Mother turned a whiter shade of pale as she stood up immediately and whisked me to the door.

"Would you schedule those X-rays soon, doctor?" she asked.

"Of course," was the good doctor's answer, ". . . but certainly not for today." The following Friday, however, seemed to be a favorable time for proceeding with an Upper GI.

Mother gave her consent and we returned to Athens. I silently thanked Jesus that I had survived my specialist's examination, and I was relieved to go home again.

The Thursday before I was scheduled to return to Dr. Blumfeld for my barium study, I wasn't allowed to have anything to eat or drink eight hours beforehand. That was fine with me, and I followed my instructions to the letter.

The more my Mother kept making statements like "You must be getting really hungry, Cheryl," or "I'll bet you just can't wait to eat something delicious when this test is over," however, the more I wanted to cancel the entire trip!

Stop obsessing over me, Mom! I said to myself. *I'll eat whenever I'm good and ready, and I wish you'd hush up about it!*

Still, I couldn't help wondering what it might feel like to gain a few pounds and look pretty--or at least normal--like other girls in school.

Would that be too much to ask, Lord?

Chapter Fifteen

I faced Friday prayerfully, though somewhat hesitantly. Mom and I left Athens around 9:00 in the morning and we arrived in Parkersburg one hour later.

"So, what are you going to want to eat after this is all over, Cheryl?" she asked.

"You know, Mom, sometimes I think all you ever think about is eating! Why do you do that, anyway?"

"Gosh, Cheryl, I'm sorry. I didn't know I talked about it all that much. I guess it's just a natural thing for a person to enjoy eating."

"Well . . . not to *me*, it isn't!"

Mom pulled to a stop. "That, of course, is why we're here!"

But . . . where were we anyway? We certainly weren't at Dr. Blumfeld's!

Mother parked our car in a very large parking lot that was roped off into several different sections. One area said "Staff Only," another said "Physicians," another said "Doctor on Call," and another said "Patients Only."

"Gee whiz, Mom! This sure looks like a hospital parking lot to me!"

It took courage to step out of the car after Mother confirmed my suspicions.

"Why didn't you tell me we were going to a hospital, Mom?"

"Because, I didn't want you to be a worrywart like your father. He nearly had a heart attack when I told him your barium X-ray was going to be done in a hospital!"

Mother explained that the machine the technicians used for their X-rays was "state-of-the-art." She said it took a lot of space just to house the metal monster, and it was imperative for the physicians to have it at the hospital when they needed it for emergency cases.

I checked in by 10:15 and a nurse hustled me into a changing room.

"And how are we today, Cheryl?" she asked--intentionally overdoing the charm routine.

"Oh, *we* feel perfectly spectacular! That's why *we're* here!" I answered back rather sarcastically.

I was told to undress and slip into a scanty, incredibly ugly blue-and-white striped cotton robe that tied in the back. I hustled to get my change over with.

"Call me when we're ready, Cheryl!" my nurse effervesced.

"Oh, *we're* ready right now, nursey!" I exhilarated in return.

I was taken to a huge darkened room with the aforementioned machine that looked as if it came straight out of a science fiction movie.

"Will that thing slice and dice me, or just keep me levitated?" I asked.

"You sure do use big words for such a little person!"

Boy, did her remark upset me!

"I think this is called *COMMUNICATION*, ma'am!"

My nurse sat me beside the humongous metal monster and hurried out the door.

"Now you be a good little girl and wait here for the technician. This X-ray won't take long at all. Then you can run down to the cafeteria and order a nice, big breakfast!"

How wonderful. Here was another person who apparently thought one of the most pleasurable things to do in the universe was to eat. Was everybody crazy?

The chair I sat in was decidedly hard and cold as a crowbar. Try as I might, it just wasn't at all possible to get comfortable. It felt like my two sitz bones were about to protrude through the seat at any moment.

"Well, hi there, chum! My name's Mike."

Here was a person who was going to go overboard to try to make me feel special, too--but *this* person was a member of the opposite sex!

"Hi there, yourself," I reciprocated.

"Are you ready for your, ahem . . . breakfast?" Mike asked, rather jubilantly.

My technician wasn't much older than I--at least, that's the way to he appeared to me. He was actually rather cute, in a maniacal sort of way.

"Oh, sure. Bring it on!" I said.

Firstly, Mike told me I'd get something delicious to drink called barium, in case I cared to put a label on it. Secondly, Mike confirmed he was going to take X-rays of my stomach and upper digestive tract.

I saw a slight smirk.

"Actually, the two go hand in hand, Cheryl. The barium *is* your breakfast! It's flavored just like chocolate, and it's pretty good--at least to me. You *do* like chocolate, don't you?"

Oh, no! Not again!

"It sounds like *you* live to eat, too, huh?" I scoffed.

It was all so humiliating. I had practically nothing on, and I was being led around like a lamb to the slaughter by some handsome dude who felt forced to make pleasant conversation . . . to soften me up for the impending kill. Thank God my nurse had managed to tie up my gown in the back before she fled the murder scene!

"Did anyone explain how this was going to work?" Mike asked.

"Hardly. Do *you* have a clue, Mike?"

Now *that* question brought on a real guffaw!

"Hey now, chum! This is my *job.* If *I* didn't know what was going on here, we'd both be in real serious trouble, wouldn't we?"

Mike positioned me standing up in front of the metal monster. Before I knew it, I was backed right up against the beast, close and personal, and it, too, was incredibly frigid.

"Man alive!" I said. "Don't any of you guys appreciate warm temperatures around here?"

"Oh, sure we do, sunshine! But we have to work really fast and can't afford to get overheated. Comfort would slow us down. Get it?"

With that, my technician handed me a large, plastic container with what appeared to be approximately one quart of white, yep--*chalky-looking* liquid.

I had been forewarned.

"Ahhh. And this would be the barium! So how much am I supposed to chugalug?"

"Why . . . ALL of it, of course!"

Yeah, right. Tell me another one.

"Okay, now, take this straw and start sipping," said Mike. "First thing we do is take a look at your esophagus. Do you know what that is?"

"What do you think?"

Gross. My "breakfast" tasted just awful!

"If this goop is supposed to be chocolate, how come it's not brown?" I asked.

Mike's answer was logical. "Haven't you ever heard of *white* chocolate, sweetie pie?"

I swallowed once more.

"Come on, now, Cheryl. BIGGER swallow. You can do it!"

I swallowed harder.

"Think chocolate cake, Cheryl!"

More and more swallowing. . . .

Mike jerked a big metal plate over my upper torso, then hurried into a small room behind a glass window. The two of us could still make eye contact.

"GOOD JOB, CHERYL! NOW TAKE A DEEP BREATH AND HOLD IT, KIDDO! HOOOOOOOLD IT--"

CLANKETY, CLANKETY, CLANK!

It sounded like the monster was thrashing and lashing out at me as I stood frozen in time and mute as a church mouse.

Oh, what a racket it made!

"There! That wasn't so bad, was it?" asked Mike.

It was a dumb question to pose, but I just had to ask it: "Are we almost done, Mike?"

"Oh, you funny person, you!"

Next, I was positioned *atop* the monster and instructed to lie perfectly still on my back. Oh! I almost left out the best part--I had to drink another large portion of barium before I reclined.

YUCCO!

CLANKETY, CLANK, CLANK, CLANK!

"GREAT JOB, KIDDO!" Mike insisted.

"Okay. I will try to be gentle here," he continued, ". . . but I've got to start kneading your tummy like you were a big chunk of bread dough. See what I've got here in my hand?"

It was really hard to see in near-dark conditions, but it looked like Mike was holding a humongous rock--and it *felt* like it, too!

He pushed . . . pushed . . . HARD . . . HARDER . . . against my upper abdomen.

"I'M GONNA UPCHUCK!" I shouted.

"OH NO, YOU'RE NOT! TAKE ANOTHER DEEP BREATH, CHERYL!"

CLANK, CLANK, CLANK! CLANK, CLANK, CLANK! CLANK, CLANK, CLANK!

"GOOD GIRL! GOOOOD GIRL!"

"N-now . . . are we done?"

But we weren't, of course . . . not until I'd drunk all of the barium and spit up at least a third of it. Mike told me my reaction was typical.

"Okay, round one is OVER! You can relax while I check your films, Cheryl."

Mike slipped away once again and was back in less than two minutes.

"Good girl!" he said again when he returned. "We're over halfway finished and we really got some good shots! I'm going to escort you out to the patient waiting room for about an hour or so till that barium moves down into your upper intestinal tract a bit. The worst part of your test is history, kiddo!"

About a dozen patients were in the waiting room besides me. All of us were clad in the same stunning attire and most of those looking at me had forlorn expressions on their faces. One woman, possibly in her sixties, decided to strike up a conversation with me: "What're you in for, darlin'?" she asked.

"Oh, I'm just here for an Upper GI. That's all."

"I figured you were enjoying a barium cocktail like the rest of us, but . . . but what kind of symptoms are you havin', girl . . . if you don't mind me askin'?"

I really would have preferred to keep to myself, but as I looked into the talkative woman's eyes, I saw fear and frustration. Maybe responding to her would relieve her anxiety in some way.

"Oh, I just have some trouble eating, ma'am. I'm not in agony or anything like that, though. How 'bout you?"

"My doctor thinks I've got a stomach ulcer." She sounded really woebegone.

"Oh, he does? My father used to have one of those, too. It hasn't bothered him for years, though. He had to stay on a real strict diet for a time, but he's all better, now."

The woman stared ahead at the bare, gray wall in front of us and became stone-cold serious.

"Well, I'm supposed to be on a diet right now myself, but giving up my cigarettes has been much harder to do. Much . . . *MUCH* harder!"

She reached up to smooth back her salt and pepper hair and I noticed her right hand was trembling slightly.

An old man who looked like death-warmed-over joined in the banter and stared directly at me.

"You don't smoke, do ya, honey?"

Oh, brother.

"No, no. I wouldn't *touch* a cigarette. I think they're disgusting!"

The woman next to me seemed almost insulted!

"You mean to tell me you never had a cravin' for a cigarette before, hon? Come on now, girlie. I find that hard to believe!"

How could I explain it? Think hard here. . . .

"Honestly?" I began. "I've been taught that the Good Lord frowns on our doing anything to our bodies that can cause us harm. The Bible says our bodies are '. . . temples of the Holy Spirit . . .' (1 Cor. 6:19), and I don't want to do anything to displease Him--since He's dwelling inside of me."

The silence was thicker than my barium had been.

"Well, I think that's a real crock," the woman asserted.

"Are you one of them church-goin' nuts?" asked another old man across the way.

I was mortified. I had been laughed at all of my life because I was skinny, but I had never before been put down because I was a Christian--at least not to my face. What was I to say?

My parents had always told me about times when my faith would be tested.

I must be bold. I can handle this. . . .

I searched for the proper words. "Actually, I don't know what I'd do without Jesus in my life. If it weren't for Him, I probably would have given up all hope of gaining weight years ago!"

Mouths were dropping!

"You *do* look pretty puny to me," said the woman.

"In fact, you look like you could use some meat on them bones o' yours, young'un!" added the first old man.

My turn! Give me the words, Jesus!

"Oh, I well know what I look like, sir. I've been this underweight most of my life, and sometimes I get really discouraged over my appearance; yet, Mark 9:23 assures me that 'Everything is possible for one who believes,' so I intend to go right on believing!"

"And you actually accept that tommyrot?" the old man questioned.

"Why, yes . . . yes, I believe it one-hundred percent, sir, and it saddens me that you apparently don't know the Lord as I do. Have you ever even been to church yourself?"

It seemed to me like all the patients in the waiting room looked up from reading their magazines at the same time. What a time for me to witness!

"I can't say that I've ever been to no church before," the man resumed, ". . . but if'n I ever *did* go, I'd be sure to take what was preached at me with a big grain o' salt! I ain't no 'hellfire and brimstone' type," he went on. "No way! That Bible stuff just leaves me cold!"

I thought back to a time years earlier in my mother's Sunday school class when she had shown little self-conscious Timothy the way of truth and salvation. Could I muster the courage to address this non-believer, now?

"You know what else I think, sir?" I continued to expound as I looked into weary, bewildered eyes. "I think our heavenly Father loves you just as much as he loves me and the rest of the people here in this waiting room, but I think if you harden your heart much longer, you may never know the great joy and happiness you can feel through Jesus' gift of salvation!"

The old man, unable to combat the power of my deep convictions, rose slowly, shook his head in disbelief, then exited into the hall. He totally left the scene!

The woman beside me reached for my hand. I extended mine, and we shook firmly in a congratulatory manner.

"My name's Marlene," she said. "You really are somethin' else, girl! What you just did took lots of guts! That old codger was a real pain in the kiester. I don't think *I* would have had the courage to stand up to him the way you did. So . . . where do you go to church, anyway? You *do* live 'round these parts, don't you?"

"No, not really. I live back in Athens--you know, Athens, Ohio. I go to the Wesleyan Methodist Church there. It's just a little church, but we've got a real good pastor and--"

A nurse appeared at the entrance and called out to my new acquaintance.

"Marlene? Marlene, it's time for another X-ray."

"Excuse me, missy," Marlene said. "Looks like it's time to party again!"

"I'll probably be right behind you, Marlene," I replied. "Good luck, now . . . and have fun!"

Marlene parted company with me, but she left me with some very encouraging words as she disappeared: "I think maybe I'll return to church myself next week. I think it's time to get some spiritual as well as medical help. I refuse to let this cigarette habit ruin my life any longer!"

I thanked God, silently, that I had made an impact on dear Marlene, and I hoped I had reached the "old codger" to some small degree, as well.

I would never know.

Chapter Sixteen

I wasn't particularly eager to tell Mom about my experiences in radiology on the way back to Athens, but it seemed she had hundreds of questions to ask me as we drove home.

"So, was the second part of your X-rays more unpleasant than the first part, Cheryl?"

"No, not really. I was able to focus my mind on more important things than the barium."

"Did Mike keep on 'kneading' your abdomen while he took pictures of your upper intestinal tract?"

"Oh sure, but not so much as when he was concentrating on my stomach."

"Did he tell you what it looked like inside when he was working on you? I mean, did he give any clues as to what looked possibly . . . abnormal?"

I kept thinking about the old men and Marlene.

"CHERYL?" Mom shouted impatiently.

Mother insisted on asking more and more about my procedure, but I couldn't get the patients I'd met off my mind.

"CHERYL?" Mom repeated. "CHERYL! Why don't you want to talk about what happened back there?"

Mom meant well, I was just somehow . . . preoccupied.

Mom drove to a little restaurant on the outskirts of Parkersburg, pulled to a stop, then started humoring me.

"Come on, Cheryl. Let's go inside and get something super-good to eat. I promised you anything your little heart desired when your X-rays were over, you know!"

The restaurant was cold, and I felt weak and sweaty. I plopped down at the table nearest the door, and Mom sat across from me.

"There now! Isn't this a peach of a place to grab a bite or two?"

I picked up the menu and tossed it down on my seat without reading a word.

"Cheryl! What you went though back at the hospital was a physical ordeal! You need to replenish your body with nutrients and get your digestive system functioning as it should again. Come on, now! You just pick up that menu and order some decent food!"

But eating just wasn't important to me.

"Okay, okay, Mom. Or how 'bout if you order something for me. Whatever you want to choose will be just fine--anything you want me to have."

I should have realized that Mother would go overboard, but I hardly heard what she told the waitress to bring me. When the waitress returned with a giant stack of pancakes, two scrambled eggs, sausage links, fried potatoes and orange juice--all for me--I had to laugh right out loud in Mom's face.

Mom was hurt.

"Oh, Mom, I'm sorry--I'm *truly, truly* sorry, but I never expected you to order half this much food for me! And . . . and you're only having one cup of coffee, yourself?"

Mom stirred two heaping teaspoons of sugar into her coffee and clanked the spoon around endlessly in her cup.

"You know, Cheryl, I have your best interests at heart and we had an agreement; you were going to--"

"I know, I know, Mom. I promised to eat and I will do what I can. But . . . could you just back off for a few minutes?"

Mother stirred yet another teaspoon of sugar into her coffee.

Boy, was she ever getting to me!

"Are you nervous, Mom?" I asked

"I'm just anxious to get you all well, Cheryl. I've been trying to help you for years and years and--"

"Well . . . you're doing a good job of making *me* nervous! When God wants me to get better, He'll help me, Mom! I know He will!"

I discovered it was quite intolerable without any conversation, so I ultimately gave in and decided to at least tell mother about the patients I'd met in the X-ray department: "One old man just refused to listen to anything remotely religious," I said. "That really bothered me a lot. I don't know exactly what he was there for, but he became so convicted listening to me that he actually got up and *left*!"

"Are you saying what you talked about convinced him that he needed Jesus?"

"Yes . . . yes, I think it did just exactly that. He said he thought the Bible was a bunch of 'tommyrot,' and he called me a 'church-goin nut'!"

Mother put yet another teaspoon of sugar into her black brew and looked positively horrified.

"Are you *certain* he called you that, Cheryl?"

"Mom--it's okay! I've been called lots worse than a 'nut' before, you know. I just kept praying silently that Jesus would give me the right words to witness with and I'm certain He did just that!"

NOW, I had mother's attention. She finally stopped stirring her coffee and put her spoon down.

"I'm really proud of you, Cheryl," she said. "Maybe the good Lord planted you there by those needy souls expressly so you could show them 'the way'!"

"You mean as in '. . . the way, and the truth, and the life,' (John 14:6) don't you, Mom?"

"Of course! You *are* very well-read in the Bible, aren't you?"

"I had a good teacher, Mom. You got me started, you know!"

Mother called the waitress over and asked for a chocolate donut.

"Get real here, Mom--I can't stuff down another bite! If I *could*, believe me I wouldn't want anything remotely chocolate after this morning's experience!"

But no, the donut was clearly for Mom.

"Oh, excuse me, Mom!" I laughed apologetically.

"So, go on, daughter. What else happened in radiology?"

I told my mother all about Marlene and her obvious addiction to cigarettes: "She really seemed like a nice person, too. I thought it was a real shame that she was ill. She said her doctors thought she might have an ulcer or something."

Mother momentarily had a far away look in her eyes. "Do remember your father used to have an ulcer too, Cheryl? Did you tell her about that?"

"Why yes, I did, Mom, and by the time I left, Marlene had pretty much decided to go back to church again--regardless of her health."

"Are you telling me that your conversation with Marlene influenced her enough to return to church?"

"That's what she said, Mother--and she actually seemed sincere about returning. I could tell."

"Your father will be really happy that you were able to spread the Word to those people today, Cheryl. Did you know he has witnessed many times to the people he works with?"

"Is witnessing easy for him, Mom?"

"Golly, no, Cheryl! Your father's always been--how do I say this--rather *solitary*, if you understand my meaning."

I forced down two bites of dry pancakes.

"You mean, he's a 'loner,' don't you?"

"Exactly. That's exactly what Ronald is, but he sets a good example for his coworkers--he doesn't swear, doesn't smoke, doesn't drink, doesn't carouse--he's really a different man from the man I met when we first started dating. You know, I never would have married him if he hadn't accepted Christ as his personal savior, don't you? He was actually pretty wild, years ago!"

"My dad was wild, Mom? I can hardly imagine him being that way."

"Then, you'll never believe this, but he sped around all over the country on his Indian Scout motorcycle and got into all sorts of trouble!"

"My dad? My dad was a biker?"

"Yes, but he never belonged to a gang, or anything like that! The important thing is that Ronald got convicted somewhere along the way and wound up at the altar where he gave his life to Christ. He was *truly* a changed man after his conversion in church and settled down. He's been a calm, devout Christian ever since!"

I swallowed two sips of orange juice and one chunk of potatoes. I loved my father very much and could hardly imagine he had experienced such a personality change when he was saved.

"Why does Dad he always seem so . . . so serious Mom?"

"Oh? Do you find him serious, Cheryl?"

"Well, sure I do. I'm not saying he's not a good father or anything like that, but he sure never acts very exhuberant . . . well, like Uncle Frank does, for instance."

"Frank's lots of fun, isn't he?"

"He sure is, Mom--and he likes the same type of music that I like, too!"

"Do you think that makes him a better person than your dad?"

"Of course not, Mother! It just means Frank and I have more in common, that's all."

"Well, your uncle certainly does love you, Cheryl, but he doesn't love you any more than your father. Don't you ever forget that!"

I pushed my plate away. She was correct, of course.

"Was Uncle Frank saved too, Mom?"

"He was, for a fact! I don't know all the particulars, but Sybil never would have married Frank either, unless he'd converted to Christianity."

Mother drained the rest of her coffee and stared silently at my plate of breakfast rejects.

"You're not going to eat any more, are you?" she asked.

"Do you want me to regurgitate on the table?"

Mom motioned to the waitress.

"May we have our check, please?" she requested.

"Well, you sure can, lady, but. . . ."

The waitress turned pertly to address me. "Was there something wrong with the food I served you, dear?"

I searched and searched for an acceptable answer to give our waitress, but I simply couldn't come up with an appropriate remark.

"No, no, of course, not, Ma'am!" Mother said as she answered the waitress for me. "Your food was just fine, I assure you! My daughter just had a procedure done at the hospital and--"

I felt a keen desire to exit. "I'll just dash out to the car, Mom. You can doggy-bag that stuff if you want, I guess."

Mother took her time returning to the car to join me. She was obviously upset as she scooted onto her seat.

"Don't you think you were rather impolite back there, daughter?" she began. "I mean, the waitress acted pretty insulted when you didn't say anything remotely complimentary about the food. The least you could have said was--"

"Where *is* my food, anyway?"

"It's still right where it was, Cheryl."

"Why didn't you bring the leftovers with you, Mom?"

"Why bother? You wouldn't have eaten them at home, either. Would you?"

Mother was correct, of course.

"Thanks for buying my breakfast anyway, Mom. It's not your fault I can't finish my food, you know."

I successfully stifled the urge to discuss the guilt I felt over having wasted my mother's hard-earned cash as we drove back to Athens. Thankfully, it seemed like time passed quickly until we pulled into our driveway.

My father acted perfectly elated to see us when Mom sounded the horn, and he greeted us at the front door with open arms.

"Well, Cheryl, tell me all about your trip to the big city!"

"Oh . . . it wasn't half as bad as I'd expected, Dad. Everything went quite well, I think."

Mother hugged my father, saying, "Cheryl did just fine, Ron. We won't know anything definite until Dr. Blumfeld calls back, but she tolerated the barium well enough."

Dad pulled out two chairs at the dining room table and motioned for me to sit down right then. "You sit, too, Clis. I want to hear every last detail!"

Mother appeared to have boundless energy as she explained to the best of her ability what my X-rays had been like.

"Cheryl," he said, "You must be just itchin' to find out what those X-rays show. I 'spect our prayers are gonna be answered soon, now. Don't you?"

I was too tired to say *anything.*

My father looked perplexedly at Mom and scratched his head.

"Oh, Ron," Mom said, "Cheryl's okay. It was just a very exhausting day for her."

I couldn't stop thinking about Marlene and the old men in radiology. I turned to Mother: "They're not going to make it, are they, Mom?"

"What's she talking about, Clis?" Dad asked.

"I think your father would be interested in hearing about those two patients you witnessed to on your trip, Cheryl," Mom suggested.

"Cheryl? Did you get to tell somebody about the Lord today?" Dad persisted. "I'd love to hear about that, too!"

"O-okay, Dad. One of them was a really old man who could hardly stand hearing the Word. He became so troubled that he walked out on me while I was testifying. That was hard for me to take."

"But you took the time to tell him about Christ before he left?"

"Of course--to the best of my ability. I told him about the way I kept on praying that I would get well, and he said all that Bible stuff was just a bunch of 'tommyrot'."

"*Tommyrot*? He called the Holy Word *tommyrot*?"

My father took the old man's reaction almost personally--almost as much as if *he* had been having the conversation with the nonbeliever instead of me.

"And there was this nice lady, too, Dad--her name was Marlene--and she seemed to have a real addiction to cigarettes. She looked very unhealthy. I felt terribly sorry for her. She had dark circles under her eyes and her hands shook and--"

"And you decided to testify to Marlene, too?"

"Oh, sure. I told her about our bodies being 'temples of the Holy Spirit' and that we are supposed to keep ourselves 'pure' for Him if we want Him to be pleased."

My father looked decidedly pleased.

"Sounds like did all you could do in the amount of time you had, Cheryl. It's not possible for us to convert others to Christ, anyway. Did you know that?"

"What in the world are you saying, Dad? I thought spreading the Word was our mission as Christians. Didn't I do what I was supposed to do today when I told those people about my Jesus?"

"Oh my, YES, you did just super, and you'll prob'ly be rewarded some day . . . but we can't save anybody by *ourselves*, Cheryl. What we *are* commanded to do is to *present* the Word--then the spirit of Christ, Himself, will jump in and take over from there."

"So, how can we know if we make an impact then, Dad?"

"That's a hard one to answer, Cheryl. You just have to learn how to eyeball people carefully and watch how they react. Sounds like that ol' guy who left the room was sure gettin' your message, though. Sounds like he was so uncomfortable that he could hardly stand himself. Now, it's up to him to accept or reject the Son of God."

"What about Marlene, Dad?"

"You really took a shine to her, didn't you, Cheryl?"

"Yes . . . and she actually told me she was going to return to church again."

"She *DID*?"

"Yes, Marlene told me she was going to go back to try to get the spiritual strength she needed to overcome her cigarette habit."

Dad seemed overjoyed!

"Well, there's your answer, Cheryl! You cared enough about Marlene to point her in the right direction and now you gotta have faith that Jesus will do His part! You're a good egg, daughter!"

My father was usually a man of few words, but on that Friday, he had tons to say and I saw him as being totally committed to Jesus.

He rose from the table, walked over to the refrigerator and opened the door.

"Here ya go, Cheryl," he said. "I saved a nice big piece of apple pie just for you!" and he sat my dessert down in front of me.

I thanked Dad, but declined.

Mother had tears welling up in her eyes.

"Now, Clis, don't you fret none! I saved a piece for you, too," he said, as he put Mom's pie gingerly down in front of her, as well.

She left the table.

"Now, why in the tarnation did she get up and go, Cheryl? Did I say somethin' wrong, or what?"

I stood up and tenderly embraced my father.

Dad hugged me back.

What difference did it make if Dad didn't appreciate my classical piano music, anyway? My father loved me deeply and I was lucky to have such a fine Christian example to follow.

"Mom's just fine, Dad," I told him. "You made perfect sense out of an otherwise stressful day, and mother just feels wrung out like I do. She'll be all better tomorrow, Dad," I assured him as I sauntered off to my bedroom.

"BUT WHAT ABOUT YOUR APPLE. . . ?"

Chapter Seventeen

Monday came. There was no message from Dr. Blumfeld. Tuesday and Wednesday—still no Dr. Blumfeld.

Thursday morning, mother anxiously phoned Dr. Woodworth, and I talked her into letting me skip school. I put my ear next to Mom's ear close to the receiver so I could hear the doctor's words firsthand: "Mrs. Kimes," Dr. Woodworth related, ". . . I was just about ready to call you. Dr. Blumfeld's report is here on my desk, and you'll be happy to learn that the barium studies showed nothing remotely abnormal in Cheryl's stomach or upper intestinal tract. He wants her to have a Lower GI, though, as soon as possible, and I agree. Would you like me to set that test up for your daughter next Friday?"

Mother hung up the receiver without giving Dr. Woodworth a definite answer. I followed her to the sofa and the two of us started to explore the possibility of another X-ray in the hospital for me.

"So . . . what flavor would *this* barium be?" I asked. "Oh, wait. I guess flavor wouldn't be much of a consideration in this test, would it, Mother?"

Mom grinned. "Hardly, Cheryl," she said.

"And I'm supposed to just casually submit to this procedure, too?"

"Well, Cheryl, Dr. Blumfeld is doing his level best to uncover whatever malady you may have. Since Dr. Woodworth respects this internist, do you think you should back down, now?"

I could just imagine how embarrassing it would be to have some stranger filling my posterior with barium.

Mother appeared to choose her words carefully as she delivered her pitch as calmly as she could.

"Why don't you look at it like this, Cheryl. Dr. Blumfeld relies on barium studies to diagnose serious ailments, and I'm sure he orders these exams several times a week for many of his patients. If *I* had to give a barium enema to anybody, it'd no doubt be very disturbing to me, but to a trained technician doing the X-ray it would seem quite routine."

"But my body is *my* body! It's private and personal and I'd be mortified to have any person do such a thing to me--even though it *is* his job!"

Mother seemed to understand my apprehension.

"Have you been praying about these tests, Cheryl?"

"Of course, Mom! Every single night!"

"Then, continue to pray. Jesus hears all our prayers . . . about everything! Ask Him to guide you in making your decision about having a Lower GI."

"You're not going to force me into this, are you?"

"No, Cheryl. I really believe you *should* have the test, but it's your decision. I know I could probably make you take it because you're my daughter, but I'd rather you come to the place where you truly feel God is directing you."

I walked outside for about two hours that afternoon . . . walked and thought. I sought a nice, secluded wooded area directly behind our house with a huge moss-blanketed boulder sheltered by trees. I climbed up on top of the boulder and lay flat on my boney back.

I am a chicken, I said to myself. *Deep down inside of me beats the heart of a chicken . . . a puny, disgusting, worthless, pathetic chicken that doesn't have sense enough to run when she's about to get her head chopped off.*

I pictured Grandma Norma back on the farm chasing a desperate hen, feathers flying furiously, trying in vain to escape its inevitable fate--Grandma wielding a hatchet in one hand and a skillet in the other. What a comical sight I imagined!

"CHERYL! CHERYL!" Mom yelled. "CHERYL, ARE YOU OUTSIDE, SOMEWHERE?"

"I'M FINE, MOM! JUST LEAVE ME ALONE A LITTLE LONGER. OKAY?"

Shoot, life would be lots easier if I'd been born a chicken. I'll bet I would be more observant than the average fowl. I would see my fate coming. I would be able to outrun my pursuer. I could change my destiny.

A tiny bird lit in a dogwood tree just a few feet away and twittered merrily. At the same time, I noticed a subtle movement in the weeds below her, and I suspected a snake might be preparing to claim its next victim.

I was right! As the grass parted underneath the unaware songster, a long, shiny blacksnake stealthily advanced towards the young fledgling. It was easy to predict the likely outcome of the unfolding drama!

I'd always been fascinated by snakes. They were despised by most Christians I knew and were terrifying to Mother and Aunt Sybil--but not to me. After all, God had created reptiles just like He'd created all creatures, and the way they slithered and twisted around was incredible to watch. They had to eat, too, didn't they?

I should have been immediately vocal. I should have shooed the unsuspecting bird away at that very moment!

At the same time that I was reflecting on the bird's plight, however, I was distracted by music coming from our television room. There, as my father was absorbed in watching the Billy Graham Crusade, George Beverly Shea was singing one of Dad's favorite hymns, "His Eye is on the Sparrow." I could hear each word distinctly: "I sing because I'm happy, I sing because I'm free. His eye is on the sparrow, and I know He watches me!"

What was I thinking! I should help that little songster survive! He wanted to live!

Quick as a wink, I yelled "FLY AWAY! FLY AWAY!" as loudly as I could, and just as quickly, the fledgling took flight! The blacksnake--no longer engaged in the hunt--never had a chance to strike. He could find another meal without much trouble.

Example noted, Lord! Thank you, I prayed. *Thank you for helping me save that little fledgling*--as the snake crawled off for another potential ambush.

I hurried inside to tell Mother I'd made my decision about the proposed barium study, and I told her about the drama that had just unfolded for what I believed was my benefit.

"I guess you identified with the birdie, didn't you, Cheryl!"

"Yes, I did, Mom--but you know the funny thing about all this? Suddenly I don't even know why I was fearful of a Lower GI in the first place! I know God wants to help me, just like I wanted to help that fledgling."

My father was moved when I told him my about my experience. He opened our Bible to Matthew 6:26 and handed it to me. I read aloud: "'Look at the birds of the air; they do not sow or reap or store away in barns, and yet your heavenly Father feeds them. Are you not much more valuable than they?'"

My father cleared his throat and told me to skip down to Matthew 6:34. "Well, go on, now, Cheryl. You're comin' to the best part!"

I continued reading aloud and wondered what lesson my father was trying to teach me:

"'Therefore do not worry about tomorrow, for tomorrow will worry about itself. Each day has enough trouble of its own.'"

No further conversation was necessary.

The next few days passed slowly. I got to the place where I was actually looking forward to have the barium X-ray so my life could return to some semblance of predictability--if not normalcy. Mother, who had been eager to take me back to the hospital in Parkersburg herself, however, was disappointed; her boss apparently needed her at the bank to finish a presentation for a board meeting on the same day I was scheduled for my Lower GI.

My father consoled her. "Just don't give my takin' Cheryl to the hospital a second thought, Clis. I don't get to spend near as much time with my little girl as I'd like, so takin' her to the hospital myself would sorta be a blessin' in disguise. Just let it be, Clis."

"But you're not a *mother,* Ron. You can't comfort her like a mother can. She may need lots of TLC when her X-ray is over. *I* should be there for her, Ron!"

My father stood his ground. "I love our little Cheryl ever bit as much as you do, Clis, but I insist you stay in Athens and look after your job. My daughter and I will do just dandy in that big ol' hospital! We'll have a good time together. I'm sure of it!"

Thursday night, I had no dinner--just a castor oil cocktail. Then, Friday morning as anticipated, my Dad and I drove off so I could have my lower bowel X-rayed.

I felt incredibly weak and could hardly keep my eyes open as we drove away. My mouth felt dry as parchment.

"Why don't you make up a story for me, Dad?" I asked while riding. My father had always been able to tell the most delightful tales to lull me to sleep when I was a youngster, and I'd savored that time with him.

"Can't do that very well and navigate at the same time, Cheryl," he said.

"Do you know any good jokes, then?"

"No, not right off . . . but I *do* know a few lines of poetry. Wanna hear 'em?"

I couldn't imagine my father reciting poetry. He piqued my curiosity, though, so, unfortunately, I gave in.

"Okay, good!" he said. "Here are a couple of my favorites, Cheryl: 'The wind blew harder, the weather grew colder, and Crusoe came home with a hare on his shoulder. Where did Robinson Crusoe go with Friday on Saturday night?' Get it, Cheryl? Get it? Pretty good, huh?"

Was he serious?

"Or, how 'bout a shorter one: 'He sat on a boxcar and his feet drug on the ground.' Longfellow. LONG-fellow. Whatcha think, Cheryl?"

Now that *was funny!*

I started to laugh, but suddenly I could feel huge knots wadding up in my stomach like steel baseballs.

This is probably what Dr. Blumfeld called 'peristalsis,' I reasoned. *It will pass.*

But it didn't.

"Pull over, Dad!" I hollered. "Pull over, quickly! I'm going to barf!"

My father signaled and hustled the car off the road as I tried to avoid regurgitating. My eyes teared and mucus shot out of my nose, but I was determined not to vomit for the life of me--and I *didn't!*

I was downright miserable.

My stomach ached.

Dad gently stroked the back of my head as I tried repeatedly not to upchuck.

"Looks like you got one bad case of the dry heaves," he said.

Then he bowed his head, and I knew he was silently praying.

"You're just nervous and hungry," Dad stated, when he looked up to reassure me. "Everything's gonna be fine soon, Cheryl. I know it is! Take in a few deep breaths and let's get on the road again. God's not gonna let you down on this day if I have anything to do with it!"

As we headed on to the hospital, I felt my abdomen relax since my father had prayed.

"Your prayers really pack quite a wallop, Dad! How'd you ever learn to pray that way?"

I think my father was embarrassed.

"Pray w-what way?"

"Well . . . *earnestly,* I guess, like you really mean what you're praying about and expect Him to answer you, Dad."

"Oh, I firmly feel God hears us when we're sincere, Cheryl. The trick is to truly *believe* He's tuned in to us when we're in prayer. There's a verse in Mark--Mark 11:24, I think--where Jesus says '. . . whatever you ask for in prayer, believe that you have received it, and it will be yours.'"

"How in the world do you remember all those important verses in the Bible, Dad? It's so hard for me to remember them most of the time, but you seem to know so many by heart!"

"How is a person supposed to witness to others if he don't know the Good Book inside and out, Cheryl? How can a person live a Christian life if he hasn't taken the time to memorize them verses, so they'll be there when he needs 'em?"

I was cramping up again.

"PERISTALSIS, DAD! PULL OVER!"

"No, Cheryl . . . I-I'm sorry, but I've got to keep on drivin' or we'll be late. You just think about our loving Savior and focus on how well you're gonna feel when your docs finally figure out what your problem is! You just concentrate on relaxin' and let Jesus take over your fears. You're gonna be fine, Cheryl. I promise you!"

Dad told me to open my car window and let the breeze blow on my face. The fresh air seemed to ease my nausea.

"*That's* the idea, Cheryl! We're almost there, now! Have faith!"

Within fifteen minutes, we pulled into the hospital parking lot where Mother and I had been a week earlier. Dad ran around to my side of the car and opened my door with a forceful yank.

"Well, just look at you, Cheryl! You did it! You made it!"

Confidently, the two of us walked into the radiology department. I thought about the three patients I had met in the same room the previous week, but they were absent this Friday. It was just my father and me.

Dad checked me in with the receptionist on duty. "My daughter isn't feelin' so good," he stated. "Is this barium test gonna take very long?"

The receptionist shook her head and told him to have a seat and make himself comfortable.

I was zipped into X-ray.

My technician, Mike, remembered me from the previous week.

"You look a little peaked today, Cheryl! Do you feel thirsty?" he asked.

For some reason I wanted to give a smart answer, but I just didn't have the energy to be on the defensive.

"I'm fine. I'm just fine, Mike. *Really*, I am."

Then . . . all was a bit blurry. I vaguely recall changing into another *beautiful* hospital gown like I had worn before and being placed atop the same noisy machine as before. I also recall being told to turn onto my left side and feeling extremely cold. A nurse assured me I'd "feel like myself again" when I got some fluids to drink.

Quite quickly, my Lower GI was all over, and I thanked God. My father put his arms around me when I returned to him and gave me a cup of hot tea from a vending machine.

"That technician of yours told me you're pretty dehydrated, Cheryl. What say we blow this joint and get some more liquids down you. Okay, daughter?"

We headed back to Athens. Dad bought me a grape soda on the way home plus a large cup of black coffee a few miles further down the road. I didn't particularly like coffee, but I drank every drop and asked for more. Then, I drifted off to sleep despite the caffeine.

"All will be well in God's time, Cheryl," was the last thing I heard my father say . . . and I believed it would be . . . sooner or later.

Chapter Eighteen

The results of my Lower GI Series came as no surprise: my intestinal tract looked perfectly normal.

I had no disease to treat.

I would continue to resemble a bag of bones.

The skinner I grew, the more friends I seemed to lose. I joined a couple of social organizations in the hopes of fitting in better with other girls in junior high, but not even Rainbow Girls--which Grandmother Amy suggested--made me feel as if I "belonged" the way my classmates seemed to.

Besides, I sensed I was being used by these clubs. No matter what other good qualities I knew I had, it seemed like the only thing most of the girls wanted me there for was to play the piano. So, in Girl Scouts I performed whenever our troop leader needed music for special occasions, and in Rainbow Girls I played the processional and recessional for every meeting.

Most people appreciated my talent, but did anyone appreciate the real me . . . *inside*?

By the middle of the eighth grade, I found riding the bus home to be intolerable. My father--clearly able to see how miserable I was--came directly to the point one snowy December day after I deboarded: "Are they makin' fun of you on the bus, again, Cheryl?"

"Of course, Dad. It's always the same ol' story."

"You know, Cheryl, if you'd be willin' to wait about half an hour after school for me, I could swing around when I'm done at work and pick you up on my way home. Would you like me to do that for a spell?"

What a break!

"Oh, would I ever, Dad! Could we start tomorrow?" And for the remainder of the eighth grade, my father was kind enough to drive me home after my classes.

Often, I had to wait outside the principal's office for my father to arrive. Talk about boredom! I began doodling on notebook paper to kill time. I sketched everything within eyeshot from wastebaskets to coats on coat racks, to overshoes, to lunch boxes, to the janitor sweeping the hall--whatever was available to me, I sketched. Duplicating my surroundings was surprisingly simple, I found, and happily filled up much of my spare time while I waited.

Why, drawing was practically as easy as playing the piano!

When the second semester started, I had become enthusiastic enough about drawing to take art class as an elective. I gathered up several pencil drawings I'd made while waiting for my father to show my prospective art teacher, Ethel Woolf.

"Did you really draw these pictures yourself, Cheryl?" Miss Woolf asked.

"Oh, sure, Miss Woolf. It was lots of fun."

"Well, you surely did a fine job, Cheryl. I think you'd be a definite asset in our art class."

Finally I found a class in school that I could look forward to attending in addition to chorus, but after only a couple of months, even Miss Woolf felt compelled to put me down and draw attention to my skeletal build.

Art Class with students Charles Douglas (far left), Rene Kirchner, Cheryl, Ethel Woolf (instructor), Susan Brophy, Carl Misner, and Lois Simpkins, circa 1957
Courtesy Athens Messenger

Miss Woolf had been showing our class how to add depth to objects we sketched on paper by using a simple technique called shading. On this particular occasion, she called all of us over to the window, pulled me close to her, then unexpectedly hoisted my arm into the air. The sunlight cast a predictably brilliant glow onto the side of my arm where it shone, and Miss Woolf held onto my arm like a referee announcing the winner in a boxing match.

I hardly felt like a winner at the time.

“Cheryl’s arm represents a pole, class!” she said cheerfully. “Note how the front side of the pole is brighter than the back side? See how the opposite side of the pole is much darker?

That contrast is what you need to show in your drawings. That contrast is what we call 'shading'."

I tried to pull away, but Miss Woolf held tightly. "Just remember Cheryl's pole-like arm as an example of shading, and illustrate your drawings like this to show contour!"

Mom or Dad would have undoubtedly confronted Miss Woolf had I told them about her inconsiderateness, but what good would it have done? She had decided to criticize me in her own special way like many others, and I was used to it--but I lost respect for my teacher that day, and I never regained it.

About three months into the semester, Miss Woolf announced a National Scholastic Art Awards Contest conducted by *Scholastic Magazines.* Any of us artists who entered the contest and won first place would receive a gold key and be honored in a special ceremony later on. To Miss Woolf, this competition was a bona fide big deal.

During this particular April, our art class had begun to study textile design, and we were learning how to print fabric in a variety of unique ways. We were all supposed to use a process known as "tie-dye," and the resultant artistic possibilities were endless.

Mostly, my classmates wrapped different objects in white cotton material, tied their bundles with string, then soaked them in dye until the desired hue was reached. When the strings were removed, *voila!* Everywhere the strings had been and the folds were tightest, the material stayed white; everywhere else, the dye penetrated. There was always a certain element of unpredictability in the outcome, making the process very exciting . . . at least in my opinion.

I struggled on my own at home to come up with a unique artistic statement and looked through several nature magazines to find ideas. I searched and searched for something unusual to imitate, and I found it: spider webs! Why God had ever created spiders had always been a mystery to me. Spiders were creepy and tortuous, and my classmates in gym had once likened me to the scary critters. Yet, spiders' web-spinning masterpieces were fascinating! In the summers I spent many hours just watching them (though never too closely) as they spun their intricate patterns and repeated their symmetry of design. . . .

Could I mimic their webs? Would it be possible to fold a piece of fabric into sections first, then dye it in such a way as to get web-like results?

I spent one entire Saturday afternoon at home using Rit dye on Dad's old white handkerchiefs. I made an absolute mess in our kitchen, but I ended up with very promising results.

My father was miffed. "You say you think you've got a good thing goin' here, huh, Cheryl?"

"Well, just look, Ron!" Mom interrupted. "Does the design on this hanky look like a spider web, or doesn't it?"

Mom could see it!

"But do you think this would work on a bigger scale, Mom?" I asked. "Do you think I could pull this off in art class and make a decent showing . . . or not?"

"I'll just betcha you could do it, Cheryl!" Dad interrupted. "Nothin' ventured, nothin' gained, right?"

So, off I trekked to art class with materials in hand--a four by four foot piece of cotton fabric I cut from a bed sheet and several strings long enough to wrap around my proposed tie-dye creation. Miss Woolf would supply the dye and a large vat.

Once in art class, I had the rapt attention of every single student trying to anticipate exactly what I was going to do next.

I lay the cotton square on a large table and smoothed out the wrinkles from the center to the edges; then I folded the square in half, then I folded it into quarters, and then diagonally for as many times as possible till I ended up with a thick triangular bundle. Next, I tied several strings around the triangle as tightly as I could. After I had finished tying the material, I emptied the recommended amount of turquoise dye into a large container of water and carefully stirred the liquid. Lastly, I introduced the prepared cloth.

What a transformation!

Almost immediately, the turquoise dye permeated the material, then I let the color deepen for about fifteen minutes.

SUCCESS! You should have seen the results when I untied the strings. "It looks just like a huge spider web!" I heard one classmate say.

"No, not to me . . . it looks like it represents a series of sound waves!" said another student.

"Anyone can see it shows ripples on the water!" voiced another artist.

Miss Woolf, amazingly enough, commended me: "Yes, Cheryl, your abstract design is truly, truly beautiful--*whatever* it represents. What do you think, class? Do you think Cheryl should enter her textile in the Scholastic Awards contest? Do you think she might win a gold key?"

By unanimous vote, all the art students shouted a resounding "YES!"

Miss Woolf helped me fill out a form the next day to resister me for the contest, and within two weeks she heard back from the judges in Cincinnati. I ACTUALLY WON "FIRST PLACE" IN TEXTILE DESIGN!

Three other artists at AHS also rated a "first," but I was the only person in junior high who did so. Incredible as it seemed, there were over three thousand artistic entries from our entire region, and yet I won the highest award given in my classification!

THREE THOUSAND ENTRIES! WOW! THANK YOU, FATHER!

Mr. Lackey, our principal, headed to art class as soon as he heard the good news and shook my hand vigorously.

"Athens High School is extremely proud of you, Miss Kimes," he said. "We're going to have an assembly in a couple of days and I'll present you with your gold key at that time along with the awards to the other three girls who placed."

"You mean in front of the whole, entire school? I wouldn't have to make a big speech or say anything, would I, Mr. Lackey? I'm not very good at talking in front of an audience. That would really frighten me, sir!"

"You won't have to say a word, Miss Kimes. Just come up on stage when I call your name, accept your award, then hurry back to your seat. There's absolutely nothing to worry about. It'll just take a second, dear."

My principal looked down at the floor and shook his head. "Playing the piano in front of everybody at school like you do seems like a far bigger source of anxiety to me, Cheryl, and you always breeze right through performing!"

Still, I remembered a time in church when I had slipped on my way up to the piano. I had looked so foolish. Could the same thing happen to me again--in front of all my peers?

The day of the assembly arrived. My parents assured me that the student body would be proud of my accomplishments and added that it was an honor to call attention to my success in the assembly.

"Please be with me today when I accept my award," I asked my heavenly Father before I went to school, "and thank you for giving me Your help along the way . . . a-and thank you for creating spiders."

My father took me to school as usual, and I grew anxious as the awards assembly drew closer. Lunchtime was impossible to cope with. How could anybody be expected to have any appetite under such stress?

I forfeited lunch.

I've got to remain calm. I am making a mountain out of a molehill. I'll just dash up to the podium and dash back to my seat. It will soon be over.

Hundreds of students filled the auditorium. I never realized there were so many students in junior and senior high.

How in the world can I make an entrance up there without having a heart attack or. . . .

I sat motionless in the auditorium while my classmates fidgeted.

"What's your problem, Cheryl?" my friend, Lauretta, whispered.

My heart was racing. "Nothing. Nothing at all," I whispered back.

"Do you think you're going to get an award today, maybe?" Lauretta probed. "You seem awfully uptight to me, Cheryl!"

I had told few of my classmates about my artistic achievement. How I hated attention! I preferred to just meld into my surroundings.

I could hardly wait to see what my gold key looked like, though. . . .

Mr. Lackey walked on stage, approached the podium, and reached his arms out over the student body like Moses parting the Red Sea. He waved his arms up and down.

"QUIET, NOW, EVERYBODY!" he yelled.

The din continued.

"I SAID BE QUIET, PEOPLE! I HAVE IMPORTANT ANNOUNCEMENTS TO MAKE!"

He had what . . . what? I couldn't really concentrate on what our principal was attempting to say. I just wanted to get my award and--

I felt a sharp elbow jab me in my right side.

Lauretta? Lauretta? What are you poking me for, girl?

Lauretta looked at me with wide eyes and a quizzical expression.

The kids in front of me turned in my direction and stared.

"CHERYL KIMES?" Mr. Lackey yelled. "CHERYL KIMES? ARE YOU NOT IN ATTENDANCE, MISS KIMES?"

Again, Lauretta shoved her elbow in my side, harder!

"Cheryl!" she exclaimed! "Mr. Lackey called you to go on stage! Didn't you hear him, Cheryl?"

Oh, no. OHHHH, no! I wanted to go home.

"Go accept your award, Cheryl!" one of the students close to me said.

"Go on, Cheryl! Mr. Lackey won't wait much longer!" said another.

Gold key. Gold key. I have to go on stage to get my gold key. Move, feet, move!

I stood erect, took a big breath, and made my way to the end of the row.

A few students started to clap.

I kept forcing myself. *MOVE feet! COME ON, legs! HELP ME, LORD!*

I kept making headway toward the principal. I kept focusing my eyes directly on him.

"Hey, skinny!" I heard in the distance.

Just what I was afraid of.

"Hey, bird legs! Whatcha gonna get? A worm?" rang out from the center of the student body.

Amidst a flurry of activity in the same section, a teacher dragged a couple verbal hooligans out of the audience. Areas of out and out laughter echoed from one side of the auditorium to the other. More teachers jerked others out of their seats and herded them into the hall.

FINALLY! I stood at the platform and faced Mr. Lackey. A few more students in the audience clapped, reservedly. Again, the principal "calmed the sea."

Mr. Lackey called four other students to stand next to me; two juniors who had won a *Key 1,* plus a sophomore who had received a *Key 2*, and another junior who had received a *Key 3.*

I didn't hear the slightest commotion when any of these recipients came onto the stage. The student body seemed silently respectful and eager to commend them for their accomplishments after they made their grand entrances.

But as for me? Why was I treated so unkindly?

Mr. Lackey made a grandiose speech attesting to the merits of our teacher, Miss Woolf, and he said the five of us winners deserved to be praised for our respective artistic abilities.

He also noted that it was extremely unusual for an eighth grader--*me*--to have won first place when the competition was so keen.

I was genuinely embarrassed.

Then, one by one, each of us winners received a large Certificate of Merit plus our individual gold keys.

Mr. Lackey allowed much applause from the student body.

Great. Just great. Now, let's get this over with!

I hurried back to my seat to avoid hearing more snickering.

I showed Lauretta my key. "Neato!" she said.

And it was . . . wasn't it?

The following Tuesday, a large article appeared in the *Athens Messenger: Students Win Coveted Awards in Annual Scholastic Awards Contest,* it read. A fine synopsis followed about the contest plus a nice group photograph to boot. Miss Woolf stated in the article, "I'm very pleased that our Athens school system, which is very small compared with many, should make such an excellent showing."

We had competed against students from much larger schools, including those in Cincinnati, Dayton, and Chillicothe, Ohio, as well as Covington, Kentucky.

Hooray for our side.

Chapter Nineteen

After receiving my award in art, I was asked to design program covers for our P.T.A. meetings as well as for our school paper, *The Megaphone.* Students and faculty alike seemed to appreciate my art work, though no amount of complimentary remarks mattered much to me. I was a talented-enough artist, but playing the piano was much more satisfying; whenever I played the piano, the literature seemed to transport me away from any personal ridicule, and I could flee to a private inner place where no derision or rejection existed.

Several piano and violin teachers in the area belonged to two different music clubs, the Junior Music Club and the Athens Woman's Music Club. Mrs. Phelps belonged to both, and she encouraged me to participate in them. Recitals were held after church on Sundays in several local churches and private homes, and performing would be "excellent exposure" for me--from Mrs. Phelps' standpoint.

How could I disappoint Mrs. Phelps?

I started performing in both music clubs on a regular basis, and I was *always* placed last in their programs, showing that I was considered the best . . . except for this *one* time.

His name was Jerry--my only real competition to date. Jerry was a slight person, a couple of years older than I, and he exuded a certain dynamic flair when he played the piano. Admittedly, I found him to be rather spectacular at first, but now that I give it more thought, it was probably his *choice* of dramatic compositions that made him seem so razzley-dazzley.

Whatever it was that made him outstanding, Jerry just galled me to death when he overshadowed me in that unforgettable Sunday recital at the Presbyterian Church.

It wasn't enough that he had chosen to play "Prelude in D*b*" by Chopin (I recalled how Dr. Blumfeld had insisted that Chopin was a brilliant composer), but Jerry had to set the piece up by first describing in *glorious* detail how Chopin had written the impressive composition to emulate rain. Often, Jerry said, the rain would be "soft and gentle," but frequently, it would be just the opposite, ". . . a veritable thunderstorm descending from the heavens with gusto and fury, ever relentless. . . ." Jerry just went on and on about it before he *finally* performed the blasted thing.

I listened intently while my competitor played the work that truly cemented my desire to pursue piano forever. Jerry was right; it *was* positively uncanny how easily a listener could hear the continuing onslaught of rainfall--the perpetual pattern of raindrops that never let up until the storm was over.

I was quick to shake Jerry's hand when he had finished playing. "I really enjoyed your performance of the Chopin, Jerry!" I said.

"And I truly enjoyed your Schumann as well, ah . . . ah . . . 'Cheryl' . . . isn't it?"

The two of us exchanged amenities for about fifteen seconds until I was pushed to the side by several of Jerry's doting fan club.

I understood my place.

Mrs. Phelps and I left.

As fate would have it, the very same Chopin "Prelude" appeared in a movie on television the following weekend while my parents and I were at Uncle Frank and Aunt Sybil's.

After a thankfully light dinner following our evening church service, I headed straight for their TV room. A 1945 movie called *A Song to Remember*--the life story of Frederick Chopin--was showing on television. The movie starred Cornell Wilde, a handsome young actor who played the role of the prodigious Frederic Chopin, a pianist struggling with tuberculosis . . . a pianist who composed some of the most emotional music I had ever heard for piano to that time.

I was simply spellbound.

At one romantic point in the movie (while Chopin and his lady friend were enjoying an afternoon together on the Isle of Majorca), there echoed the very same "Prelude" that Jerry had performed the week before. This time, instead of being played on a piano, however, the raindrop melody was performed by a symphony orchestra.

Immediately, I wanted to master the piece myself--as soon as possible!

I could hardly wait to ask Mrs. Phelps if she would allow me to learn the Chopin.

"You know, Cheryl," she responded with cool reserve after I voiced my request, ". . . Chopin wrote other 'Preludes' and 'Mazurkas' that might be more on your level before you try the raindrop composition, but most certainly we can find some appropriate Chopin for you if we look around."

"But . . . but I'm *absolutely sure* I can play his 'D*b* Prelude' if I practice, Mrs. Phelps. Could I just begin it, at least, and see how it goes after a week or so?"

I had already made up my mind to play what I had chosen. Mrs. Phelps could see that I was dead set in meeting my objective, so she offered little more resistance. Instead, she opened her piano bench and pulled out an old tattered copy of a large collection of Chopin's works called *Chopin Favorites for the Dedicated Pianist.* She handed it to me and I eagerly glanced through the table of contents. There were not only "Preludes," but many other works by Chopin plus a concerto movement and . . . and . . . what *was* a concerto, anyway?

"You've never heard of a concerto before, Cheryl?" Mrs. Phelps asked. They're just wonderful compositions featuring a soloist--perhaps, a pianist--plus an orchestra playing at the same time. Almost all major composers wrote a piano concerto or two, even Beethoven did. In fact, Beethoven wrote five piano concerti and they're all just fantastic pieces!"

"Could I learn a concerto then, Mrs. Phelps?"

"Now, now, let's take it one step at a time, Cheryl. Why don't you start with the 'Prelude' you said you wanted to learn, and then we'll see how it goes at your next lesson?"

I could hardly wait to start learning the piece that had so appealed to me. Every day for the following week, I occupied the piano bench at home for hours at a time and probably came close to driving my parents mad while doing so! Whenever I could, I'd practice Chopin--not only the "Raindrop Prelude," but his other "Preludes" as well--and I sightread two "Nocturnes" and toiled with an "Etude."

When my next piano lesson came around, I was more than adequately prepared to play Chopin's "Raindrop Prelude" . . . *without* the music!

Mrs. Phelps was impressed.

Was there a greater piano composer than Chopin?

Not to me!

By the beginning of the ninth grade, I had become quite proficient at the piano. I usually detested every single day spent at school, but my love of classical piano literature managed to distract me from the name-calling that continued to permeate my existence. "Bones" . . . "Skinny" . . . " Bird Legs" . . . were the most customary nicknames several of my classmates called me, and it seemed I heard those horrific handles nearly every time I turned around.

Yet, I knew I had another name as well; it was "Child of God," and in me, my heavenly Father somehow saw potential, and yes, perhaps . . . perhaps . . . even beauty.

It was deeply hurtful to be laughed at by my peers, but I felt secure in my faith, and I felt secure in the talents I knew the Good Lord had given me.

Jesus was my friend.

At the end of ninth grade, on June 2nd, 1959, I was promoted to Senior High, and the *Athens Messenger* told how I had "presided at the piano" for the graduation ceremony.

Presided at the piano! That phrase made me feel so special! I'd played "Marche Militaire" by Chopin for my class' processional and recessional, and I'd also performed another piano solo by Chopin, his "Revolutionary Etude, Op. 10, No. 12."

Neither Mrs. Phelps nor Uncle Frank ever hinted that particular "Etude" might be far beyond my capabilities, so I believed I could conquer the piece from the very start, and I did exactly that!

After the promotion exercises, several people shook my hand and told me that I'd made one incredibly powerful pianistic statement despite my being so tiny. But after all, Chopin, as well, was frail and underweight. He and I *did* have that much in common!

I couldn't have been remotely successful, of course, without Jesus. I visualized Him during every note I played . . . sitting right there beside me . . . right there on that very same piano bench during my performance . . . all the time I was playing.

Upon entering high school, I took a growth spurt. Even though I was barely able to eat enough to sustain my weight, I grew several inches taller . . . then taller . . . then taller . . . and I kept on reaching upwards till I actually loomed a couple inches above Cousin Fred.

I was five-foot-nine and one-half inches tall.

I weighed eight-nine pounds.

About the time I was ready to try my hand at another Federation Music Contest, Fred invited me out to White's Mill for an "important announcement," as he called it. Would I care to accept his invitation?

Silly question!

Fred hadn't been driving very long when he picked me up at my front door, and he drove up in Robbin's brand new, bright red Thunderbird. When I opened the door to greet him, there he was--in military clothes! WOW! He looked just magnificent, I thought--much like the picture I'd seen of his father in the Marines.

"Gosh, Fred! Are you going off to war, or something?" I asked.

"That's what I wanted to tell you about, sunshine! Well . . . are you comin' or not, sugar?"

Fred proved to be a great driver. He handled Robbin's car with skill and ease, negotiating curves like a NASCAR professional on a jam-packed track.

"Where'd you ever learn to drive with such finesse, Cousin?" I asked him as he alternated hand over hand for a suave left turn.

"I mean," I continued, ". . . you're . . . you're so smooth and all! I tell you, you're just a natural behind that wheel! I'm really amazed!"

And I *was* . . . but I was also confused.

"What *are* you dressed like that for, Fred? What's going on here?"

When we arrived at White's Mill, Fred parked the T-Bird close to the entrance of the old historic mill-turned-restaurant and politely came around the car to open my door for me. He wasn't my date, of course, but he treated me like a princess for some reason. What in the world. . . ?

Once inside White's Mill, Fred ordered an alcoholic beverage.

"Want a near-beer?" he asked, winking.

"Of course not, Fred. You *know* I don't believe in drinking!"

"Well . . . I know you seem to enjoy barium, so I just thought. . . ."

I stared at my cousin and simultaneously raised my right eyebrow.

"Cool it, Cheryl! Cool it!" he reiterated, as he ordered a soft drink for me instead.

The aroma of freshly ground corn and other grains filled the atmosphere. Crushed peanut hulls covered the floor where patrons had trampled them under foot. The place certainly had a casual atmosphere.

"It's kinda nifty here, isn't it, Cous?" asked Fred.

I agreed.

The two of us could clearly see the bridge my Grandfather Earl had built from our window seats. I pointed to it, admiringly.

"Earl was responsible for that right over there, Fred," I gestured.

"Earl? Earl . . . *who*?"

"My Grandfather Earl, of course!"

"Your grandfather built bridges, sugar? Are you kidding me?"

I nodded confirmation.

"Well, I never knew that, Cheryl. I guess there's a bunch I don't know about you and your Dad's side of the family!"

Making conversation was usually extremely easy for my cousin, and he was often quite jovial, yet I could tell Fred was preoccupied with something personal that afternoon.

We talked a bit about my upcoming piano contest. Fred encouraged me to "give it my best shot" and aim for a "superior" again.

He ordered another drink while I took a swallow of my pop. As usual, he could get away with nearly anything.

"That stuff'll destroy your liver, ya know, Fred," I said. "It's only a matter of time."

"Lay off. Okay, Cous?"

I could hear the mill wheel as the water continually drove the round structure, and the splashing became increasingly annoying.

"Well, Cheryl. You had enough?" he asked.

I screwed my face up and cocked my head to the left.

Was he kidding me?

"W-well, no . . . hardly! Why did you bring me here, anyway?"

Fred rose and started to pull me and my chair out.

"Let's go, chum!"

"I'M NOT BUDGING, Fred!"

I held onto the table legs with both hands and gritted my teeth.

"GET IT?" I said.

Fred sat back down.

"What's wrong with this picture, Fred?" I asked. "You brought me here all dressed up like a soldier . . . and you went on and on about making an important announcement about something or other--then you just totally finked out! I'm prepared to sit here till the cows come home if you don't fess up. Well?"

Fred ordered another drink.

I succeeded in shaming him. He sent his drink back and decided to get down to the matter at hand.

"Okay, okay," he said. "I'm leaving, sugar. My sainted mother is sending me away to 'school' as she likes to call it."

That statement sure got my undivided attention!

"What? Why in God's holy name would she do a thing like that, Fred?"

"Because . . . oh, you know, Cheryl. My father was a Marine and all--it's kinda like she wants to carry on the family tradition through me, I guess."

The smile on my cousin's face told me he was unquestionably proud of his father and his intentness told me he wasn't kidding about the subject.

"Where, Fred," I asked. "Where are you headed, Fred?"

Fred cleared his throat.

"Culver," he said, matter-of-factly.

"Culver? Where . . . where *is* Culver, anyway? I never heard of it before."

Fred sat erect in his seat. "You . . . you never heard of Culver, sweets? Honestly? Well, Culver's a military academy that's supposed to make a *man* out of you. It's in Indiana--Culver,

Indiana--and it's right by a big, scenic lake called Lake Maxinkuckee."

"Lake *Whats-in-kuckee*?"

"Lake Maxinkuckee . . . Max-in-kuc-kee . . . and they say it's really beautiful there."

No trace of a smile returned.

"When are you leaving? How . . . how long will you be gone?"

"I'm going in a week, and I'll be gone . . . don't know for sure . . . several months, perhaps . . . I guess. But I'll get to ride horses and stuff like that. That'll be one good thing about the place, I suppose."

In an instant, I could imagine what life would be like without Fred to lean on. What a letdown.

"We better go, now." Fred concluded, and before I knew it, he was pulling me and my chair out from the table, again.

Somehow, for some reason, I felt like I'd never see Fred much after that evening. Was this his final "good-bye"?

"But . . . but Fred, what if I have an important question to ask you, or need to. . . ."

"Didn't you ever hear of 'taking leave,' sweets? I'll be back now and then just to check up on you. How's that sound? Well?"

I sniffed back the tears. "Do you promise, Fred? Do you really think you will return . . . someday?"

"You have my word, Cheryl. Yes, of course! You can count on me!"

Cousin Fred and Cheryl, 1960
Ronald Kimes, Photographer

Chapter Twenty

Life was never quite the same after Cousin Fred left for Culver. My father was quick to assure me that God would send another friend to fill Fred's shoes, however, so I busied myself at the piano, trying my best to rate a "superior" in my third Federation competition.

I still got an "excellent" on piano, though, and Mrs. Phelps was at a loss for words.

Fred would have known what to say.

I became a member of CMC Society, a social sorority, and Tri-Hi-Y Christian Fellowship. Mother said the more clubs I belonged to, the better it would look on my record for entrance into college so I joined--but mostly to please Mom. I also joined Future Homemakers of America, because my mother thought it would be "the thing to do."

I entered a teenage dressmaking contest sponsored by the Singer Sewing Machine Company and won second place. First place would have felt much better to me. Fred could have buoyed my spirits.

I competed in an American Legion Contest and wrote an essay about the United States Constitution and won an award.

Oh, goody. Another accolade.

I accompanied musicals and continued to play for AHS choruses and ensembles throughout high school, but no matter how much I performed I never felt quite as secure as I had when Fred was around.

I gave the National Federation of Music Clubs competition one final shot when I was a sophomore, but try as I might, I *still* couldn't achieve a "superior" rating.

But hey . . . I had another award to decorate my bedroom wall.

Eleventh grade . . . twelfth grade . . . graduation was upon me and Principal Burke asked if I would care to play a solo for our graduation ceremony, on June 8th.

Oh, sure . . . why not?

Mrs. Phelps was positively joyous that I had been asked to perform a solo for graduation. I had heard a spectacular piece by Rachmaninoff called "Polka de W. R." (a polka written on a theme his father, W. R., had composed)--an arduous composition requiring incredible strength and technical prowess. It'd be a great change from my Chopin infatuation. Would she agree to teach it to me?

I bought a copy of "Polka" and took to Mrs. Phelps so she could see it.

"Cheryl, Cheryl," she said. "I have great faith in you as a pianist, but this piece . . . this particular piece is incredibly daunting. Are you *sure* you want to tackle this particular one? Once you start it, you won't have time to turn back, and there are only two months left until you graduate. Do you realize how hard you'll have to practice, dear?"

Once again, I assured Mrs. Phelps that I was strong enough physically to succeed in conquering Rachmaninoff's masterpiece, so she reluctantly gave me a "thumbs up."

My parents doubted my ability, too, when they heard my first feeble attempts to practice "Polka," but I refused to throw in the towel! "Polka" was by far the most difficult piano piece I had ever heard, and I wanted to prove to myself that I could master it. On days when my practicing seemed to yield little progress, I'd repeat Philippians 4:13 over and over: "I can do all this through Him who gives me strength. I can do all this through Him who gives me strength. I can do. . . ."

I knew, deep in my heart, that Jesus knew no limitations.

The closer I got to graduation, however, the more I could feel my heart racing whenever I practiced. In truth, playing the Rachmaninoff almost wore me out, though I tried to hide that fact from my parents.

It must be my nerves. My heart must be acting up because I'm nervous about my approaching performance. I must have more faith.

Sometimes, I felt as though my pulse was going to pound an exit through my temples. One evening, I took my pulse because I felt particularly exhausted following a practice session. While watching the second hand on my alarm clock, I counted my heart beats at over one hundred eighty per minute.

Admittedly, I was alarmed.

The following day after school, my father picked me up as usual. "How's that Rachmaninoff progressin', Cheryl?" he asked while driving me home.

"Oh, it's coming along just fine, Dad."

"Sounds awful hard to me, daughter."

"It is . . . a . . . a *little*. The thing is, Dad, I'm just crazy about 'Polka.' It appeals to me more than any piano composition I've ever heard before in my life."

"That's not he first time I've heard you say that about a piano piece, Cheryl!"

"I suppose that's true, Dad, but I just can't perform something, well . . . if I'm not *wild* about it at the time. It just doesn't work for me to start a piece if I don't think it's the most incredible piano piece I've heard up to that time. I *know* I can do the Rachmaninoff. I'm ninety-five percent certain I can, at least!"

Yet, I had an difficult time focusing on Rachmaninoff's "Polka" for the next four weeks. How I wanted to talk to Fred for that extra little five percent boost of confidence that I needed! Of course . . . Fred was gone.

Then, one afternoon, Mom got a phone call from Robbin that somehow jarred me back to reality: "I understand your cousin's doing very well at Culver and is really committed, Cheryl," Mom said. "Robbin told me he's joined a group of cadets there called the 'Black Horse Troop,' where he gets to ride saddle horses and is reponsible for their tack and grooming --well, you remember how he always loved to ride, don't you?"

"He *did*?"

"Sure! He used to go down to Macafee's stable on Route 50 and ride whenever he had spare time. He was really good with horses and treated them with respect. Sounds like he's pretty committed, now, doesn't it?"

I needed to apply myself! I needed to force myself to live up to my obligations or suffer the consequences of an ill-prepared performance. Did I want to let my graduating class down?

"Shape up, kiddo!" Fred would say. "PULL YOURSELF TOGETHER AND DO YOUR JOB! YOU'VE STILL GOT TIME! YOU *WILL* SUCCEED! I'M ABSOLUTELY CERTAIN YOU WILL, COUS!"

I continued to toil over the Rachmaninoff intensely for the next several days, much to the disgruntlement of my mother as I often skipped dinner. Periodically, while I was seated on the piano bench, my father would pat me on the back as he dashed down the hall for one thing or another. I knew I had his support as well as Mom's, and by the time graduation came around, boy, oh boy, was I ever ready to perform!

Graduation night proved very emotional for me. I had played Elgar's *Pomp and Circumstance* on the piano for several other graduation ceremonies at Athens High, but *this* time *Pomp and Circumstance* was played *for me* and the rest of our Class of '62.

It was time for change.

A large chunk of my life was over.

Our speaker, Jesse Stuart, poet laureate of Kentucky, told us that we graduates were about to enter a competitive world and that we should act without fear as we faced our individual tomorrows. I listened intently and took his words to heart as I tried to ignore the butterflies in my stomach.

When our distinguished speaker had finished, three other classmates performed solos on trombone, trumpet, and violin, ending with the fourth performer--me on piano.

I played "Polka" well enough, I thought, and nobody shouted "WAY TO GO, SKINNY," or "ATTA GIRL, BONES," or "YOU SHOW 'EM, BIRD LEGS". . . then I took my bow.

Cheryl after high school graduation piano solo, 1962
Humphrey's Studio

Of course, I didn't have a date for the dance that night. Nope. I'm certain I was the only senior who didn't attend the celebration, in fact, but then . . . did my absence matter in the total scheme of things? Did it matter that I wasn't part of the jubilation and festivities on THE MOST IMPORTANT NIGHT OF MY LIFE?

I stayed up late after returning home and played "Polka" two more times in succession—just because I *could.* Summer would be here soon and something exciting would surely happen to compensate for my feeling like a complete social misfit.

Yet, summer proved pathetically pointless, and I couldn't have been more eager to enter college than I was by September.

Mother and I went shopping together just before freshman orientation, and she was nice enough to buy three new blouses for me to wear for my first week at Ohio University. I was tempted to let her cut my hair as well, but my father thought I looked more feminine with long hair—"more feminine like God had intended"—he said, so I adorned my ears with big, shiny earrings and hoped they would call attention away from my hollow cheeks. All in all, when I left for orientation I felt as secure as I probably could have despite the fact that I was so grossly underweight.

"Well, li'l froshie, how did orientation go?" my parents asked when I returned after my first day at O.U.

"Oh," I shrugged, ". . . everything went just fine, I think. I definitely know what classes I'll be taking now, and I'm quite certain college is going to be a piece of cake!"

One thing *did* concern me, though, and that was my Rachmaninoff piece. I knew I hadn't practiced "Polka" nearly enough over the summer to bring it back to the secure state it had been when I graduated, but I felt reasonably certain it would still be acceptable. Still, I had to audition for a piano professor at the School of Music—

"Are you going to try out for that new professor from Juilliard?" my parents questioned. "We hear he graduated at the top of his class!"

"Of course, I am! His name is George Katz and if he says he doesn't want to teach me, I'll just go to one of the other piano profs instead. Everything will all work out swell one way or the other. I'm sure Jesus will help my audition go beautifully."

It was Thursday around 11:00 in the morning when I went to the music building and rapped on Prof. Katz' studio door. I could hear him practicing fast and furiously as I knocked, and I'd never before heard such difficult piano literature *anywhere.*

I was understandably overwhelmed.

How in the world could I expect him to agree to teach someone on my level, as prodigious as he obviously was? So much for this idea!

I turned around and started to leave when the Prof. Katz' door swung abruptly open with an enthusiastic "Well, come in, there! COME IN, I said! ARE YOU WAITING FOR AN ENGRAVED INVITATION?"

There he was--larger than life--wearing khaki trousers and a short sleeved undershirt with deep rings of perspiration soaking through the fabric.

He wiped his brow fervently with a large handkerchief.

"Well . . . WELL?" he bellowed. "Do you have a NAME?"

I introduced myself and told Prof. Katz the obvious: I was a freshman who wanted to major in applied piano and study with . . . with HIM!

"Yes, yes, YES--go on and play something for me, then. ANY thing! What's it going to be? Well? WELL, NOW? What did you bring for me to hear, Cheryl? Let's get on with it!"

Prof Katz' degree of excitability made me feel exceedingly nervous. I had never been around anybody nearly as energetic as he.

After I told him I intended to play the Rachmaninoff, Prof. Katz hurried across his studio and anchored himself in a chair. He leaned forward like a puma ready to pounce at my slightest mistake. My heart surely must have been beating up to two hundred beats per minute!

Slow me down, Lord! I prayed silently. *Lord Jesus, please slow me down!*

No sooner than I started the piece, however, Prof. Katz bounced to his feet!

"Cheryl . . . CHERYL! You've never played on this grand piano before, HAVE YOU?"

I stared straight ahead and made no reply.

"Don't you want to warm up on a couple of scales to get the feel of the action before you proceed any further?"

HA! NOT THIS TECHNIQUE ROUTINE, AGAIN! WAS HE KIDDING?

"I'm . . . I'm actually ready to start right now, sir! I'm sure I'll get the hang of the keyboard after just a few measures."

Prof. Katz sat down again, and I started . . . once more. I played approximately one and one-half pages of "Polka" before he stopped me again.

Uh-oh. I must have sounded terrible!

"FINE! FINE! OKAY, CHERYL!" and he was on his feet, again.

"You need me. I think I can help you. That's enough playing!"

Did I need . . . help?

"You mean, you're . . . you're accepting . . . *me*?"

And he did! Prof. Katz started teaching me the following Monday--weekly hour lessons--and I was never so disappointed in my life. Oh, he was a *marvelous* instructor, and I felt he might have the potential to make me a somewhat better pianist than I already was--but the piano literature he assigned me was nothing at all like Chopin's music or Rachmaninoff's.

Instead, Prof. Katz gave me, of all things, an easy piece by Mozart! Prof. Katz actually had the audacity to tell me to learn the first movement of what appeared to be a simple Mozart Sonata plus an equally easy Bach Invention—*the first one in the book no less*--before my next lesson. Why, I could have played either of those two pieces when I was in grade school!

What was he thinking, anyway? I'd hoped for way more challenging music, more on the order of the "Polka" I had just performed--or rather, had *begun* to perform for him. I had to bite my tongue.

"I'll bet you don't even know what a piano phrase is, do you, Cheryl? he asked.

I pointed to one.

"So?" he said. "Exactly how are you supposed to *show* a phrase, then?"

"What do you mean? All the notes belong together and are played smoothly like . . . like one complete thought or sentence!"

Absolutely. I was certain that was an accurate response!

"Good, very good, Cheryl. But again, how, *precisely*, do you show a phrase? HERE! LET ME DEMONSTRATE!"

Prof. Katz clapped his hands together twice and motioned for me to vacate the bench immediately.

Then, the esteemed professor performed the first page of the Mozart he had assigned me, but the piece didn't sound at all like I expected. He was falling and lifting his hands gracefully, and his expression was simply . . . it was simply . . . well . . . I guess it must have been the *correct* way to play Mozart!

I was astounded by his sensitive touch.

"We have lots of work to do here, Cheryl. DO YOU THINK YOU CAN TAKE IT?"

"Well, well . . . sure, but I was hoping for harder music and--"

"Don't you know you have to CRAWL before you can WALK? WELL?"

I left Prof. Katz' studio feeling exactly like my father would have described—"lower than a snake's belly." Could I ever, *ever* please George Katz?

At my next lesson, Prof. Katz instructed me to buy two rubber exercisers for my hands and squeeze them several times a day, as hard as I could, without fail.

"You've got to build up your weak muscles so you can play MUCH more intensely!" he insisted. "Power at the keyboard comes from many parts of your body--your back, your shoulders, your arms--but your fingers need to be much stronger, too!"

So, I did what he asked. I went to a local sports store and bought special hand exercisers and used them religiously without fail, day after day after day. I practiced my assigned pieces along with a host of other technical studies, too, until I started to sound a bit more powerful than the frail young woman I was.

I did my best to please Prof. Katz.

At the end of the first semester, I had to perform my piano jury exam which involved playing for the entire piano faculty of Ohio University. My Mozart and Bach were memorized and my fingers were no doubt stronger--but would I play adequately? If I didn't please the faculty, I'd have to change my major!

First, I was asked to play a couple of scales, which I did, grudgingly.

"Don't you practice scales and arpeggios every day to warm up?" Dr. Jennings questioned.

I was honest. "No, truthfully, not really. But I *do* enjoy playing exercises by Isidore Philipp and Hanon . . . if that counts."

"So, George," said Dr. Longstreet, ". . . is there some reason scales are not being stressed here?"

"All in due time, Bill," Prof. Katz responded. "Cheryl's got phenomenal fingers and innate musical talent, but apparently none of her former teachers had the temerity to insist that she incorporate scales into her daily practice regimen."

"Well, I know you're going to teach her to phrase well, George, but--"

Prof. Longstreet looked most alarmed. It was the familiar look I had observed years earlier from other hard-nosed adjudicators!

"Scales will come, Bill." said Prof. Katz. "Scales will come!"

The following week Prof. Katz informed me that I had earned a "B" in my jury.

"Gosh! That's just awful!"

"Well . . . you know what to do to make a more favorable impression next time, don't you, Cheryl?"

So, little by little, or should I say *very* little by *very* little, I tried to force myself to learn a few major and minor scales and arpeggios, but deep down inside I continued to see them as a total waste of my valuable time.

Scales were for incompetents--not me!

I made the Dean's List the first semester, and my parents were proud of me.

I made the Dean's List the second semester, too, and I continued to practice piano in the manner which seemed to keep Prof. Katz cordial--though without scales. Consequently, I still received a "B" in my second semester jury.

Summertime was a welcome change and a chance to enjoy a break from college. Oh, Prof. Katz did give me a Beethoven Concerto to take a look at, but it was monstrous in length, and I intended to lounge around in my backyard for three months.

"Browse through this in your leisure before fall, Cheryl," he advised.

"But it's so . . . so *thick,* sir!"

"What do you EXPECT? IT'S A CONCERTO!"

I took the foreboding piano work home and shelved it in the back of my bedroom closet. Occasionally, I'd dig it out and finger through its forty-two pages, but I never played it conscientiously. I had once told Mrs. Phelps I was eager to learn a concerto, but--

You've got to be kidding.

Give me a break!

It's summer!

Chapter Twenty-One

My parents and I went to Lake Hope several times in June, and I made every attempt to foster a hearty tan. By the first of July, my skin tone had deepened considerably, and in gaining more color I appeared to be somewhat healthier--at least in my parents' opinion.

My annual visit with Dr. Woodworth, however, showed that my weight gain was still not keeping up proportionately with my height.

What else was new?

Dr. Woodworth, rather reluctantly, suggested, "You know, Cheryl, there's a wonderful gastroenterologist at Ohio State University Hospital in Columbus who has a marvelous reputation as a diagnostician. I'd be happy to arrange an appointment for you, if you'd like."

I had heard this spiel before. Was he serious?

Mother seemed almost insulted when she heard Dr. Woodworth's advice and projected negative feelings about his suggestion. "I really don't see the point, doctor," she responded.

I, apparently like my mother, had no desire whatsoever to experience another Dr. Blumfeld encounter.

"No . . . no, doctor," I replied to Dr. Woodworth, myself. "I'd rather not. I'm having a nice summer and I'd hate to ruin it with a bunch of medical tests and hypothetical speculations. If you could maybe prescribe something for my cramping, though, I'd appreciate it."

It was as though I had tossed a live grenade at my physician. He sprang to attention!

"CRAMPING? WHAT cramping, Cheryl?" he asked.

"Why . . . why the cramping I get when I eat, sometimes."

"You never told me about this before, Cheryl. Just how often do these cramps occur?"

"How often? Oh . . . oh, just now and then, a few bites after I start to eat and. . . ."

"Why haven't you mentioned this to me either, Cheryl?" Mother cut in.

"What could you have done, Mom? When it happens, I just stop eating for a bit till the cramps leave. Just forget I said anything. It's no big deal."

Dr. Woodworth leaned forward, rested his elbows on his desk and cupped his weathered face in his caring hands. "This puts a whole new light on your situation, Cheryl," he said. "Having *any* degree of cramping while you're eating isn't normal. Cramps just aren't normal . . . *at all*!"

So, I gave in. I agreed, at that very moment, to let Dr. Woodworth arrange an appointment for me to see Dr. Floyd Beman at Ohio State University. I would get my visit out of the way before fall and hopefully enjoy my second year studying piano at Ohio University all the more.

My parents took me to Ohio State University Hospital in three weeks.

"This campus sure is a whole lot bigger than ours in Athens, Clis," Dad noted. "Looks like they have a thriving university here. Did you ever see so many students in your life?"

"It's a Big Ten college, Ron," Mom told him. "The medical school here is a huge teaching school, too. They train interns to be some of the most respected physicians in the Untied States."

Oh, really? I was rather impressed.

My father parked our car as close as we could get to University Hospital, and the three of us walked in together to see Dr. Beman. Hordes of young men in white uniforms rushed everywhere--serious-faced souls, all obviously concentrating on their business at hand. Several spoke to us as we stepped onto the elevator.

"Are all these people interns, Mom?" I asked.

"Apparently so, Cheryl. They look very focused, don't they?"

We had to take the elevator up eight floors to get to Dr. Beman's office. When we arrived, he was waiting for us outside his door in a starched white medical uniform with a scowl of sorts on his face. He was portly--even heavier than Uncle Frank--and he projected an air of intensity and authority when he looked our way. Also, much to my chagrin, Dr. Beman had a mild cough that struck me as being nothing less than a smoker's hack!

Dr. Beman extended his right hand to shake my father's, then he shook mother's hand in the same manner, then lastly, mine.

"I'm Dr. Beman," he said, ". . . and you obviously must be Cheryl. You'd better get all your paper work done right away so I can have plenty of time to grill you, young lady. I swear, the amount of red tape circulating in this place is despicable! The rigmarole around here never ceases to amaze me."

Dr. Beman thrust some papers at me, grumbled indistinctly, and motioned for us to join him inside his office.

He slammed the door behind him.

No sooner had I begun to chart my medical history when a kindly nurse knocked on the door, opened it, approached me, smiled dutifully, and handed me a blue and white gown to wear for my examination with Dr. Beman.

"See what I mean, Cheryl?" Dr. Beman said. "It's just one thing after another in this place. Oh, well . . . well . . . HERE! Give me those worksheets and you can finish them later. I'll find out what I need to know about you in a couple of minutes, anyway."

Before I had a chance to even fill in the date, the nurse led me to another room where a novel examination was about to occur. Dr. Beman joined me almost before I could jerk my gown on--jabbed me here, probed me there--it felt like a repeat of the eposide with Dr. Blumfeld! This time, however, my examination was much more thorough and . . . and Dr. Beman used a stethoscope *to listen to my lower abdomen.*

What?

"Excuse me," I interrupted, ". . . but isn't my heart a lot *higher*?"

I received no response, as Dr. Beman continued to press around on me for about twenty more minutes.

"Meet me right back in my office after you get dressed, Cheryl," he ordered gruffly as he left, giving me little chance to catch my breath or ponder my circumstances.

Dr. Beman looked deep in thought when I returned to his office. My parents, in the same way, seemed particularly serious . . . and quite tense.

I sat down across from Dr. Beman though he kept his back towards me for the next ten minutes. I kept my eyes glued to his clock, so I could keep track of all the time he was wasting--*my* valuable time.

At last, he faced me.

"I understand you're a pianist, Cheryl. I understand you're a perfectionist, too. Is there much truth to that?"

I turned quickly to Mom.

"I DIDN'T ASK YOUR MOTHER, CHERYL," he chided.

"Just answer his question, Cheryl," Mom said softly. "Just tell the good doctor the truth about how you feel and everything."

"Well . . . yes," I addressed my interrogator, ". . . I *am* a pianist," I responded, ". . . and I suppose I am *also* a perfectionist, but how else is a musician supposed to be when she's trying for a scintillating performance?"

"'Scintillating,' you say! Now there's a twenty-thousand dollar word I don't hear every day!" Dr Beman replied, unable to conceal a grin over my precise way of expressing myself.

Dr. Beman smiled at my parents, too, then reached into his top desk drawer and pulled out a pack of cigarettes. Deliberately, he lit one, *extremely* . . . deliberately . . . savoring its taste and aroma while inhaling away . . . then releasing a huge projectile of disgusting smoke and particulate matter in our direction . . . directly at *us*, his *GUESTS*!

The sight of his smoking sickened me. I just couldn't keep quiet. "That stuff'll kill you, doctor!" I said, boldly.

"CHERYL!" Mom shrieked.

Dad was so embarrassed, he nearly keeled over.

"It's okay, Mrs. Kimes," Dr. Beman acknowledged. "She's right, you know. Smoking really *is* a bad habit!" and he pounded the tip of his cigarette repeatedly into his well-worn ashtray, occasionally glancing up at me with a mischievous air.

I stared again at the clock.

I was truly irritated.

Dr. Beman rose to his feet and started to pace in front of his big picture window, simultaneously lecturing as though he were speaking at an important seminar.

"There's nothing wrong with being a perfectionist to a point, Cheryl," he said, ". . . but you *can* carry your behavior to extremes. If, when you sit down to eat, for example . . . if you have to make certain the silverware is perfectly positioned along the side of your plate and all the ice cubes in your glass of water are exactly the same size, then you *obviously* have a problem!"

He sat down with a thud.

I looked away.

"I'm over *here*, Cheryl!" he exclaimed.

I looked directly at him.

"You shouldn't *ever* be a concert pianist," he went on. "I treat several of them here in the area and *believe* me, concert pianists live a physically demanding life!"

BOY, WAS I ANGRY! HOW DARE HE TELL ME I SHOULDN'T BE A PIANIST! WHAT RIGHT DID HE HAVE TO TELL ME HOW I SHOULD LIVE MY LIFE? WHO DID HE THINK HE WAS, ANYWAY?

"But . . . but that's what our daughter's always wanted to be, Dr. Beman!" interrupted Mother, forcefully.

"Then," said Dr. Beman with assurance, "your daughter should choose another career, Ma'am."

My father was totally silent. I needed someone to be in my corner!

Dad? Dad? Why aren't you saying anything? Why can't you come to my rescue here?

Dr. Beman penned a prescription for me on paper and pushed it across his desk in my direction.

"Here you go, Cheryl. I want you to take three of these pills a day with your meals and report back to me in a couple weeks. If they help, I won't need to see you again for another year or so. Do you think you can do that?"

FINALLY, my father spoke up! "Exactly how are those pills supposed to help my daughter anyway, doctor?" Dad asked.

"Cheryl's all tied up in knots, Mr. Kimes. Her abdomen is as tight as a drumhead and her pulse rate is sky-high. These pills--I call them 'purple pills for pale people'--should relax her and help her function in a more placid manner. They're smooth-muscle relaxants. We'll see if they make it any easier for her to digest her food and make eating more tolerable. Hopefully, she might even be able to gain a couple pounds."

"And that's *it*?" asked Mom.

"I don't have a crystal ball, Mrs. Kimes, and I refuse to subject your daughter to a plethora of tests unless they're absolutely indicated. Somewhere in the future, I may advise her to have more extensive studies done here at the hospital, but in the meantime . . . let's start with something simple. She's already had an unusually large battery of tests and radiation for someone so young."

Dr. Beman rose quickly after answering his page.

"But . . . but . . ." I started . . . and he was out the door.

My parents stood, likewise, and headed into the hallway. I trailed behind.

"I, TOO, had a question to ask him!" I persisted. "I wanted to know why he was using his stethoscope so much on my abdomen. That really didn't make one bit of sense to me! I wanted to know--"

"He was listening to your heart, of course, Cheryl," said my father.

"But my heart's not way down *there,* Dad!"

"You'll just have to ask him about it the next time you see him, then, daughter!" my father concluded, and the three of us returned to Athens.

For the next two weeks, I took Dr. Beman's prescribed drug as directed. I *wanted* to see a difference in the way I felt . . . I *tried* to see a difference . . . but I just *couldn't.*

Mother called Dr. Beman at the end of my medication's trial period and relayed his advice to me in the matter. "Your doctor still believes you should take the muscle relaxant, but he also wants to give you another drug as well to augment its effectiveness. The two drugs working together may have a more beneficial effect."

I took Dr. Beman's advice and thanked God for my doctor's expertise and apparent interest in my behalf.

But I still had subtle cramping when I ate, and I didn't gain one single, solitary pound.

Chapter Twenty-Two

My sophomore year at Ohio University began with an unexpected letter from the Ohio University School of Fine Arts Scholarship Committee: "Dear Cheryl," it read. "We are happy to inform you that you have been awarded the following scholarship for the coming year. . . ."

The letter went on to say that the award was based on student musical performance and participation as well as scholastic record and financial need, and it was signed by the Director of the School of Music, the Director of Student Financial Aide and the Chairman of the Music Scholarship Committee.

PRAISE GOD!

I could hardly wait to show the letter to my parents! Although I wouldn't receive a tremendous amount of financial aide, the award proved to me that the quality of my musical and academic performance in college was commendable.

My mother and father were overjoyed!

I was quite certain that Prof. Katz was aware of my award and had no doubt given the Scholarship Committee his recommendation for me. He seemed pleased with me as his student and continued to devote most of my lesson time to concentrating on piano phrasing and touch. Little by little I could tell my hands were becoming far more responsive and controlled, and I was starting to become more capable of expressing sensitivity. Several of my peers even said their goal was to play the piano as well as me!

By the middle of October, George Katz told me I was ready to play in a student recital--without music. He said I should memorize four pieces I had been studying by Prokofiev from a collection called *Visions Fugitives*, but when I closed my book during a practice session at home--hey! They were already memorized!

Play in a student recital . . . play in a student recital . . . play in a. . . .

If my two prescribed drugs were helping me, I couldn't tell. All I could think about was how scared I was going to be in front of my college peers, and I was worried that if I forgot and made a mistake I'd never be able to find my place again. How I wanted my first showing at Ohio University to be a good experience.

On November twenty-first, the day I was scheduled to perform *Visions Fugitives*, I couldn't eat a bite. I had no breakfast, no lunch, and in general felt as if the "Gates of Hell" were beckoning me.

"You're acting perfectly silly!" Mother scolded. "You are obviously doing a very commendable job at O.U. and you've got to get ahold of yourself. God wouldn't let you mess up this afternoon when your piano prof has such a high regard for your talent!"

I put on my best Sunday-go-to-meetin' dress, took a tablespoon of antacid, and drove myself to college, praying as I went.

When I arrived at the Music Building, it was nearly 2:45.

EEK! The recital would start in only fifteen minutes!

As I walked into the recital hall, a student usher recognized me as he handed me a program.

"Good luck, Cheryl," he said courteously. "You must really be doing well with Prof. Katz!"

I took a nearby seat and looked at the program.

What? Lo and behold, there I was, *last* in order following a clarinetist, a baritone soloist, a saxophonist, and a trombonist.

I had actually been placed in the most revered spot in the recital as in my high school years, and seeing my position there helped me summon some confidence.

I listened intently as the musicians before me performed admirably.

I clapped sincerely for them.

Then, I rose to do my musical duty.

My first piece, "Lentamente," went well. I had good control of the phrasing, I demonstrated warmth and contour in the melodic lines, and I was pleased with my overall sensitivity.

"Allegretto," the second piece, made a satisfying statement--delightful and peppy, lots of dynamic contrast--and I thought I stated the humorous moments comically enough.

"Animato," perhaps the most difficult of the four *Visions*, went spectacularly! I had been obsessing over its large jumps and huge chords--but I hit every single note on target.

One more to go, Lord! Only one more to go! Don't fail me now, Jesus!

"Molto giocoso" was a one-page movement that would be over in "two shakes of a dead sheep's tail," my father would have said, and then I would dash off the stage!

I DID IT! I TOTALLY DID IT!

THANK YOU, JESUS!

Before I heard any clapping, before I had time to swallow hard or try to stop my knees from shaking, I heard "BRAVO! BRAVO!" from the back of the auditorium.

Now *that* was Prof. Katz!

I bowed as gracefully as I could manage and rushed into the hall.

Had I made even one mistake?

Not that I was aware of.

Had I successfully performed in a way that endeared me to the audience?

Why yes, judging by the volume of my applause, the audience was very impressed!

Could I have performed so well without Jesus' help?

ABSOLUTELY NOT!

I was eager to tell my parents about my successful debut when I returned home. "Honestly, Mom and Dad," I said enthusiastically, ". . . honestly, I don't think my performance had one single flaw anywhere! Can you believe I did as well as I did? Well, CAN YOU? And can you believe I was actually the very last one to play in the whole shebang?"

"Cheryl, Cheryl," said Mother approvingly. "You really are progressing well under the tutelage of Prof. Katz, aren't you?"

"Yes, Mom, I think so. He certainly is teaching me how to play the piano with much more finesse than I was ever taught before. I just thank God he accepted me last year as his student. I've learned so much from him."

My father entered the conversation with a modicum of hesitation. "There's just one thing I . . . I wonder, Cheryl," he said. "In all your enthusiasm over your college career, don't you think you better be careful not to neglect your place in our worship service at church? I mean, unless I misremember, I don't think I've heard you and your uncle play duets together in several months, have I? If you really believe the reason you're doin' good at the School of Music has anything at all to do with your Lord and Savior, well--"

Dad was right. I hadn't given performing in church much thought in some time. I had been so busy with my college classes and my recital that church had definitely taken a back seat. But . . . did I have ample time to play at church while simultaneously continuing to practice my Beethoven Concerto?

I phoned Uncle Frank the following day.

"Well, hey there, Cheryl!" my uncle answered. "I've been wondering when my long lost, prodigious niece might have time to call her neglected ol' Uncle! How's Ohio University treating you these days?"

What followed was a sorely needed overdue conversation with my uncle. After I filled him in on my recent success in the music department, he told me he'd been asked to prepare a Christmas contata for our church.

"But is there enough time to make a contata feasible, Uncle Frank?" I asked.

"Oh sure . . . *sure* there is, Cheryl! Besides, Christmas music is always fun to sing so it never seems like a burden to learn. I'm sure we can pull it off in time with the right li'l accompanist."

Christmas? Was Christmas coming? I'd hardly noticed.

"Well . . . please don't ask me to help out at this frantic time in my life!" I cautioned my uncle.

"You? Did you think I was going to ask you? Why, I would never, ever, *ever* ask you to drop your responsibilities at college and overextend yourself at church."

Oh, wouldn't you, Uncle? Wouldn't you?

"Where is the regular accompanist, anyway?" I asked.

"Oh, Bernice is still going strong, but if you just had time to fill in for a rehearsal or two, it'd be a big relief to her--you know, to have a little break around the holidays."

This was exactly what I was afraid would happen. Once I contacted my uncle, I'd get all saddled up with extra duties at church and my college life would suffer. I would have keep my priorities straight.

"Uncle Frank, I thought I told you there was no way I could possibly--"

"Well, *okay, okay,* Cheryl. I just thought *if* you had any spare time you might give our choir a gander. I'm certain the music would be sight-readable for you . . . but if you don't have any extra time, I *do* understand."

The subject of our playing a piano and organ duet during a service never entered the picture. Now *that* might have been a nice change of pace, but as for accompanying? I'd done more than my share of accompanying from grade school through high school. Why would I want to help Uncle Frank at church now as busy as I was--just to be nice?

My father corralled me before I flew out of the house to go to my first period class the next morning.

"Was that who I think it was on the phone with you yesterday, Cheryl?" Dad asked.

"Perhaps," I answered.

"Well . . . are you two going to do a duet some time in the future, maybe?"

"Dad, honestly, I wish we could, but Uncle Frank just wants me to help out with accompanying his choir in rehearsals. That's all."

I didn't feel like I needed a Bible verse that morning, but I got one anyway: "From everyone who has been given much,

much will be demanded; and from the one who has been entrusted with much, much more will be asked (Luke 12:48)."

"For cryin' out loud, Dad! Don't you understand? I just feel like I've got my hands full to overflowing at this time in my life and there you go--making me feel terrible over not giving a little more *here* and a little more *there* and . . . where *DO* you get off anyway, Dad?"

Of course, as soon as I'd lambasted my father, I felt like dirt.

I jumped into my car and sped off to campus, never offering the first hint of an apology to my father for my outburst, never comprehending that he was only trying to protect his daughter from an ugly human vice--*selfishness.*

Thankfully, a piano lesson was not scheduled for me that day. In fact, what would be wrong with my skipping a class or two, anyway? I probably wouldn't even be missed.

I turned my car in the direction of the towering old elm trees that flanked the entrance to campus, drove slowly towards their beckoning branches, then parked off the side of the road under a couple of their awesome spires.

Most students were in class. Only a handful were scurrying about . . . those obviously late to class . . . frantically trying to beat the bells they feared had already rung . . . conjuring up excuses to tell their professors in case they didn't make it to their classes in time. . . .

I should be in class myself this very minute. I'm just as bad as the rest of these slackers. I'm just a misguided fool who's keeping up a frantic pace to nowheresville because I'm a good little gal who doesn't want to disappoint anybody.

I rested my chin on the steering wheel and reminisced about being at Lake Hope. What a spot to fantasize about!

How I longed to be back in the woods at that very instant with the gentle breeze blowing . . . and the birds singing . . . and the waves tickling the beach by the lake.

Two students walked in front of my car, holding hands, deep in thought, no doubt in love--not caring about assignments or commitments--just thinking about each other.

They paused, briefly, for one soft, solitary embrace, totally oblivious to my presence, totally engrossed in their special moment together.

How beautiful.

How utterly foreign to me.

I closed my eyes.

I wonder what that would feel like? I wonder how different my life would be if I had a loving young man or husband to share my time with? Would I dream about escaping to a nearby lake for solitude with nature, or would I dream about cooking scrumptious dinners for my someone . . . or designing a house together . . . or planning a family . . . or. . . .

I opened my eyes and looked at my spindly fingers and boney knuckles as they gripped the steering wheel white-hard. My fingers weren't much bigger than the metal spokes holding up an umbrella, actually. They were pathetic.

Who was I kidding?

Who would ever want me.

Chapter Twenty-Three

About the time I had all of the notes down in my Beethoven Concerto--all forty-two pages of them--my uncle asked me once again to rehearse with his choir at church.

"This Christmas cantata I've decided to use, Cheryl, is a well-written collection of contemporary songs that tell the story of Jesus' birth. It should have lots of appeal to our young people."

"But, Uncle Frank, the Word of the Lord is supposed to remain changeless, isn't it? I mean, even though the text is modern, God's Word should never deviate from the Holy Scripture, should it?"

"You're right, of course, Cheryl--and the text doesn't stray in this music. The thing is, today's youth are conditioned to hearing much more rhythmic music and off the wall chords than the kids twenty years ago ever listened to. How can we win young souls to Christ if we don't tell the Christmas story in their own, unique musical language?"

"But, I am so *swamped* Uncle. Might I help you out, maybe . . . for just *one* rehearsal?"

Uncle Frank was understanding and assured me he wouldn't ask for my assistance again unless it was truly necessary. He said it would be a "kind gesture" to offer Bernice a little "time off" during the Christmas season.

I told my uncle that I would gladly serve as temporary accompanist, though in my heart I wasn't very enthusiastic.

Frank's choir was relatively small, but eager to sing. It consisted of a typically strong soprano section, a louder than usual alto section, three very bold tenors, and five bellowing basses. All in all, he had around fifteen well-meaning Christians, bent on doing their level best and lifting their voices as dramatically as necessary.

Singers in the soprano section included both my mother and Aunt Sybil. *How could this be? They didn't even read notes!* Yet, somehow, with repetition and desire, both my mother and Auntie learned their parts quickly, and gave it their all.

I was impressed.

The first half of my uncle's rehearsal went well, and several people came down from the loft to shake my hand during the break.

"I'm so, so happy you could take time to help us out tonight, Cheryl!" Rose said.

"You really sight read well, too!" added Gilbert, her husband.

"I don't know how we'd manage without your being here," Goldie concurred as she gave me a tight squeeze then put her hands on my shoulders.

"Are you feeling well these days, Cheryl?" she had to ask.

"Why sure, Goldie. I couldn't feel perkier if I tried!"

Goldie squeezed me even more tightly, then shook her head pitiably.

"I keep you in my prayers every night, you know, Cheryl. I don't know what else I can do for you. One of these days I expect to see those little shoulders of yours covered with padding--and you won't be able to keep the fellows away from you door!"

I knew Goldie meant well, but I was what I was! Maybe I should go to a sports store and buy some football gear to wear under my sweaters. I might look top heavy that way, but if I stuffed some cotton in my cheeks and perhaps wore two pairs of trousers to augment my legs--maybe my overall appearance might be less alarming to others who had to look at me!

The second half of the rehearsal started out without many hassles, I thought. I tried to act enthusiastic despite the drop in my morale. *Goldie was a sweet lady. I knew she was trying to help. She could turn her head away if my physique was demoralizing to her.*

The choir continued to practice, but somewhere in the composition, where baby Jesus was assumedly lying quietly in His manger, one of the tenors stood up in a huff and started to spout off at the director--*my uncle!*

"I don't feel like the tenors are making a very strong musical statement here," Edward proclaimed. "Are you certain the balance of parts is correct, or don't you think we tenors could sing out a bit louder?"

Uncle Frank had a bit of a problem with Edward. Try as he might, the tenor had a tendency to sing way off key with horrific vibrato, yet my uncle didn't want to kick him out and risk damaging his faith or sincerity. Edward had a sensitive ego.

"Well, no . . . no, Edward," Uncle Frank placated. "The tenor section is coming through loud an clear and you all sound just beautiful the way you are! Isn't that right, Cheryl?"

I could see Frank's dilemma when he asked for my opinion, and I knew how I had to respond. "Oh, I think the whole choir sounds incredible--just incredible--better than I ever expected, to tell the truth! It's a lovely cantata, too . . . just lovely!"

"Well," Edward started in again, ". . . to me, I don't think the tenors are ever going to be heard above the rest of the choir. I think we all need to be lots more forceful, especially in the last ten measures on page thirty-six."

Frank motioned for Edward to sit back down and told everyone to turn to page thirty-six. Everyone did.

"Well, now . . . you see there at the top of the page, where you've got those dynamic markings and all . . . there's that *mezzo-forte* written for the tenor line. Do you see that, Edward?"

Edward said "of course" he saw it, and understood that sign to mean medium-loud.

Frank tactfully commended him for his musical knowledge, then went on.

"Now . . . now right there above that sign, there's an obvious *forte* written for the sopranos. See that, too, Edward?"

Edward said he saw that *forte* "plain as day". . . but again, he voiced his utter disagreement over the balance. "There are how many sopranos in this choir, Mr. director? I think the sopranos probably out-number us tenors by about three to one! Wouldn't that mean we tenors would have to overdo our parts to come through strong enough?"

"OH, BELIEVE ME, YOU'RE COMING THROUGH LOUD AND CLEAR!" I butted in.

I just couldn't help myself! I knew I shouldn't have said anything, but who needed Edward's atonal yodeling to spoil the rest of the choir, anyway?

Frank scowled at me.

Edward got up promptly and stomped out of the church, head held high!

"NOW, EDWARD," Frank yelled as the tenor pompously exited the building, "EDWARD--DON'T YOU DARE DESERT

US NOW! WE NEED YOU UP HERE TO DO THE LORD'S WORK!"

Edward departed anyway, much to the good of the other choir members, in my opinion.

Frank rapped his baton on the music stand and apologized for the disruption. "I'm sorry about this, folks," Uncle Frank said. "He'll come back again," he assured the choir, convincingly.

But if he doesn't, it'll be nobody's loss. . . .

The remainder of the rehearsal seemed subdued and lackluster. Oh, *I* did a bang-up job at the piano, but the depleted choir somehow seemed less joyful than before the Edward incident.

Frank came over to see me after the last song was rehearsed. I didn't appreciate the stern look on his face.

"Look here, Cheryl," he began. "I realize you're a music major and what you told Edward was absolutely correct . . . but *I'm* the director here and *I* should be the one to decide who stays and who gets dismissed! I value your input--in fact the whole choir probably agrees that Edward wasn't doing a stellar job--but Edward *is* part of our group and believe me, Edward was doing the best he could!"

"But . . . but Uncle Frank . . . his best wasn't good enough! Do you have any idea how much more in tune the choir sounded after he walked out?"

Frank frowned momentarily, took off his glasses, then wiped the lenses excessively with his handkerchief. *Boy, did my uncle ever look perturbed!*

"Run down there and grab a Bible out of the pews, please, niece."

Boy, was I beginning to feel put-upon. Still, I forced myself to do what Uncle Frank told me to do.

"Now, Cheryl, open to Proverbs 3:9-10. Tell me what it says, please. Go on, Cheryl, read the verse out loud."

Frank's no different than Dad--always making a federal issue out of every slip I make, always convinced that the answers to every problem in life are found in the Bible. They're both so predicable!

I started to scan through the verse quickly. "Proverbs talks about your firstfruits . . . about *tithing*, basically. What are you getting at anyway, Uncle? How does this possibly relate to Edward?"

"Out loud, Cheryl. OUT LOUD, I said!"

I felt like a child.

"Okay, OKAY! It says to 'Honor the LORD with your wealth, with the firstfruits of all your crops; then your barns will be filled to overflowing, and your vats will brim over with new wine.' What in the world does this have to do with--"

"Did you ever look very closely at Edward, Cheryl?" my uncle asked.

"Can't say that I did!"

"Well . . . well next time he comes to choir, take a good look. He's not exactly what you would call white collar!"

"So?"

"So, since Edward doesn't have much to give monetarily, he tries to compensate by contributing his talents!"

"*What* talents?" I scoffed.

My uncle's forthcoming reaction to my assessment of Edward seemed surprisingly harsh. I had merely stated the obvious, that's all! Edward's vocal "contributions" were despicable. Anybody who wasn't tone deaf could plainly hear that.

Nonetheless, Uncle Frank lambasted me. "We all strive to be Christians here in the Wesleyan Methodist Church, Cheryl, and we sing to the Lord because it's the way we praise Him and show Him how much we appreciate His goodness. Certainly even *you* must be able to think of numerous times when He guided you or came to your rescue, or answered your prayers or did *something* to let you know that He cared for you. Haven't there been times in your brief lifetime when you received a blessing or a gift from God and you knew it was given because He cared for you and loved you? Or . . . or are you somehow oblivious to His mercy?"

I didn't have to think very hard to remember the numerous times I knew Jesus had been on my side; but on the other hand, no matter how many years my folks and I had prayed for Him to help me gain weight, the requested pounds had never materialized. Wasn't He ever going to give me what I truly wanted?

Whatever. The simple truth was that Edward couldn't carry a tune in a bucket, and the choir would sound one-hundred percent better without him messing everything up. Why was this such a hard concept for my uncle to grasp?

Again, Uncle Frank continued to ramble. "God has been extra good to you," he said. "He gave you an inquisitive mind, gobs of talent, and a supportive family. If you had been less fortunate and didn't have half the musical ability that you have--would He love you any less?"

I didn't need to respond. The answer was obvious.

"WELL?" Frank pushed. "WELL, CHERYL? WOULD HE LOVE YOU ANY LESS?" he repeated once more as his voice thundered.

I felt dispossessed.

"What's your point, Uncle *dear*?" I said sarcastically.

"My point is that a Christian gives back to the Lord in the same degree that he is given. Just because Edward doesn't have the same amount of talent that you do, Cheryl, he still wants to return something to God that is from his heart, and Ed's voice is his most personal possession!"

"But, Uncle Frank--"

"NO MORE DISCUSSION! IF YOU THINK FOR ONE MINUTE THAT I'M GOING TO DEPRIVE EDWARD OF HIS HEARTFELT DESIRE TO SERVE CHRIST THROUGH HIS SINGING, *ESPECIALLY* AT THIS SACRED TIME OF THE YEAR, THEN YOU ARE SADLY MISTAKEN . . . EVEN IF YOU *ARE* MY NIECE!"

I drove home as fast as I possibly could and bit my lower lip to keep from crying.

Just see who Frank can get to help him in a pinch the next time he needs an accompanist. I don't deserve his bawling out! If Jesus isn't helping me gain weight, why should I help Frank with his stupid ol' choir, anyway?

I poured myself into practicing Beethoven's Piano Concerto the following week. In case Prof. Katz had an inkling to go on a tirade about any possible lack of diligence on my part, I wanted to be prepared for his onslaught.

I became a member of the Ohio University Chorus and Music Educator's National Conference near the end of the semester and was inducted into Sigma Alpha Iota, an exclusive honorary music fraternity. In short, I filled most of my time with piano practice and musical activities and finally received an "A" in applied piano, which I felt was long overdue.

Uncle Frank didn't ask for my help any more at church, but *had* he asked, I would have truthfully been able to say, "Heavens, no! Are you kidding me? I'm positively deluged with college work!" and it would have been the Gospel truth.

Christmas break afforded me the luxury of being an observer in our congregation when Bernice returned to accompany the choir. For many reasons, I wouldn't have missed their performance for the world, and I was so sick of practicing my concerto that I really needed a diversion.

To say that Mother and Sybil were excited about singing in the cantata would be the understatement of this chapter. Since the choir didn't own choir robes, all members were personally responsible to wear their best. Sybil, naturally, felt obligated to purchase a new dress for the occasion, and she had no qualms about doing so. Frank had money to burn, and Sybil seemed to enjoy using every opportunity she could to make herself look pleasing in God's sight. My uncle was happy to oblige her, and my father, likewise, told Mother to buy something "suitable" for the church production.

Mother was happy to comply.

Consequently, the weekend prior to the Christmas cantata, both Mother an Sybil went shopping at a local dress shop and returned with lovely new clothes to wear in the cantata. Mother purchased a beautiful, conservative light green suit--tailored and quite understated--and Sybil promised Mom she could borrow her long strand of cultured pearls to spruce it up a little.

Sybil, on the other hand, bought a contrasting dark green dress with a lovely "V" neckline--but not so plunging that it would make the congregation gasp. Why, she would have been totally shunned by our church had she drawn any undue attention to any part of her body except her *face*. Sybil was so elated with her purchase, in fact, that she also bought a new undergarment as well--a tight-fitting, shiny white girdle to wear . . . well, ah . . . to wear where it . . . where it *belonged.*

Christmas Eve, the night of the Christmas cantata, arrived with an extra appropriate bonus--an incredible amount of unforecasted snow which had commenced to blanket the Athens community around one-thirty in the afternoon. By the time we left home at seven o'clock to hear the cantata, the streets in town were completely covered with the unpredicted white fluffy fleece. Talk about the right atmosphere for the Yuletide!

When we arrived at church, the pews were filling quickly with people of all ages--many from other churches as well--and Uncle Frank was understandably delighted.

"Just think what a powerful impact our cantata will have on all who come to hear the Christmas story tonight, Cheryl," he said. "Our presentation could be a turning point for those who yearn to hear more about the little baby in the manger whom God sent to save our world!"

"I certainly hope you're right, Uncle Frank," I said, "and I hope it all goes well for you and your hard-working choir."

By seven thirty, the church was completely full. Several kind souls from our congregation gave up their seats for guests who had no place to rest their chilly bones, and it was so cold that the pastor ordered an usher to dash downstairs and make certain the furnace was operating properly--that the auxiliary fans were set to blow plenty of hot air up from the basement. Heat was especially necessary, Frank explained, for the choir to feel warm and relaxed. That way they could sing their very best.

Frank ascended the stairs to the podium and greeted the congregation with an appropriate Christmas salutation. "I want to extend my personal welcome to each and every one of you who came hear our dedicated little choir on this cold, blustery evening. I hope you'll enjoy our musical message!"

Trickles of whispers and an aura of general gaiety filled the air.

The old furnace clicked on: *BANG, BANG!*

Everyone looked around in their pews to make certain the obtrusive noise was not a threat of any kind. No . . . no . . . all appeared to be well.

Auxiliary blowers began to puff away, sending copious amounts of hot air up through the old metal floor grate below the choir loft. One by one, each choir member--dressed in his or her finest--strode over that floor grate to take their assigned seats. Subdued smiles of astonishment quietly emanated from every member as each one savored the fleeting warmth of the gusts from below.

Oh, dear! Rose almost got her heel caught in the grate! Now, *that* would have been tragic! Then came Goldie, carefully . . . then Mother . . . then Sybil. . . .

OH, NO! OH, NO! OH, NO!

Not in a million years was the congregation prepared for the fate that befell my pretentious aunt. For as soon as Sybil stepped blithely onto the worn old grate, the back of her new green dress blew up over her head exposing her beautiful new girdle and, well . . . well . . . it all happened so fast that none of us in the congregation had time to even consider looking in the opposite direction!

Predictable snickers and numerous coughing "attacks" abounded.

Ol' Mrs. Kenny grabbed her paper fan and fluttered it rapidly in front of her face, although she certainly couldn't have been remotely over-heated!

Not only did the incident expose Aunt Sybil's new undergarment, but the skirt of her dress decided to momentarily adhere to her stiffly-sprayed coiffeur most obstinately, while Sybil frantically tried to push it back in place where it *should* have stayed!

I watched my aunt carefully as she continued to walk to the choir loft while smoothing out her dress, then faced the audience demurely, then gracefully took her seat--displaying the greatest amount of poise I have *ever* witnessed from any human being to this very day!

Aunt Sybil showed absolutely no detectable emotion whatsoever as she assumed her post, waited for Uncle Frank to lift his baton, and then joined in with the other voices for what turned out to be one incredibly successful performance!

Even Edward, of all people--whom my uncle had charmed back into his choir at the last minute--seemed to blend in harmoniously with the other choir members, and the congregation seemed remarkably moved by the holiday presentation.

Uncle Frank's Wesleyan choir set the stage that Christmas for the start of great musical expectations, and before long much of Athens was buzzing about how he'd formed one of the finest little church choirs in the whole community!

The following week, just before college resumed, my uncle wanted to know if I'd "shoot him" for asking if there was any way I would consider *temporarily* helping him out at the piano--just a little longer.

"But you promised--" I said.

"I know I did, Cheryl, but--"

"I told you there was no way I could possibly--"

"It's only for one Thursday night a week, though and--"

I knew Prof. Katz would not be at all happy if I told Uncle Frank I would assist him, but I had to admit I *did* have fun accompanying his choir. The music was easy, the congregation didn't make me nervous, and the experience of performing was good for me. *I* understood that, even if Prof. Katz would *not.*

"Okay, okay, I'll do my best," I told my uncle. "I'll do it--but you *do* understand I won't have time to practice at all--I'll just play the best I can on Thursday nights. That's all I can promise."

Chapter Twenty-Four

The Saturday morning of the concerto competition, I dressed down. I wore trousers to hide my bird-like ankles and a bulky sweater to make my upper torso appear as plump as possible. I wore no jewelry--particularly no rings--so I could concentrate better on how the piano keys would feel under my excitable fingers. Then, I entered the music building at Ohio University where the competition was to be held.

It will be over soon. God is with me, and He will help me do the best I can.

I sat down in the back row of the auditorium and bit my nails. The music faculty sat front and center.

Diane sang her solo first, and did very well.

Prof. Katz, who had been sitting with the rest of the professors, hurried over to greet me after Diane had finished, smiled knowingly, then said "You don't have a thing worry about, Cheryl. Trust me on this. It's in the bag!"

I started my concerto strongly and made certain my phrasing was as perfect as my professor had taught me.

LIFT THOSE FINGERS HIGH! ARTICULATE! I could hear Prof. Katz say inside my head as I forged ahead with the Beethoven. *YOU CAN DO IT! YOU CAN DO IT!* I continued to hear. *CONCENTRATE, CHERYL! CONCENTRATE! YOU CAN WIN THIS! I KNOW YOU CAN!*

Was I making any slips? I didn't hear any--

Then, it happened. Somewhere in the slow and expressive second movement, I felt a twinge of discomfort in my abdomen. My muscles tightened.

Keep going, Cheryl! Keep going! I told myself. *I mustn't dare let a little uneasiness stop me now! Help me Jesus,* I prayed silently.

I faltered slightly . . . then kept right on playing.

This is only my nerves. I'm almost finished. I must keep going! Stay with me, Jesus!

Finally . . . came the cadenza. Finally . . . the last chord. Finally . . . I was finished.

There was no clapping.

Everyone seemed so serious!

"You may go backstage and wait there, dear," a faculty member instructed.

I went behind the curtains and Diane and I grasped each others' sweaty hands tightly.

"You've won it!" Diane said.

"NO, NO, I haven't!" I replied. "You did a fantastic job, Diane. I'm certain YOU'RE going to be the winner today!"

Yet, deep down in my heart, I knew the difficulty level of my concerto was quite a bit greater than my competitor's aria (not to mention much longer), and I somehow sensed my life was about to become far more laborious.

When the two of us were called back on stage, I held my breath for the outcome.

"We want to thank both of you for the brilliant job you've done this morning. We recognize the fact that you are both superb musicians, and it was not easy for us to choose between you."

That was the director of the whole school of music speaking, Dr. Ahrendt!

"This spring, however, we can have only one winner, and that winner will be . . . Miss Kimes!"

What? What? Did Dr. Ahrendt say what I think he said?

Diane embraced me as tears rolled down her cheeks. "Congratulations, Cheryl!" she commended. "I know the faculty made the right decision!"

She didn't realize it at the time, but I was so unsteady on my feet that I think Diane was partially holding me upright!

"Miss Kimes, you will begin rehearsing with the orchestra in three months," Dr. Ahrendt declared. "You will perform the Beethoven Concerto on April 12th in Memorial Auditorium, and I hope this will prove to be one the high points of your college career at Ohio University. Congratulations, Miss Kimes! Congratulations!"

Prof. Katz jumped up on the stage and rushed to meet me. "SEE, CHERYL, SEE-- JUST LIKE I SAID!"

"But . . . but I just don't think I can--"

"There is no place for negativism, now, Cheryl! You won this competition legitimately, and as a result, you will play your Beethoven with the Ohio University Orchestra! This is an incredible opportunity for you and you'll be a better musician when it's over."

I swallowed hard and tried not to bend over from lower abdominal cramping. *What was going on inside of me, anyway?*

I hurried into the hall and bowed my head. *Thank you, Jesus! I know I couldn't have done this without You. Thank you so much for being here with me to help me perform! Thank you for being my Lord and Savior!*

I drove home immediately. Apparently, I must have beamed success when my parents saw me, for they knew the outcome of the competition before I opened my mouth!

"So, He came through for you again, did He, Cheryl?" Dad said.

"And now we get to pick out a beautiful, long evening gown for you to wear," Mom added as she wiped away her tears with a hanky. "How soon do you want to go shopping for one?" she asked. "We'd better go to Columbus for the best selection, I think. Sybil will be overjoyed to help us pick out one for you, too. We could even go this very afternoon, if you like!"

A gown? I'd never gotten that far in my thinking. I just assumed I'd wear a nice church dress . . . I guess . . . if I won . . . but an actual evening gown? Was my mother kidding me?

More to the point, would we be able to find a gown that would fit me? As skinny as I was, would any store in Columbus have clothes that would cover up my tiny frame and make the rest of me look halfway presentable?

I'd never enjoyed shopping for dresses, and I could just visualize spending hours and hours listening to rude comments about how frail I looked and how impossible it was going to be to find *any* gown *anywhere* that would work magic on my so-called figure. Why couldn't I just wear jeans, anyway? The important thing was how I performed at the piano, wasn't it? Perhaps I could have the stage manager lower the lights during my concert and I could play in the dark! Franz Liszt did that a time or two, I'd read. Liszt thought it made him sound much more dramatic when he performed in the dark . . . and darkness would obscure my body and--

"Mom," I spoke up, ". . . I really *do* need to practice."

"But your concert is still three months away, Cheryl!"

"Yes, I know, I know . . . but I just don't think this is the right time for me to go on a shopping spree. Would you and Sybil try to comprehend that, please?"

"Well, I suppose if *I* were preparing for a gala event like yours I'd feel like practicing extra hard so I'd be truly prepared," Mom said.

"Exactly, Mom, so what's the chance of your going to Columbus without me and bringing back a couple gowns on approval, then? That'd surely be a relief to me!"

I could see Mother was disappointed, but I was going to stand my ground.

"It's just that I thought we could make a day of it together, Cheryl. I thought it would be fun to shop around and spend some time with Sybil and . . . are you still praying about all this, Cheryl?"

"About my concert? Of course!"

"What about your health issues? Are you praying about them, too?"

"Not . . . not so much, Mom. I just decided to accept who I am and make the best of what God has given me."

Mother seemed horrified!

"What? Why did you stop praying, Cheryl? The Lord answers prayers in His time, not in ours! *I* certainly haven't stopped praying about you! *I* still believe that some doctor will cure you some day, and I intend to have faith until that happens!"

Mom was a good Mom, but I wasn't sure she was being realistic.

"But, I'm not really *sick,* Mom! I'm just . . . I'm just *thin*! Look. You know I wear a size eight, and I trust your judgment. You and Sybil can have a wonderful time shopping for me while

I spend the day here at home at the piano. I'll be happy with whatever you decide to buy for me. I promise."

With my closing remarks, Mother soon headed off to Columbus without me.

I didn't practice very much that afternoon. My father spent nearly three hours in our storage unit outside, tinkering with some fishing gear while listening to his favorite country music station. Every time I'd hear him reach for the screen door to come inside, I'd hop onto the piano bench and concentrate on Beethoven's cadenza--otherwise, I wasted time.

When Mom arrived back home, it had been several hours since she'd eaten. My father, bless his heart, hugged Mom and told her to take the rest of the day off--that he was going to be responsible for fixing the evening meal.

"Why, Ronald!" she exclaimed. "Did you actually have time to prepare a dinner today for your wayfaring wife?"

"What a thoughtful thing to do, Dad!" I added. "I never heard you lift a finger in the kitchen once, Dad!" and I hadn't!

"Well, that must be because you were practicing that fancy cadenza of yours so much!" he replied, tongue in cheek.

"Oh, Cheryl!" Mom was quick to inquire. "How *did* your practicing go!"

"It went just . . . fine . . . Mom. But, aren't you going to show me what's in that big Lazarus package you've got under you arm?"

Mother called both Dad and me over to the sofa and pulled out the most beautiful, long pink evening gown I could ever imagine! It had a gorgeous embroidered bodice with an equally gorgeous full length skirt plus a large flowing pink bow in the back.

"Why, Mom!" I said. "An opera diva would be happy to perform in this!"

"Well, you just run along and try it on, then," said my father, "while I rustle up some vittles and give you girls some energy!"

I'd never witnessed any of my father's prowess in the kitchen before, and I was eager to see what he'd cooked for the three of us, so I declined to try on my new gown before we ate. It probably wouldn't fit, anyway.

Mother freshened up quickly and returned to Dad's bountiful banquet.

Dad prayed before we began: "Thank you, Lord, for bringin' my lovely wife safely home to me. Thank you for this food, too, and please bless it to the use of our bodies. In Jesus' name, Amen."

After he prayed, my father set out some kind of minute steaks with thick, tomatoey gravy, a bowl of mashed potatoes crowned with several large pats of melting butter, a dish of mixed green peas and pearl onions, and a dish of rolls with a jar of his mother's homemade strawberry jam on the side.

"Oh, Ronald!" Mom said. "I never had any idea you could cook like this! I'll make sure you get your fair share of opportunities to help out in the kitchen from now on!"

I tried to eat, like always, but couldn't get more than my customary few bites into my uncooperative stomach. Besides, I should try on my pink gown. Why wait any longer? I excused myself politely, dressed, then returned to stand by the table, modeling what turned out to fit incredibly well and seemingly needed no alterations.

My father gasped when he saw me.

"Daughter, you look heavenly in that gown!" he said.

"He's right," Mom added, ". . . you're . . . you're simply elegant, I tell you! Do you like it, honey? Well, you *do* intend to keep it, don't you?"

"Sure, Mom, sure--if I truly look as presentable as you say."

My father consented to let me bypass dessert, but I didn't exit before I caught a glimpse of his final delectable.

"Is this apple betty?" I heard Mother ask as she sampled it enthusiastically. "Boy, you really outdid yourself here, Ron! Honestly, this dessert is positively tasty!"

Long about 10:00 that evening, I returned to the kitchen to have another look at my leftover dessert. I took two small bites and felt I was going to lose them.

My parents were watching television at the time, as I managed to softly slip the remainder of my father's culinary finale into the garbage can. There, on the bottom of the can, mostly concealed by paper towels and other debris, lay three boxes labeled "TV Dinner"--and therein lay the secret of my father's cooking triumph.

This will be our little secret, Dad. You put your heart and soul into fixing a special meal for us and Mom never needs to know how you finagled it.

Only my grandmother's jelly was homemade.

You almost totally got away with it, too, you sly fox! You went to all the trouble of scraping out the individual servings from the aluminum TV trays and piling them neatly into larger serving dishes . . . and Mom never caught on! You're an absolute genius, Dad!

I thanked my heavenly Father for giving me a parent who cared enough to go to such creative ends for my mother and me, and I thanked Him, as well, for helping me swallow as much of Dad's "cooking" as I had managed to do. Fortunately, my dad had no idea how miserable I had felt when I was forcing down each morsel. Neither he nor mother had the remotest idea how stuffed I became every time I even *sampled* food--but this problem was hardly new.

I practiced piano as little as I could get away with over the remaining weeks leading up to my April concert. Prof. Katz urged me to do far more than I was doing, but I felt in my heart that I was as ready as I needed to be.

At the same time, I continued to accompany Uncle Frank's enthusiastic choir, and I always had a sense of gratification whenever I helped him.

Prof. Katz was by no means pleased with my assisting my uncle, as I'd anticipated, when he ultimately extracted the truth from me about my musical moonlighting. "You can't graduate from church, Cheryl!" he chided. "NOW is the time you should be spending extra hours practicing your Beethoven! NOW is the time you need to be certain your Beethoven is a part of you! NOW is the time you must force yourself to refine what you have learned and REHEARSE and REHEARSE until you could perform your concerto standing on your head if necessary!"

BEETHOVEN, BEETHOVEN, BEETHOVEN! How I longed to never hear his name again! How I wanted my concert to be over--to be a memory--so maybe my life would be normal once again!

But what *was* normal, anyway? Most of the day my stomach was churning and my intestinal tract felt tied in knots. Occasionally, I'd have horrific abdominal contractions as well that produced such intense pain I felt I couldn't stand it.

"That sounds like spastic colon to me," Dr. Beman assured Mother when she called him at Ohio State. "A spastic colon will wear itself out in about an hour," he said, "then she'll be as good as new until the next attack comes. Her Lower GI study *did* appear to be normal, though, as you recall. . . ."

I was advised to take several pain killers and wait out the spasms when they occurred. I was also advised that when the semester was over I should return to Ohio State University Hospital for further tests.

Help me, Lord Jesus! Help me, Father! I need to feel better for my April 12th concert!

The week of my concerto performance, Prof. Katz informed me that I would have two rehearsals with the orchestra.

"WHAT? *ONLY TWO?* DID YOU SAY *ONLY TWO REHEARSALS?* HOW IN THE WORLD WILL THAT EVER BE ENOUGH TIME TO GET EVERYTHING COORDINATED?"

My piano professor explained that all I had to do was concentrate on *my* part, but I was still anxious about the orchestral ensemble.

"BUT . . . BUT THERE ARE ALL THOSE *OTHER* MUSICIANS, TOO, AND THEY'LL ALL HAVE TO PLAY THEIR DIFFERENT PARTS AT THE CORRECT TIME AND--"

"But those other musicians will have to follow *you*," Prof. Katz said, "and if there are any problems, the conductor and the orchestra will be responsible for *themselves*!"

Concentrate! Concentrate! It will all be over soon, I kept thinking--and I never stopped praying: *Father God in Heaven, please, PLEASE help me to be successful in my debut with the Ohio University Orchestra. PLEASE just take control of my nervous insides and help me relax. THANK you for giving me this talent, Lord, and guide me as I use your gift to perform this beautiful concerto. I will give you the glory, Father. Amen.*

I noticed a certain intensity in my prayers that I'd never felt before when I went to my Lord. I was just plain frightened to death--far more than I had ever been during all my piano juries or at any other time when I had performed. Without His help, I knew I had no chance of my representing myself well. Without His help, I knew I would likely fall flat on my behind and be the laughing stock of the entire music school.

In addition, something was just not right inside me, nerves not withstanding. I was beginning to believe, for certain, that some elusive malady was seriously in need of attention. Playing the piano seemed to exacerbate this uncomfortable feeling, but I knew there was no way out of my commitment on April 12th.

Was I going to survive my concert, or succumb?

Tuesday afternoon was my first rehearsal with the orchestra. The Steinway grand was moved front and center on stage in Memorial Auditorium.

"Isn't there any way we could shove the piano *back* a little bit more, Prof. Katz?" I questioned.

"Well, certainly, Cheryl!" my professor scoffed. "We *could* put it all the way backstage behind the curtains . . . but wouldn't that make it rather impossible for you to see the conductor?"

I took my place on the piano bench and tried to focus on the Steinway's gigantic, toothy grin. *Boy, did I ever feel self-conscious. Man alive--I'd never before realized how many musicians there were in an orchestra, anyway!*

Maestro Sanov, the conductor, had to rehearse the introduction four times before he even allowed me to play my first note! The intro was three pages long. Brother! *How much longer would I be expected to wait!*

Prof. Katz strode quickly over to me with his typical invincible air.

"Do you think you might be able to stop squirming, Cheryl?" he whispered in my ear.

Oh. Is that what I was doing?

"I just want to play this daggone concerto and get it over, sir!"

I scooted the bench backwards and forwards a couple times. It made a terrible screeching sound on the freshly polished stage floor.

Maestro Sanov had to stop the orchestra and restart . . . *again.*

Prof. Katz grimaced.

"Look here, Cheryl," he said. "It's not like you're going to have one superb run through and everything will fall tidily into place, you know! You're going to be here a long time today no matter how much you want to leave the stage. Now get a grip and try to lose yourself in the Beethoven!"

At last, Maestro Sanov nodded for me to enter.

Here goes--

DRAT! I MISSED MY ENTRANCE!

I heard the sound of Maestro's baton tap repeatedly on his music stand.

"Don't worry about that false start, dear!" he said. "Performing is a nerve-wracking experience until you've done it a couple hundred times or so, and I'm willing to stay here all day if necessary!"

The orchestra groaned.

Prof. Katz marched back into the audience.

We tried once again . . . and that was all I needed!

Before I knew it, the first movement ended with an unexpected twist: "I think we can just skip over your cadenza, today, Cheryl!" said Maestro. "You're obviously in fine shape and the orchestra knows where its weak sections are. We will proceed to the second movement at this time. You're doing great!"

The orchestra members clapped! Prof. Katz clapped! I'd made it through round one!

Thank you, Jesus!

Beethoven's long, endearing second movement went far better than I'd expected, with no hitches. Then, came the final rollicking third movement--my favorite.

Oops! We weren't together!

"Prof. Katz?" Maestro shouted into the auditorium. "Does Cheryl always take this movement at such a breakneck speed?"

"Well, the last movement *does* say *Allegro,* I believe!" replied Prof. Katz.

"But . . . but we just can't--"

Prof. Katz seemed delighted to have to tell me to slow down for the *orchestra's* benefit, and he assured me the musicians would be motivated to increase the tempo by the next rehearsal. It was a good lesson in pianistic control, he said, for me to have to slow *anything* down . . . so I relented.

When we rehearsed the last movement a second time--even though I felt I was restraining the force of twenty Lipizzans within me--Beethoven was finally exonerated.

"BEAUTIFUL! JUST BEAUTIFUL, Cheryl!" Maestro commended.

The orchestra clapped for me, again.

"I think our first rehearsal together was outstanding!" Maestro told the orchestra. "Cheryl performs like a pro already, and after another rehearsal or two we'll all sound as professional as the Chicago Symphony!"

I was flattered, but terribly self-conscious.

And . . . I was *bushed.*

"We'll meet back here again Thursday night at seven o'clock and then decide how many more rehearsals are necessary. In the meantime, you all practice as though your very lives depend on it!"

Once again, Prof. Katz lent some input. "Are you okay, Cheryl?"

"You wouldn't want to know."

"I never said this'd be easy, did I, Cheryl? I was certain you could handle it, though, and believe me, you are doing superbly!"

I couldn't wait to leave. I was simply exhausted, and I wondered how in the world I had been talked into entering the stupid competition in the first place.

Oooooh . . . right. This was Prof. Katz' idea.

Thursday night's dress rehearsal went somewhat better than our first one, with little need for repeating sections and no ensemble concerns. At the conclusion of our rehearsal, Maestro announced that unless someone felt a particular need for one last rehearsal together he felt certain we could all just bide our time until the 12th.

WHAT? NO MORE REHEARSING? WAS HE KIDDING?

I just wanted to scream!

Prof. Katz assured me that for a college orchestra and student soloist, we made a wonderful presentation. Before I could open my mouth and ask for just a little more time with the orchestra, my professor shook Maestro Sanov's hand and stated very audibly, "Cheryl is READY! She sounds just SPECTACULAR and I'm sure the concert on Saturday will be a grand success!"

Was that it? Was there nothing more to do before Saturday but twiddle my thumbs and fantasize about the myriad of calamities that could befall me in two days? Was there no way for me to get a fix on reality and stop the gnawing butterflies in my stomach and the persistent abdominal cramps?

My drive home that evening was fraught with a profound lack of confidence.

I tried to give myself a pep talk. "I CAN DO THIS!" I said aloud in the car as I drove. "I WON THIS COMPETITION FAIR AND SQUARE AND I CAN DO THIS!"

I must be capable enough or I would have had noticeable problems at my rehearsals.

My rehearsals had gone very well, however. The conductor was pleased, the orchestra was pleased, and my piano professor was pleased.

Yet still--I felt insecure. Was I going to live through April 12th, or was I going to embarrass my family and make a complete fool of myself?

There must be help for me, somewhere. There must be some Bible verse. . . .

Chapter Twenty-Five

When I arrived home after my rehearsal, it was nearly 9:00 p.m. I managed to be as quiet as *pianissimo* when I turned the house key in our front door then tiptoed softly to my bedroom without waking my parents.

Predictably in my bedroom, on the nightstand where it belonged, lay my Bible--the Good Book--the book my mother had taught me from as a child in her Sunday School classes, the book my father and uncle had used to keep me in tow as a teenager, the book I had sometimess, regrettably, tired of.

Yet, the Bible had always helped me when I had needed it and I had relied on it whenever I had conflicts. I needed to know if God would direct me to a verse, somewhere, *anywhere*, that would strengthen my faith, help me have peace, and give me the physical and emotional resolve to carry on for my concert.

I picked up my Bible, expectantly, and did something I had always done when I wanted a quick answer--something haphazard to a non-believer, but something reliable to a person in Christ who has the faith to trust her instincts: I opened my Bible to a random page, closed my eyes, and let my index finger fall at will on a random verse to give me the strength I needed to overcome my self-doubt.

My index finger pointed to 1 Peter, 1:6: "In all this you greatly rejoice, though now for a little while you may have had to suffer grief in all kinds of trials. These have come so that the proven genuineness of your faith . . . may result in praise, glory and honor when Jesus Christ is revealed."

I dropped to my knees. *Forgive me Father, for doubting You. I praise You, Lord, for making me exactly who I am, and I praise You for the help that I know You are going to give me Saturday when I perform my piano concerto. Thank you, Lord Jesus, for allowing me to come to You like this. Thank you, Father, for Your mercy and steadfastness. Amen.*

I had absolutely no problem falling asleep that night. I felt relieved and blessed by having read the Bible, and I felt surprisingly calm over my approaching concert in two days.

God would see me through.

Friday passed entirely too slowly. I played my concerto none at all--after all, if I didn't know it well enough by now, what amount of practicing would help?

Saturday morning came speedily, and with it my hair appointment with Laura Sapp. "Do you think you could gracefully pile most of it on top of my head so there won't be any stray locks dangling down as usual?" I asked her. "I don't want anything in my peripheral vision to distract me from seeing the keyboard or the conductor clearly."

My hair-dresser obliged, and I was pleased with her artistry!

"Will you be coming to hear me tonight, Laura?" I asked.

"No, probably not . . . but I'll be sure to say a prayer for you, Cheryl!"

Neither Aunt Sybil nor Uncle Frank were planning on attending my concert, either. I was disappointed on the one hand, but my uncle seemed to have a logical reason for their staying home. "I hope you'll forgive us, Cheryl," he told me. "Sybil tries never to do anything that might cause her to have cardiac problems. We would both love to hear your performance, but it might be too emotional for Sybil. Her heart can't take any undue stress, you understand."

"Would you say a prayer for me anyway, Uncle?"

"Of course, Cheryl! We both fully intend to!"

Then, before I knew it, I was dressed, ready to go to Memorial Auditorium, and surprisingly at ease.

My parents seemed shocked at my composure.

"Don't you want to go over any of your concerto one last time, Cheryl?" Mom asked.

"MOTHER, PLEASE! I am just FINE!"

My father, likewise, thought I might have some last minute musical details to address, but when I convinced him I was confident, he suggested the three of us pray before we drove to the event. We held hands by the kitchen door and bowed our heads. Dad did his prayerful duty reminding us "For where two or three gather in my name, there am I with them (Matthew 18:20)."

"He will accompany you tonight, Cheryl," Dad assured me. "Have no fear!"

As soon as we arrived at the auditorium, I dashed backstage and took a quick peek from behind the curtains into the audience.

The seats were really starting to fill up. It was possible for the auditorium to hold up to two thousand people or so, yet I felt sure I could handle the situation.

Then, almost before I realized, the orchestra made its way on stage.

The audience quieted down.

The lights dimmed.

"GO, CHERYL!" Prof. Katz urged backstage. "GO, CHERYL--RIGHT THIS MINUTE! YOU'RE ON!"

I don't remember walking to the piano that night. I don't remember anything significant about the orchestra's introduction either, in fact. *Mostly* what I remember is that I was determined to enter on cue--and *precisely* on cue, I did!

I was doing wonderfully, I thought, until all of a sudden--during an exposed solo part in the first movement--I stopped. I totally stopped.

There came what felt like an eternity of silence.

I looked at Maestro Sanov.

Maestro looked at me.

HELP ME, FATHER! HELP ME, LORD!

I pictured Jesus sitting beside me . . . then, as though absolutely nothing irregular had transpired . . . I resumed.

Whew! That was a close call!

My abdomen felt like two iron bookends were pushing my hip bones together. *JESUS, DON'T LEAVE ME NOW!*

At once, my mind cleared, I released all doubts, and I concentrated on giving the best performance I could give.

I never played the second movement with more sensitivity than I did that night--not like a seasoned professional, of course--but as expressively as I knew how from my years at the piano. There were even moments when I felt positively at one with the keyboard. What a great sensation!

I never played the last movement any faster, either, but the orchestra kept right up with me as I knew they would--and when I struck the final chord of the concerto, I felt a sublime sense of satisfaction, relief, and . . . *exhaustion.*

Dad could hardly wait to take a photograph of me and the beautiful red roses I was presented following the concert. "You will always remember this evening with pride and thankfulness, Cheryl," Mom said as he snapped the shutter of his camera in our living room. "Don't ever forget that God heard you when you called on Him!"

Cheryl after Beethoven concerto concert, 1964
Ronald Kimes, Photographer

For the next several days, lovely cards and congratulatory notes flooded my mailbox. Perhaps my most cherished handwritten note--which I will always treasure--came from my favorite English teacher at Athens High School: *Dear Cheryl,* she penned. *Last Sunday afternoon I was looking forward to seeing and hearing you in the symphony concert. Now I am still enjoying your lovely performance and the 'so-pretty' pink dress. Thank you for a tuneful and proud evening. Congratulations on your recognition and success, and continued progress to you. Sincerely, Irene Hand.*

I was overwhelmed that someone of Miss Hand's advanced age and stature would have made the effort to attend my concert, and I was very touched that she had obviously enjoyed hearing me. I respected her so much.

My mother and father, as well, received numerous compliments from their friends after my successful performance. The following week, however, when I overheard Goldie talking to Mother after church, her words struck me as being a potential sign from above. "Bless her heart, Clysta," she said. "Cheryl is such a tiny little wisp of a human being. She reminds me of a fragile China doll. God must surely be helping her along or she'd never have the stamina to pound out all those notes on the piano like she does!"

My mind raced back eight months earlier during the final days of August, right before the fall semester had started at Ohio University. Dr. Beman, at Ohio State University Hospital, had examined me briefly and decreed that I "should never be a concert pianist and should find a different career," and he emphasized that concert pianists led an extremely demanding life.

I'd always known that--but I intended to forge ahead and play the piano, anyway!

I had to admit, however, that I felt physically overwhelmed after I performed the concerto. I felt tired, I felt weak, and actually . . . I was beginning to feel quite confused.

Had my Heavenly Father been helping me more physically than I had been willing to acknowledge? *Had* my strength at the keyboard been greatly magnified through grace from a higher source?

I labored over my circumstances for several days.

Both my mother and farther confronted me one night after I'd attempted to eat dinner. They couldn't help but notice I was preoccupied.

"Got any plans for the summer, Cheryl?" my father asked, trying to be cheerful.

"No, not in particular, Dad."

"Summer's almost upon us, you know," said Mom. "Maybe you should think about getting a job somewhere."

"Maybe not," I replied.

I stared out the dining room window and watched a pair of robins gather twigs and assorted materials for their nest. Soon, they would boast colorful turquoise eggs, and the sounds of little songsters would fill our breezeway.

"What would be so bad about a job this summer, Cheryl?" questioned my father.

"I . . . I'm just . . . *tired*, I guess, is the word for it. I feel too tired to do much of anything for some reason."

Mother drummed her fingers on the table.

"Don't you suspect you're feeling a bit let down after your big concert, Cheryl?"

"That's probable, Mom, but I think maybe there's something else going on, too."

I forced a drink of water down and swallowed the routine pills that Dr. Beman had prescribed for me over the past year. Then I stared at my glass as I swirled the ice cubes around aimlessly.

"I'm not sure this medicine is worth the money," I stated. "I keep right on taking these pills month after month just like

Dr. Beman prescribed--and they *do* slow my heart rate down a bit--but I still can't eat half as much as I'd like . . . and I still look like a beanpole."

My father spoke up right away: "I thought you looked lovely in your pink gown, Cheryl."

"I really appreciate your compliment Dad, but my gown covered up most all of my body. Underneath it was still the same ol' skeletal me I've always been."

Mother started to clear the dishes off the table but sat back down and resumed her drumming.

"Please, Mother! Must you insist on that incessant drum roll?"

I apologized like a good daughter, then Mother said a mouthful. "Okay, Cheryl, here's what I wonder. Since you brought up the subject of Dr. Beman a moment ago, didn't he say he'd like to see you again in about a year--that'd be this coming August, wouldn't it--for more tests and observation if those pills weren't making a remarkable difference in your health?"

Wow! Mom was right. I had forgotten. But did I want to return to Ohio State?

"I thought Dr. Beman was a wonderful doctor, Cheryl," Dad said.

"I KNOW . . . I know, Dad, but with all those interns and doctors racing around all over the place plus the physical examinations and--"

"What happened to your faith all of a sudden, Cheryl?" Dad asked. "I mean, before this concerto deal took over your life, I seem to recall you had a remarkable amount of faith in the Lord goin' for you. You testified to others and you never hesitated to spread the Word. Do you remember that?"

"Let me tell you something, Dad, if it hadn't been for my strong faith, I *never* could have made it through my concert!"

Mother smiled in agreement, but added, "I can understand Cheryl's reluctance to go back to the hospital in Columbus, Ron. It sure wouldn't be what *I'd* want to do over my summer vacation. To me, at least, Clinical Research would be downright scary. It's hard to tell what all those doctors would want to put our daughter through."

I left the table and went to my room.

Did I want to be cured, or didn't I? If one chance in a million existed that any disease could be discovered that was making my life less comfortable than it could be, did I want to find out its name and fight it, or should I continue to give in to whatever my malady was and accept a less-than-fulfilling existence?

Was I all talk and no faith . . . like my father suggested?

I agonized for the rest of the evening.

Dad knocked on my bedroom door just before I turned out the lights that night and said my prayers.

He noticed my closed Bible.

"Do you read the Good Book very much, Cheryl, or just let it sit around and gather dust?"

"What do you think, Dad?" I answered, deeply offended.

"Well . . . if you *really* want to know what I think, I think you're not gettin' much good out of it or you wouldn't be in the pickle you're in tonight."

"I'm in a pickle, am I?"

"I'd say so."

Sometimes it was nice to be alone. This was one of those times.

I turned away from Dad, but he persisted in talking about the Bible.

"You know what I read when I want to relax, Cheryl?" he asked.

Did I want to know? Oh, good. He was going to tell me anyway.

"I read *The Psalms,* Cheryl."

"That's nice."

"How many do you know by heart?"

"Honestly, Dad, probably half-a-dozen."

"I see. Well, maybe sometime you ought to take a look at a few more of them. Several of them are very helpful when you're in a fix."

In a pickle? In a fix? I didn't want to be rude, but I really needed to be alone.

Dad could tell.

He left.

I prayed for answers that night. I prayed that the Good Father would help me take courage in hand and show me what to do next. I felt adrift . . . alone in a boat . . . just floating aimlessly around. . . .

The next morning in my Bible, I found a bookmark labeled Psalm 36:7. It was carefully positioned between pages 306 and 307.

My father was not known for his subtleties. Since he had obviously taken the time to call my attention to a specific Psalm, however, I thought I probably should take a couple seconds to glance over it. The passage read, "How priceless is your unfailing love, O God! People take refuge in the shadow of your wings."

How, exactly, was I supposed to apply Psalm 36:7 to my circumstances?

Does God love me enough to protect me from danger or distress? I asked myself. *Silly question. His love is unfailing!*

Does He want me to be malnourished and underweight for the rest of my life?

Of course not! He is able to hide me from whatever I fear!

I jumped out of bed and headed for the kitchen.

"MOM! MOM!" I yelled frantically. "WHERE'S MY DAD, ANYWAY?"

"Why, he's gone to work like always, Cheryl. What's so urgent, honey?"

"I've made a decision, Mother. I'm ready to go back to see Dr. Beman. Whenever he can schedule me for more tests, I'm willing to go. Whatever he says I should do, I'm ready to do it. Could I call him this morning, Mom? Could I go back to Ohio State University Hospital soon?"

Mother's predictable tears coursed down her flushed cheeks as her chin quivered.

"Are you certain you're are up to this . . . this adventure, Cheryl?" she asked.

"Oh, YES, Mom! I believe it's what my heavenly Father has planned for me, in fact, and I believe He's going to be there for me--just like he was there for me when I performed with the orchestra. All I need to do is trust Him!"

I grabbed a tissue and blotted the tears from my mother's face.

What a blessing it would be for my parents if they didn't have to worry about my well-being any longer. They had labored over my health for years.

Mother made her way over to our spinet piano and began to peck out a melody on the keyboard. She seldom played the piano, but when she did, it was always easy to figure out what the tune was.

Mom played by ear--mostly old hymns that we had enjoyed since I was a little girl on my grandparents' farm. Those great old standards had real content and important verses that were the substance of our family's entire faith!

The hymn Mother played was memorable, although I hadn't heard it in church for years. I took out our hymn book and followed the words of the second verse of *Trust and Obey* while she continued to play it:

Not a shadow can rise, not a cloud in the skies
But His smile quickly drives it away;
Not a doubt or a fear, not a sigh or a tear,
Can abide when we trust and obey.

Trust and obey, for there's no other way
To be happy in Jesus, but to trust and obey.

Mother was too emotional to speak. She handed me the receiver of our phone, and I took it unquestioningly. That very moment, I dialed Ohio State University Hospital and made an appointment to see Dr. Beman the first part of August.

Not till August? That was almost three months away!

I relayed my conversation with Dr. Beman's nurse to mother.

"The nurse told me I'd need to purge myself with castor oil before I came, Mom."

"Well, you're an old hand at that routine, aren't you, Cheryl?"

"She also said Dr. Beman would want to do a sigmoidoscopic to be certain there are no obvious problems in my lower intestinal tract b-before--"

"Before what, Cheryl?"

I was afraid I'd spoil Mother's day.

"Well," I continued, ". . . she said I should pack a bag and be prepared to stay over for a couple weeks if necessary for . . . for more intensive tests in. . . ."

Mom made an audible gulp.

"You mean stay over in . . . in the Research Clinic, don't you, Cheryl?"

I placed both my hands firmly on my mother's shoulders and turned her slowly to face me.

"Yes, yes, Mother. She *did* say in Research."

I thanked the Good Father silently for giving me the strength to do what had to be done. I thanked Him, as well, for His steadfastness and love, and I prayed that He, in His infinite wisdom, would give me and my parents the endurance we were going to need to tackle the scenario before us.

Dad was ecstatic that I was willing to return to O. S. U. "I have a notion that Dr. Beman will be the doctor who finally gets to the bottom of your problems, Cheryl!" he said when I filled him in on my August plans. "I'm just sorry you'll have to wait so long before he can work you into his schedule. This proves two things, the way I see it: number one, you don't have no life-threatenin' problem or he'd take you tomorrow, and number two, since Dr. Beman is a sought-after physician--you're gonna be in good hands, Cheryl. I see this doctor as a positive answer to prayer!"

I thought my father was being overly optimistic, but I admired his faith.

"If you don't get a job this summer, though, how are you ever gonna pass the time until August?" he asked.

What was I going to do? Well . . . I was going to practice!

"You know I'll have to give a junior recital at O.U. next year, don't you, Dad?"

"No, Cheryl, I didn't know that."

"Oh, sure. In order to fulfill the requirements for my Bachelor of Fine Arts degree, I have to give a junior recital, then a senior recital the following year."

My father had apparently thought I was going to fritter away my time over the summer, but that had never been my intention and it was time I set the record straight!

My mother, on the other hand, thought I should just take the summer off and have fun.

"You know what they say, Cheryl," she interjected. "All work and no play makes Jill a dull girl!"

"I guess Jill must not be a motivated pianist like me then, Mom! You know, I've never really seen the point of hanging out much--I mean, the parties I've been to were pointless, most movies I've seen were a waste of time, and my college friends have gone home for the summer, anyway. I suppose I do have different aspirations than most students, but Prof. Katz has high hopes for me in piano, and he was pretty pleased with my concerto concert, so--"

"But Cheryl . . . don't you ever intend to date or at least have friends of the opposite sex or--"

I stared at Mother while stating the obvious. "Look at me, Mom. What man in his right mind could ever find me attractive enough to want to get to know me?"

My father, who had been silent for several minutes, hurried over to me and gently cupped my face in his hands. "Now, you just look here, Cheryl," he said. "You are a beautiful Christian woman inside and out and *any* man worth his salt is gonna be lucky to have you. He may not have come along yet . . . but God *is* gonna send him to you one of these days when you're in the right frame of mind to accept him!"

I pulled away from my father.

"I love you, Dad, but I'm beautiful to you because . . . because I'm your daughter, that's all."

I walked over to the piano and started to read through my new music.

I could always tell when I managed to upset my mother, and I was certain she'd left the room in tears once again. That made me feel just terrible.

Dad was probably right about one thing, though. I *wasn't* ready to develop a relationship with the opposite sex. God just wasn't motivating me in that direction.

I'd know when He did so.

Chapter Twenty-Six

By the first week in August, I had learned all the notes in Beethoven's *Thirty-two Variations in C Minor*, Debussy's *Pagodes*, and Chopin's *Scherzo in B flat Minor* for my Junior piano recital. My uncle and I continued to perform sacred duets in our church once in a while, and by throwing myself into my music, I was reasonably successful in keeping my mind off returning to Dr. Beman.

On August the 9th, however, I had an appointment to keep. Dad, Mom and I drove to Ohio State University Hospital.

By 9:30, I was in Dr. Beman's examination room, lying mostly unclad on another cold, steel table. His nurse stood at the foot of the table, and on an adjacent stand lay a long, straight tube of some kind attached to what appeared to be an air hose.

What? An air hose?

"Have you ever had a sigmoidoscopic before, Cheryl?" the nursed asked.

"Fortunately NOT!"

Get that torture device out of here! It must be at least two feet long!

How I wanted to be back in Dr. Beman's office where my parents were waiting--and hopefully praying--for me.

"If I might give you one important piece of advice, Cheryl," the nurse offered, "try your level best to relax your muscles while the good doctor is scoping you. Think about some *thing* or some *place* very pleasant, and travel there in your mind. This is not an enjoyable procedure, but Dr. Beman does it many times a week and it will be over before you know it."

The nurse pulled on a squeaky pair of sterile latex gloves and snapped them noisily into place on her fingers. Next, she took the cap off a humongous tube of petroleum jelly. It bubbled and popped disgustingly while she squeezed it onto the sigmoidoscope.

"That's the most obscene noise I've ever heard in my whole put-together!" I said.

"I'm sorry, dear. Dr. Beman wouldn't put you through this if he didn't think it was one-hundred percent necessary."

She lubricated the long inflexible tube thoroughly and kept her back towards me, trying to conceal, unsuccessfully, its foreboding length.

Dr. Beman bounded confidently through the door.

"Cold enough in here for you, Cheryl?" he asked, almost chuckling.

It seemed to me like he had the most inappropriate sense of humor!

"How long is this going to take, doctor?" I asked.

Dr. Beman muttered something under his breath and coughed a time or two.

"That depends entirely on you, Cheryl. Now turn over on your left side there," he added rather gruffly, "and let's see what's going on inside of you."

I rolled over reluctantly.

Something that sounded like an air compressor started to sputter around like the one at my father's garage. *BOY, did that sound make me apprehensive!*

"You're going to feel something very cold now, Cheryl. I want you to take a deep breath and I'll tell you exactly what's happening as I go along."

Dr. Beman stuck the tube into my posterior.

WHOA! TALK ABOUT FRIGID!

"H-how do you doctors w-work in temperatures like this, anyway?"

Dr. Beman ignored my question.

"I'm going to start inflating you with some puffs of air, now. . . you're going to feel pressure . . . here we go. . . ."

"OUCH!" I yelled as I jumped!

The tube ceased to ascend inside my colon.

Dr. Beman spoke up. "It is *REALLY* essential that you lie *perfectly* still, Cheryl! I know you and your folks would probably rather be out shopping this afternoon, but I've got to have a clear look at what I'm dealing with inside your intestinal tract. In case you're wondering, this is not what *I'd* prefer to be doing with my afternoon, either!"

I felt severe abdominal cramping like I'd never experienced before.

"YOU'VE GOT TO RELAX, CHERYL!" Dr. Beman was adamant.

Relentlessly, he probed.

I clenched my teeth.

"I don't see any . . . any polyps . . . no tumors . . . no inflammation . . . we're halfway through already . . . your walls are nice and smooth. . . ."

I wanted to pray out loud so badly! It just didn't feel holy to talk to my heavenly Father in my . . . my *position.*

"Everything looks completely normal, Cheryl," Dr. Beman said, still pushing the tube further into my intestines.

"One more peek and we're done!"

I imagined gentle waves caressing the shore at Lake Hope. I visualized fluffy, white cumulus clouds rising above the trees, butterflies gliding over my head, and woodland flowers popping up among the maples and oaks.

HELP ME FOCUS, FATHER! HELP ME FOCUS!

Suddenly, without notice, the machine clanked nosily and withdrew its air with one mighty *whoosh.*

I sighed deeply, but was determined not to cry.

"There, there," Dr. Beman consoled me, his steady hands pushing my sweat-soaked hair off my forehead.

"I wish I could make this exam more tolerable, Cheryl," he said, "but I do the best I can with what current technology gives me. The day will come when there'll be a better tool to replace this rigid scope, but so far this is the only diagnostic instrument I have to offer."

Dr. Beman reached for the stethoscope around his neck.

"You did a fine job for me, Cheryl. Now just lie very, very still." Dr. Beman pushed his stethoscope forcefully against my abdomen, just below my navel. "I promise this won't hurt you at all."

Once again, Dr. Beman listened intently to my abdomen with his stethoscope like he had done twelve months earlier.

A look of optimism enveloped his face.

"Bingo." he said softly. "BINGO!" he repeated, louder.

"Dr. Beman? DR. BEMAN!" I raised my voice. "WHAT ARE YOU LISTENING TO DOWN THERE, ANYWAY? THIS IS MY BODY AND I HAVE A RIGHT TO KNOW WHAT YOU'RE DOING!"

Then Dr. Beman--though I doubt he was in the habit of doing so--slipped the ear pieces of his stethoscope into *my* ears, while continuing to hold the business end of the instrument tightly on my abdomen.

I listened with all my might.

"Can you hear that, Cheryl?" he asked. "It's a metrical "swish, swish, swishing" sound. I believe that's your blood struggling to get through your celiac artery. Isn't that amazing?"

I heard it clearly!

"I . . . I *guess* it is, doctor . . . but what, exactly, does that 'swishing' mean, anyway?"

Dr. Beman took his stethoscope slowly back out of my ears and methodically repositioned it around his neck.

"It means you're about ready for the 'blue plate special,' kiddo!"

Dr. Beman cleared his throat and acted as though he was trying to suppress some amount of emotion. So was I, but I was emotional from *frustration.*

Dr. Beman's nurse told me to hurry and get dressed again, then to join the doctor and my parents back in his office.

When I returned to see him, he was ready to light up a cigarette.

Oh, no. Here we go again!

I arched my right eye brow and did my best to show disdain.

"Oops!" he said, chuckling once again, as he placed the unlit cigarette back in its pack.

"How could I have forgotten!" he laughed, as he winked at my parents.

I saw nothing remotely comical about smoking cigarettes, but this was obviously not the best time to crusade against the unhealthy habit. Mother reached over and put her hand forcefully on my left knee as she attempted to scoot me around to face my doctor.

Ahhhhh, yes. It was time to serious up.

Dr. Beman took his time getting around to the heart of his findings, and when he did, my parents and I were in for a royal shock.

"I can't say for certain without admitting Cheryl to our Clinical Research Unit, but it sounds like she *might* have a rare congenital condition we call a celiac artery constriction. It's sort of my pet project here at Ohio State, and several of my colleagues and I have been collaborating on researching the disorder for some time."

"Would you please explain what you're talking about, doctor?" Mother asked.

"Yes, of course, Mrs. Kimes. *If,* and I emphasize *if* . . . *if* your daughter does indeed have this disease, she would qualify for corrective surgery which might completely cure her eating disorder. She might even gain a few pounds afterwards."

Did I hear Dr. Beman correctly?

"Are . . . are you saying, sir," I just *had* to make certain I'd heard correctly. ". . . are you telling me I . . . I might be able to look like a regular human being after--"

"Cheryl," my doctor answered, "this is a *research* clinic here, and there are no guarantees. However, based on the fourteen patients so far who have benefited from this operation, I would say you have at least a fifty-fifty chance of gaining a little weight. Considering your genetic background, I can't honestly predict you'll ever be plump and buxom, but I *can* foresee your being healthy and willowy some day."

Healthy and willowy? I could be satisfied with healthy and willowy!

Dr. Beman grew more serious and resumed addressing my parents about the Clinical Research Unit. "For me to help your daughter," he said ". . . it would require that she be admitted to C.R.U. for around two or three weeks."

"Two or three whole weeks, you say?" queried my father. "Wouldn't that be awful expensive?"

"Unquestionably, Mr. Kimes, under *usual* conditions, but in C.R.U. we have a special grant where all the diagnostic tests and surgeries are totally free."

Dad was speechless.

"Is surgery the only option, Dr. Beman?" interjected my mother.

"Yes it is, Mrs. Kimes, again . . . *if* the need for surgery can be proven. With Cheryl's hypothetical malady, there's a little muscular band that grows out from her diaphragm--much like a rubber band--and wraps itself around her celiac artery. That band constricts the flow of blood through the artery making it nearly impossible for her digestive organs to function properly. *If* that band is your daughter's problem, we have a fine surgeon who simply goes in there and cuts the constriction away."

My father was fidgeting.

"I'd offer you a cigarette, Mr. Kimes," joked Dr. Beman ". . . but I'd never get away with it!"

Nobody laughed.

"What you all need to do is talk this over and decide if you want Cheryl to undergo more tests. It's not like you have to make your decision right away."

"But . . . but I WANT THIS SURGERY!" I exclaimed. "I don't need further discussion, Dr. Beman! I am willing to do *whatever it takes* to feel like a normal human being! Honestly, sir . . . I WANT THIS SURGERY ASAP!"

Dr. Beman glared at me as though I were the only patient he had ever seen who was capable of making up her mind on the spot.

"Is your daughter always so impulsive?" he asked my parents.

For some reason, my father suddenly became very much on the defensive. He sat tall in his chair and acted as though he was ready to do battle with the one professional we had ever met who might conceivably change my life.

"Excuse me, doctor," Dad said, ". . . but I wasn't aware that my daughter was *required* to hem-haw around. I figure since she's spent the last twenty odd years prayin' for a miracle, she's entitled to be pretty excited over your offer. Now, if you *require* her to chew this matter over for the next day or so . . . we can arrange it!"

Way to go, Dad!

"Otherwise, Dr. Beman," Dad concluded as he stood to his feet, "Cheryl's made her decision and we'll go with it!"

No further discussion was necessary. Boy! When my father put his foot down, he thrust it down with all the force of a Ringling Brothers' two-ton elephant!

"I can't *believe* you talked to her doctor that way, Ron!" Mom chastised Dad as we walked to the car.

"Well, she's *my* daughter, and I never intend to stop prayin' *or* fightin' for her, Clis!"

"But all Dr. Beman wanted for us to do was to take some time and *consider* his suggestion. He didn't want us to make a hasty, rash decision that she might regret later . . . that's all, Ron!"

When we reached our car, my father turned on the ignition and sped out of the hospital parking lot.

"How 'bout if we live it up tonight, Cheryl?" he said as he momentarily turned to face me with what he thought was a colossal idea. "You've got to officially check in back there by 11:00 tomorrow morning according to the admittin' office. From then on, until you're *healed,* you're gonna be eatin' bland hospital food that's not very tasty. What say we call Frank and Sybil up and see it they'd like to join us for a celebration at a fancy joint downtown? Would you like that, Cheryl?"

"What are we celebrating, Dad?" I asked.

"Why, your up-and-comin' miracle, of course, daughter!"

"You . . . you really believe I'm going to be healed, don't you, Dad?"

"Of course, Cheryl, of course! Don't you think it's about time?"

Mother and I both thought Dad's suggestion was a good one, so Dad found a pay phone, pulled over, and placed a quick call to Uncle Frank. He and Sybil were anything but reluctant to meet us at the Kahiki.

"The Kahiki, Dad?" I asked with a trickle of trepidation.

"Sure, Cheryl! The guys at work have been tellin' me all about the place. It's a genuine Polynesian restaurant with phenomenal food and fish swimmin' around in wall-to-wall aquariums and--"

"What's the food like, Ron? asked Mom.

"They tell me it's really unusual, Clis, and there's real live island music from a steel drum band and--"

I'd seldom seen Dad so excited. He was obviously trying to keep my mind off the notion of possible surgery, and he was doing a pretty decent job of sidetracking me!

We reached the Kahiki around five o'clock.

Frank and Sybil were already inside.

Wow! The whole restaurant was shaped like the inside of some kind of ship from the South Seas, and as we entered we had to pass through a rocky hallway with waterfalls cascading all around us.

"Gee, Dad," I said. "This place is totally unreal!"

Many patrons inside were toting around martinis and other fancy drinks, but my father said we should just ignore them . . . that drinking was not a necessity for a delicious meal, *or* a happy life.

I already knew that, Dad!

Dad also told our waiter that he wanted us to sit close to the live music so we could see the steel drum and really "get an earful."

How entertaining! I had never before heard such exotic music, and it, well . . . it all reminded me of music from Gardner McKay's *Adventures in Paradise*--my favorite television program!

When we finally were seated, it was difficult to hear exactly what our waiter was asking when he took our orders, but it sounded like he was saying "Do you want flied lice or steamed lice?"

Uncle Frank became really amused and started imitating him. Sybil was simply mortified. "Frank, FRANK!" she said, trying to silence him. "You know very well he meant *fried rice,* not *flied lice*! Now you be courteous to that dear person and help us decide what to order!"

After my uncle settled down, the five of us unanimously decided to try appetizers called *kapopo*--succulent pork meat balls on individual skewers, plus a thick oyster bisque called *bonko bonko*--soup laced with heavy cream and delicate sweet Polynesian spices.

As the *kapopo* was delivered to our table, our waiter also placed a bowl of combustable material in front of us, then actually lit it--and we were told to brown our meat balls just as though we were around a miniature campfire! I had never had so much fun in my life!

Then, for the main entrée, I chose a chicken dish with Polynesian vegetables and cashews which was just incredible! I could eat little, but my father understood my malady and didn't heckle me. *Thanks, Dad!* My family was occupied with new sights, sounds, aromas and incredible-tasting food.

We were all so engrossed in the unique environment, in fact, that my father totally forgot to pray.

Two bites into our main course, I leaned respectfully over to him and questioned, "Dad . . . DAD? Aren't you forgetting something very important?"

Almost immediately, my father put his soupspoon down and asked our party of five to join hands.

We did.

"Father, in Heaven," Dad prayed aloud, "Thank you so much for this opportunity to experience the joy of our family dinin' and fellowshippin' together, and . . . and thank you, Lord, for the wonderful doctors you've provided to heal my lovely daughter at Ohio State University. May this be the last meal she ever has trouble completin'. Amen."

I had learned to ignore the attention we received in public when we held hands and prayed. Let people gawk! We loved the Lord, we weren't afraid to show it, and if we motivated any nonbelievers to investigate the power of the Holy Spirit . . . Jesus be praised!

None of our family hurried with our dinner that evening. We laughed and joked together for nearly two hours well into the dessert course, and when our banana cake came to climax the festivities--all artfully positioned on large, dark green banana leaves--I had to admit, it *was* the best food I had ever tasted!

How much more fun could I have had if I had been able to pack away every single bite?

We drove back to Frank and Sybil's after dinner that night. Frank and I had no difficulty summoning the enthusiasm to make music in his music room--he on his Hammond organ, and I on his grand piano. We played together for over an hour.

Soon thereafter, we all went to our separate bedrooms after viewing the evening news on television, though none of us would be able to remember one single local or national item of any significance the next morning.

My family was small, and we were close. When one of us had an issue to face, we all faced it as though it were happening to each of us personally.

The next morning, I ate nothing. Frank cooked special buckwheat pancakes and smothered individual stacks of them with scoopfuls of butter and hoards of sugary maple syrup.

I apologized for my lack of appetite. "I just want to hurry and go to C.R.U., Dad!" I told my father.

At 10:00, my parents took me to the hospital. By 11:00, I was all checked into my room--a ward to be shared with three other patients. At 11:10, my parents left.

"Now, don't you hesitate to call us, Cheryl!" Mom said as she trudged off with my unusually preoccupied Father. "We can drive up here from Athens *any* day, at *any* time, so whenever you have anything at all to report . . . please call!"

"You promise, now!" Dad added.

My parents managed to leave me and head for the elevators with dry eyes.

No sooner had they left, when a nurse of noticeable determination and resolve motioned for me to take the vacant bed by the big picture window.

"Gosh! It's beautiful way up here, isn't it, Miss . . . Miss. . . ." I started.

"My name's Miss Mott," she said bluntly. "You can meet these other ladies on your own time later. For now, Miss Kimes, hang your sweater up over there in locker number three, and get to know your roomies after you put this hospital gown on," she said, tossing a predictably drab gown in my direction.

I looked down at my suitcase, clutched tightly in my right hand. Miss Mott grabbed it forcefully and stuck it into my locker.

"May I not wear the gown that I brought from home, Miss Mott?"

I saw no smile.

"Certainly, if you like, Miss Kimes--just so long as it has short sleeves. They'll be in here early tomorrow morning and draw your blood before you eat breakfast. Lab technicians don't want to fuddle around with long sleeves and fancy-dancy distractions!"

"Oh. Well, I'm a pretty reasonable person here. I'd just be more comfortable in--"

"I UNDERSTAND, Miss Kimes!"

Miss Mott pushed a tall food tray on wheels over the top of my bed. "See these menus here, Cheryl?" she asked.

Several sheets of paper were dated, labeled with my name, and covered with a week's worth of meal suggestions.

"I see."

"You may order anything you like on a daily basis. Your dietician will be your own private cook and she'll bring you whatever you request from these menus. And, starting with your first trip to the bathroom after lunch today, make sure you void in the urinal with your name on it. SAVE EVERY SINGLE DROP OF URINE THAT YOU VOID. It is CRITICAL that every drop of your urine is accounted for accurately! See the label?"

"Of course."

"Whatever you do, make sure you always void in *your* container, not in someone else's."

"Obviously."

"Any questions, Miss Kimes?"

"Yes, Miss Mott--just one."

"Well?"

"When will my doctor be in to see me?"

"Your *DOCTOR*, Cheryl? Who knows! Maybe not for several days . . . but you better get changed quickly, 'cause your troop of interns is liable to show up any minute now."

Interns? Nobody had ever told me about a whole troop of them!

"What interns are you talking about, Miss--"

But Miss Mott was already out the door.

I stood by the end of my bed, oblivious to the other three patients in their separate beds.

I felt isolated.

"Think about this place like it was summer camp," a patient across the room said courteously.

"You probably won't be here very long," she went on, ". . . but it'll be a unique experience and you'll never be the same when you leave."

I'd only been to summer camp once when I was in grade school, and I didn't have a particularly good time.

I wasn't sure I was going to enjoy this place either.

Chapter Twenty-Seven

Around 2:30 in the afternoon, eight young men and one slightly older man, all dressed in white lab coats, greeted me as I lay quietly on my hospital bed. Each of them was carrying a clipboard and pencil. Each of them looked extremely studious. The eldest man introduced himself as Dr. Lobo, Resident-in-Charge, then proceeded to talk about me to his subordinate interns as though I were a deformed cell under a microscope.

"This is the enigma of the ward, class. Her name is Cheryl, and our job is to discover what disease has kept her so skeletal all of her life. Note how thin she is."

One of the interns, without giving me any prior warning, grabbed the corner of my bed sheet and with one fell swoop yanked it completely off my unsightly body.

"DO YOU MIND?" I yelled.

"Classic Marfans!" a second intern blurted.

"No . . . no," speculated yet another, ". . . I think it's probably thyroid insufficiency!"

"Or . . . or anorexia nervosa" I heard, "or--"

I reached for my sheet and successfully jostled it back up around my giraffe-like neck.

Dr. Lobo continued: "So, here are her presenting symptoms; little or no appetite, inability to completely finish a meal, inability to gain weight, poor muscle development, occasional cramping--but on the plus side, her prior blood work is phenomenal and Dr. Beman says she apparently has a very high I.Q."

I felt far more self-conscious than usual'

"Why not just hang a sign on the end of my bed that says 'too difficult to cure' and save yourselves a lot of work?" I suggested.

One of the troop took hold of my left foot under the sheet and squeezed it empathetically.

I jerked away!

"Has her blood been drawn yet, today?" an intern asked.

Dr. Lobo addressed me slowly and loudly. "HAS ANYONE TAKEN YOUR BLOOD THIS AFTERNOON, CHERYL?"

"NO, THEY CERTAINLY HAVEN'T!" I responded, raising my voice in the same manner while simultaneously lifting both eyebrows.

The entire group of interns exuded embarrassment and looked quizzically at their resident.

"Additionally, Dr. Lobo," I added as softly as I could, ". . . you should take note that my hearing is superb, thank you!"

A tinkling of glass test tubes out in the hall signalled that "my special someone," as anticipated, was indeed approaching to suck some precious life out of me. Dr. Lobo, while exiting with the others, assured me the he would return later in the day to take my complete medical history.

My blood-letter entered my room and prepared to do his dastardly duty. He was carrying a metal basket filled with numerous empty test tubes, and I (having just been identified as being above average) was instantly suspicious that a couple of those tubes were about to be filled with *my* corpuscles!

"Hey there, beautiful. You may call me Dracula, if you like. Did you have your breakfast or lunch yet today, Cheryl?" he asked, then proceeded to laugh as maniacally as possible.

Was this character for real?

"No . . . is my fasting a requirement of yours?"

"Actually, it *does* work better for me if you haven't eaten before my analysis. That way, I can check your glucose levels most accurately."

"Dracula" screeched a chair over to my bedside and wrapped a long rubber hose around my left arm above my elbow.

"I was hoping you might hold off coming until tomorrow," I said.

"I vas hongry!" he winked.

Oh. So this was supposed to be fun-and-games time?

I tried to relax. "How many of those tubes a-are you proposing to fill?" I asked, reluctantly.

"Why, *all* of them, of course!"

"WHAT? GOOD GRIEF! YOU MUST BE KIDDING ME! I WON'T HAVE ANY BLOOD LEFT WHEN YOU'RE FINISHED!"

"Aux contraire," my lab tech assured me. "You have several quarts, Cheryl, and your body will manufacture more blood immediately after I withdraw my *teeth*--I mean, my syringe. Now, please lie still."

I hardly felt the needle as Dracula inserted it deep inside the blood vessel in my arm. He was good at his craft.

"Have you ever passed out when this was done, Cheryl?"

"Gee. I never parted with this many corpuscles before. I'll surprise you!"

As Dracula began to draw my blood, I looked away to avoid becoming nauseous.

"Do you visit us patients here in C.R.U. often, Dracula?" I asked.

"It all depends on my supply on hand, Cheryl. I get *urges* according to what phase the moon is in, and if my provisions are running low, well, then. . . ."

Ol' Dracule continued to suck away.

"So . . . do you have to share your bloody booty with your family back in Transylvania, or can you discretely upend a tube or two on the way back to your coffin?"

"Now, that was a pretty good one!" Dracula said, again *attempting* another sinister laugh.

I stopped counting my vials of blood after Dracula had filled the eighth or ninth tube and flinched slightly when he withdrew his syringe at last. He placed a large wad of cotton on his "fang marks," then tightly wrapped my bite-site with a long elastic bandage.

"Press on it there for about five minutes or so, sweetness," he said as he pretended to throw his imaginary cape around his neck and started to fly away. "You must be pretty hungry, I'll bet!"

He just couldn't leave without mentioning food like everyone else in my life!

"No, actually, I'm *not*--but I can see you've drawn enough to satisfy *your* healthy appetite!"

"If I don't see you again, Cheryl," he concluded, ". . . you enjoy your stay here at C.R.U. Someone else will be in here in a few more hours to steal more of your delicious red libation if I'm not the lucky one!"

"Don't you know *when*, for certain?"

"No, darlin', but you can handle it! You're made of strong stuff. I can tell!" and away he flew.

I heard an obtrusive sound heading towards my room at the same time the patient across from me finally introduced herself as Barbara. She also apologized for the others who had so far chosen to only observe me.

"That scrawny one over there is Sue," Barbara pointed out. "She's only twelve, aren't you, Susie?"

Susie never uttered a word, nor turned to acknowledge me.

"And the lady beside you--that's Shelly. Shelly's in quite a lot of pain and is heavily medicated 'round the clock. If you have any questions while you're here, better just ask *me*."

"Thanks, Barbara," I said, as an orderly entered our ward with a noisy wheelchair.

"MISS KIMES? ARE YOU MISS KIMES?" he questioned, staring at me.

Was everybody deaf in this place?

Before I could confirm my identity, he'd read my wrist band and asked me to hop into his small chariot.

"Where are you planning to take me anyway, if I might inquire?"

"Oh, this is just for a routine chest X-ray. I imagine the exciting stuff'll start in a couple more days."

"The *exciting* stuff?" I repeated as I hesitantly approached the chair.

"Yeah, you know, like kidney X-rays or stomach X-rays or . . . what *are* you in for anyway, sis?"

I wanted to tell him it was none of his business, and it wasn't, of course, but--

Think this through. I'm probably going to be here for several more days, and it wouldn't be to my advantage to irritate the staff, would it?"

"Oh, I'm just in here 'cause I'm a tad underweight. It'd be nice if I could gain a few pounds, I think. That's all."

He eyed me thoroughly--much like Dr. Beman had scanned me at our first meeting.

"Yep, I'd say you could most definitely use a few pounds, sis. I can surely see why you're checkin' this place out here--but don't you worry! We'll all treat you real fine."

I sank down into my orderly's wheel chair and tightly gripped its padded arm rests. Before long, I'd had a chest X-ray and was returned promptly to my room.

"I see you made it through with flying colors, Cheryl!" Barbara said when I was deposited. "Get used to it, girl," she continued. "They check all of us out like you'd never believe here in C.R.U. I figure since it's all free, there's no reason to get bent out of shape. I've been here for two weeks to date, and nothing's been totally unbearable or too alarming. You'll adjust to the place in no time at all. You'll see!"

I sat down on the window ledge and peered out over the city again.

"It truly is an awesome view out there, isn't it?" said Barbara. "At Christmastime, they leave the lights on in certain windows over there in Levec Tower to form a big, bright cross. When night falls, all you can see in the distance is that glorious symbol up in the sky. It really is a comforting touch, especially when you're sick."

I looked carefully at Barbara's profile. Her huge abdomen was grossly out of proportion to the rest of her body.

"You've been here during Christmas, then?" I asked.

"Yes, oh my, YES, girl! But it really wasn't so bad. The nurses all decorated the hallways to the hilt with pretty red and green bows and sparkly ornaments, and they sang Christmas carols together and brought us holiday treats, too. Actually, it was quite festive, Cheryl."

Before long, dinner arrived--some kind of beef goulash, a side of green beans, a dinner roll, plus lime jello with whipped cream for dessert.

It tasted fine. I wished I could have eaten all of it.

About 8:30 that evening, Dr. Lobo returned as promised. "Well, Cheryl, it does look like you survived day one!" he said.

"I certainly did, doctor. You didn't doubt that I would, did you?"

"I never doubted it for one second, Cheryl."

I stared out at my picturesque view. "What does one do for entertainment around here, anyway?" I asked.

Dr. Lobo wondered if I'd like to have a small television to watch. "TVs come with earphones and you can plug into them and listen without disturbing the other patients around you. Would you like me to order one for you?"

"Thanks, but no thanks. I can just read some from my Bible."

"Well . . . okay, then, but down on the third floor there's an old piano and some board games and--"

"A piano? Did you say 'a piano,' Dr, Lobo?"

"Yes, that's right. It's not very much in tune but some of the patients seem to enjoy dinking around on it now and then. Do you play, Cheryl?"

"Oh . . . just a little."

I was given a thorough examination from head to toe. It must have taken all of fifteen minutes before Dr. Lobo finished.

I sat up.

"What have you got against food, anyway, kiddo?" the doctor asked.

I flared up!

"CRI-MUN-IT-LY! I have absolutely NOTHING against food! And you made an error today when you introduced me to those med students, too, doctor!"

Dr. Lobo focused on staying professional.

"I get *just* as hungry as the next person!" I continued, "and I DO have an appetite--only I feel STUFFED as soon as I've taken a couple mouthfuls!"

"You feel full?"

"RIGHT ON!"

"You feel like you can't swallow another bite?"

"Do *YOU* have a hearing problem, doctor?"

Dr. Lobo went over to the window and studied the view for several minutes.

"Did you ever see a psychiatrist, Cheryl?" he asked, without turning around to face me.

Did he think my malady was all in my head?

"Heavens, no--but I *did* take a couple semesters of psychology in college and am convinced that Dr. Freud would have benefited from a good dose of religion!"

Dr. Lobo turned quickly to face me, and we both shared a good laugh.

The merriment didn't last for long.

"Look. Here's the thing, Cheryl. Your records all indicate that there's absolutely nothing physically wrong with you, except for the fact that Dr. Beman heard that *bruit* in your abdomen once."

"I heard it too, doctor. It was coming through loud and clear!"

"*You* heard it, Cheryl?"

"Yes! Dr. Beman let me listen to it while he held the stethoscope in place. *I* thought it was a real hopeful sign that he'd found the probable cause for my being so skinny all my life."

Dr. Lobo smiled, skeptically. "Dr. Beman apparently has a soft spot that I've never observed before."

"Well . . . supposing there *is* a constriction around my celiac artery, doctor. Why can't I just have a test to prove it and get out of here ASAP?"

Dr. Lobo wanted to make very certain that I understood C.R.U.'s position. "Okay, here's the way it goes, Cheryl. Ohio State University Hospital is a teaching hospital, and we strive to teach our future doctors exactly how to be scientific in their approach to medicine."

"That's understandable. I would expect you to operate that way."

"So, Cheryl, in order to make certain that there are no other contributing factors to your particular malady, we attempt to rule out all other possible diseases before we subject you to the last definitive test."

Definitive test? Definitive test?

"What test is *that,* Dr. Lobo," I asked, almost afraid to do so.

"It's called an aortogram, Cheryl."

"But . . . but why not just let me have an aortogram and get it over with, doctor?"

"Because the aortogram that you will be given--assuming we find no indication of a different disorder first--is not an examination that is to be taken lightly."

"Do you mean there is risk involved?"

"There's *always* risk whenever one performs an invasive procedure on any patient, Cheryl, there's just a little more risk with an aortogram than there is with some of your other tests."

Did I want to hear this? Did I want to hear about something that would make me squeamish and defensive and . . . and scared?

"If, on the other hand, we can prove that there might be something other than a celiac artery constriction causing your problems, we need to address that issue before you are subjected to the aortogram."

I thought back to Dr. Beman's persuasive conversation in his office with my parents and me a few days earlier.

"Dr. Lobo?"

"What is it, Cheryl?"

"It's just that Dr. Beman and I *both* clearly heard a 'swishing' sound in my abdomen. That's what motivated me to come here for further tests."

"I am aware of that."

"Well . . . didn't *you* hear the bruit, yourself, Dr. Lobo?"

"No, Cheryl . . . I honestly didn't hear anything abnormal when I listened."

"Are you thinking what Dr. Beman and I heard might have been misinterpreted?"

"Perhaps . . . or maybe it was wishful thinking on your part, Cheryl."

Dr. Lobo just wasn't making any sense!

"But why would I want to hear a defect? That doesn't seem logical to me at all, doctor."

"It doesn't, Cheryl? I've been told you've prayed all of your life that some physician, somewhere, would find your specific disorder and miraculously wave his magic wand and heal you on the spot."

"Aren't you being a little overdramatic, Dr. Lobo?"

Dr. Lobo shrugged his shoulders and looked out the window again, turning his back to me.

"No. No, I don't think I am, Cheryl. I think you may want to gain weight so badly that anything remotely deviating from normalcy will loom significantly out of proportion in your mind. See where I'm going with this line of reasoning?"

"Do you go to church anywhere, Dr. Lobo?"

"What could my attending church possibly have to do with this conversation?"

I got up from my bed and went over to the sink to get a glass of water. My roommates watched every single step.

"Want a drink?" I asked him.

"No, thank you," he replied. "Straight H2O is a killer!"

I returned to the window and drank my *lethal* beverage.

"Well, *do* you?" I repeated.

"Do I go to church, you mean?"

"Of course."

"Sometimes . . . I go to church, Cheryl. This is a pretty busy time in my life and I really don't have the time to make it to church regularly."

"I see. In other words, you don't *frequent* church."

"All right, then--I *don't.*"

"Well, Dr. Lobo, what I've been taught all my life and what I've found to be *true* is that everything is possible if you *believe* it is. I've studied the Word as long as I can remember, and there have been many times when I know others in my shoes might have given up hope . . . but I've just refused to be pessimistic."

"Why?"

"Because I believe that Jesus intends to heal me, and I believe He has brought me to this very hospital to do exactly that, with the help of you capable doctors here."

Dr. Lobo grew uncomfortable.

"I know, Dr. Lobo. I'm not very scientific, am I?"

He looked at his watch. "I've got to be getting back to my quarters. Tomorrow morning, you're scheduled for a glucose tolerance test."

"How delightful! That's where I drink about ten gallons of sugar water and try not to spew for the next several hours."

"Right! Have you ever had this test before, Cheryl?"

"Why, sure, Doctor."

"Well, then, take the test with the understanding that it's confirmation of the obvious! Hopefully, the results will be the same as before, and we'll go on from there."

"Might I be able to have a snack before bedtime under the circumstances, doctor?"

"Certainly, Cheryl. What would you like?"

"How 'bout a nice, big, thick, chocolate milkshake?"

"That sounds like a plan, Cheryl. I'll tell the nurse on my way out to have one sent over later. Just make sure you finish all of it by midnight. You don't want to foul up your sugar test now, do you?"

And Dr. Lobo bade me goodnight.

Chapter Twenty-Eight

I was awakened at 6:30 in the morning by a bit of a ruckus in my room.

"Shhh!" I heard someone say in a hushed tone.

"There now, Barbara. You can turn back over. That shot'll make you sleepy in about twenty minutes, and by that time we'll have you all situated down in--"

"But . . . but the paperwork. Is it--"

"Everything's all in order. Everything is just fine, Barbara," an orderly said as Barbara was rolled out of the room.

By 7:00, the rattle of food trays in the cart outside my door assured me that it was time to rise and shine, and the accompanying squeak of the cart's wheels was somewhat disturbing.

My dietician brought my breakfast over to me, personally.

"Here's what you're getting, Cheryl. Hope something on the tray appeals to you."

It all smelled so good! There was a delicately poached egg, two pieces of whole wheat toast, a cup of steaming hot tea, a bowl of--

"WHOA, GIRL!" my dietician added snappily. "I'm so very sorry, Miss Kimes, but this is your big glucose tolerance day, isn't it? None of this good stuff!" and she whisked my breakfast from under my nose with a second apology.

"You should be seeing a nurse directly," she said. "I'm truly, truly sorry I brought this breakfast in by mistake!"

I straightened up in bed and looked around. Susie was still asleep. Shelly, too, was sleeping. Barbara was . . . Barbara was. . . .

Where was Barbara, anyway?

A nurse approached me with a large glass of ice cubes and a huge bottle of glucose. "Are you ready for your breakfast treat now, Miss Kimes?" she asked.

"Sure! Sure! Bring on the eggs Benedict!"

She upended the glucose over the ice cubes and commanded me to swallow it as quickly as possible--all in one gulp.

"Good job!" she praised. "You've done this before haven't you, Miss Kimes?"

"Why do you ask? Is it starting to run out of my ears, already?"

I swallowed forcefully, once more, just to stifle my gag reflex.

As my nurse headed out the door, Dracula, again, rushed in to proceed with more blood-letting.

"I wasn't sure you'd be the one to return today, Count," I told him.

"Yes, I know--but I just couldn't let you down, Cheryl. I want you to be as comfortable as possible, and if some other vampire fills in for me, you might not fare so well."

I was rather happy Dracula had returned.

"You know what you're supposed to do next, don't you, Cheryl?"

"Drink lots of water and prepare to donate to you for the rest of the morning?"

"OHHHHH, YEAH! You got *that* straight, girl!"

"Isn't my arm going to be pretty sore by this afternoon?"

"You've got *two* arms there, dontcha?"

"So . . . so you're going to alternate between them?"

"Precisely! And if your limbs become too sensitive, I can always use your foot, or neck, or. . . ."

I could tell. He was serious!

Dracula did his deed and left for the hall. He turned back, curiously. "Where's your buddy today, Cheryl?"

"Who, Barbara? I haven't a clue."

7:30 came. Dracula returned as promised. He drew blood from my other arm like I'd anticipated, and I was thankful he'd had lots of practice.

"See you in half an hour, again!" he said, as he departed.

At 8:00, ol' Dracule showed up again and repeated his routine. The aroma of my roommates' food was nauseating.

Why should I have to suffer by staying in the same ward with them when I could be elsewhere? My vampire's sonar could locate me easily enough.

Just a few feet from my doorway was an isolated area for patients to use whenever they needed a change of scenery. The chairs and sofa were padded, four end tables had magazines to read, and a couple of lamps gave the area a somewhat homey feeling--if one used one's imagination.

I sat down and picked up a women's magazine. I would be able to see Dracula easily when he returned. It was far more relaxing out here.

I found a little article to read about matriculating to a private girls' college. I'd never given much thought about going anywhere except Ohio University, but for some reason, the idea of a private school looked remotely interesting.

I started to read.

"Are you thinking about Vassar?"

The voice behind me had an unfamiliar ring. Gosh, this person was practically breathing down my neck! I juked forward to avoid conversation.

The voice returned "... 'cause I can really see you at Vassar. Yep! You've got what it takes so far as I've observed. I'm just *sure* you could be a Vassarette if you wanted to . . . easily."

"DO YOU MIND?"

I moved, taking my magazine with me and turned to a different section of the periodical. Unfortunately, I sat down at the end of a row where there was a vacant seat beside me.

It wasn't vacant for long.

I sighed deeply.

"Oh, come on, now. I can't be all *that* objectionable, Cheryl!"

This person actually knew my name!

I pretended to be excited over another article, to no avail.

"Call me silly, but I've . . . I've always found it far easier to read a printed page if it isn't upside down. Somehow, just rotating it a spec. . . ."

His unfamiliar hand reached over to right my magazine.

I glanced up at last.

"Well, hi there, finally! My name's Tom. I stay just a couple doors down from you, Cheryl," and Tom held out his hand to shake mine.

I'd never before had any man be particularly forward with me. Men usually seemed to avoid me like the plague, so my previous experiences told me Tom was probably up to no good.

"So," Tom said as he continued to hold his hand within easy reach, "are you going to make me keep my paw in this position for the next ten minutes, or do you think you might humble yourself long enough to make contact, Vassarette?"

That was more than enough introduction for me! I stood up immediately, said "EXCUSE ME!" loudly and sped back to my room like greased lighting.

Brother. Where did he get off, anyway?

At 8:30, Dracula came at me again. More blood was drawn.

"I understand you met my buddy, Tom, Cheryl," he said.

"Maybe," I answered coldly.

"Tom's a nice person. Hope you can be kind to him. He's pretty sick, I'm told."

So, what was I supposed to do about that fact? We were all "pretty sick" or we wouldn't be in research, would we? Life wasn't always peaches and cream. Sometimes, a person had to deal with a few pits. At least I had Christ in my life. Jesus was compensation.

I had blood drawn every hour, on the hour, for the next five hours. I felt wiped out, but I survived.

After my glucose test was over, I managed to force down about a half-cup of potato soup and two crackers that I had selected from the hospital menu the day before.

The food was tolerable.

At 3:00 in the afternoon, Barbara returned. GOLLY! She had been in surgery!

Surgery? How come I hadn't known? How come she hadn't said anything about an operation?

I felt rather left out, but Barbara obviously felt infinitely worse.

Miss Mott marched into the ward dictatorially.

"This woman just had MAJOR surgery," she announced. "I want all of you to keep it down in here. I don't want any talking above a whisper, and I want you guys to try to put yourselves in Barbara's shoes. Surgery is no picnic, but I intend to see that this patient recovers completely! You all bear that in mind and try to sympathize with her. She'll come around in another couple of hours or so. UNDERSTAND?"

Poor Barbara. Her large protruding tummy was totally gone, at least on one side of her abdomen. I didn't know what her problem was, but I surely felt sorry for her.

I pulled the curtains around my bed and prayed silently: *Please, Lord, please help my roommate, Barbara, to recover completely from her surgery. Please help her have no complications--and please show me, Lord, how to be kind and caring to the other unfortunates I meet here. Thank you, Lord, for your guidance. Amen."*

Dinner arrived at 5:00 sharp. How could *any* person be hungry so early in the afternoon?

I ate two spoonfuls of green peas, approximately five noodles, and one thin slice of corned beef. I couldn't identify the dessert, so I returned the suspicious-looking brown concoction along with the rest of my meal to the food rack in the hall. I saved my carton of milk to sip leisurely, and walked over to the window ledge to brood.

"Didn't your mother ever serve you chocolate cake with your milk when you were a little pea-picker?"

Oh, brother. It was Tom, again--and Tom had the gall to walk right into our ward unannounced, waving the piece of chocolate dessert I'd just rejected directly under my upturned nose.

Barbara groaned.

"See what you've done, now, Thomas?" I scolded. "You've awakened my roommate!"

"Sorry . . . sorry. . . ." whispered Tom as he motioned me to follow him into the waiting area where we'd met earlier. I went with him halfheartedly, toting my milk for security but pitching my cake into the wastebasket under the sink.

The two of us sat exactly where we had sat before.

"What's a pea-picker?" I asked.

"A pea-picker? One who picks peas, obviously!"

"Why did you call me that, anyway?"

"Oh, I don't know . . . I guess I thought I might get a rise outta you, perhaps."

"A *rise*?"

"You know, a *reaction*, pea-picker."

"WHAT DID YOU JUST CALL ME AGAIN?"

"*Pea-picker? Pea-picker* . . . I . . . I guess. Why? It's just a nickname, isn't it? To tell you the truth, Cheryl, I'm not sure *how* I should address you! You're really a hard nut to crack, Vassarette!

"Please don't call me *that*, either!"

I reached over for the same magazine I'd pretended to be absorbed in earlier.

"That must be a pretty fascinating magazine. That's the same article you read before, isn't it?"

"Perhaps. Probably. . . ."

"I thought you didn't want to be called Vassarette, either. But there you go reading all about them, again. SEE? SEE HOW CONFUSED YOU MAKE ME?"

I put the magazine down and looked directly into Tom's blue-gray eyes. His eyes were very unusual and rather sad-looking, but a gorgeous, incredible blue hue--somewhere between a powder blue and a steel gray. They were actually quite compelling. I hadn't noticed them before.

I stared at Tom for a second or two, then broke away.

"What do you want, anyway, Tom?" I asked assertively.

"What do you *want* me to want, Cheryl? I mean, I've got no ulterior motive here--I'm just bored to death and I figured you might be, too. I thought if we just talked occasionally to relieve our mutual boredom, that'd be better than sulking around in our respective rooms worrying about what our doctors are going to pull on us next. Really. That's all."

Tom rose in bewilderment. His hair was on the blond side, I noted, and his features were quite handsome. He reminded me, somehow, of my cousin, Fred.

"I promise I won't bother you any more," he continued. "Maybe if you glance through the other magazines here, too, they'll be enough companionship for you, Cheryl. So long."

Then Tom trudged dejectedly back to his room.

Well. I certainly hadn't been very kind to Tom like Dracula had requested. I'd hardly even been civil, if I admitted it to myself.

Drat. I hated to apologize to *anybody*--I'd almost rather die than apologize--but I figured I owed Tom a big one.

I forced myself to go to Tom's ward and stood quietly in the entrance. His three roommates turned in my direction.

"Tom? Tom?" I spoke softly.

Tom turned away from his window and smiled gently.

"Whatcha want, pea-picker?"

"Do . . . I mean . . . would . . . would you like to go downstairs and grab a soft drink from the pop machine or . . . or something?" I asked, hesitantly.

His roommates grinned.

"Why, sure, pea-picker!"

Tom seemed terribly surprised. He grabbed some loose change from his nightstand and started to put it in his hospital pant's pocket.

"That's not necessary, you know," I told him.

"The coins? Don't you have to have change to get those pop machines to operate?"

"Well, yes. Yes, you do . . . but this treat's on *me*, Tom. I owe it to you."

"What? How do you figure *that*, pea-picker?"

Tom's roommates were following our conversation attentively, turning their heads back and forth in unison to face each of us when we spoke, like spectators at a ping-pong match.

I was embarrassed.

"Oh . . . oh, I just acted like a real snot out there today, Tom." I mumbled.

Tom reached the doorway and put his hand on my left shoulder.

"You've got a lot spinnin' around in your head these days, pea-picker. We *all* do. No matter how brave all of us guinea pigs try to be here in C.R.U. --it's still Tension City."

We walked casually to the elevator. Tom pressed the button for the third floor.

"You're just fine," he reassured me. "Don't you fret about anything that goes on here. It's all gonna work out just super for you. You'll see, pea-picker. You're gonna be one of the lucky ones who make it!"

Tom sounded almost prophetic.

"How would you know such a thing, Tom? Where would you get any such information like that about me, for heaven's sake?"

"Oh, pea-picker . . . let's just say I have my sources, okay?"

I glanced briefly back at Tom's hospital bed. Stacks of medical books formed veritable pillars around his bedside.

Did he read all of those books?

We rode together down to the third floor vending machines. I bought each of us a token soft drink.

"Could you do me a special favor, Tom?" I asked. "Could you *please, please* drop the pea-picker routine and just call me by my given name--Cheryl?"

"Why, sure . . . sure, Cheryl. I forgot. I'll be happy to call you anything you want. I certainly never meant to offend you."

"Oh, I'm not exactly offended, Tom, it's . . . it's just that I've been called so many ugly names in my lifetime, and I actually like my God-given handle. Its what my Mom and Dad chose for me and I don't feel quite so *different* when I'm called Cheryl."

"I understand, Cheryl. Say no more."

Tom assured me he would respect my feelings, and the two of us enjoyed our drinks silently for about five minutes.

"So, Cheryl, where are you from, anyway? Didn't I hear you were a student at Ohio University?"

"Yes. I'm majoring in piano."

"Piano, huh? You plan on being a concert pianist some day, do you?"

"I hope so, or I could always teach piano in college, you know, and give recitals on the side and play in church, and so on."

"You're a churchgoer, huh? Man, that's where you leave me cold, kiddo!"

"You don't know the Lord?" I asked

"Hey. I don't wanna hear any of that religion stuff!"

"Why not?" I replied. "Jesus is the one person I can always count on!"

I was shocked. I had taken Tom for being a warm, giving, Christian type, but he turned away and clearly didn't want to discuss anything remotely spiritual.

"So, you? How about you, Tom? Do you live close to O.S.U?"

"Yep. I've got a little apartment off Fifth Avenue, Cheryl."

"Wow! That's really close."

"Yes, it is, so I can come and go easily while talking some classes on campus."

"That sounds great, Tom. What are you planning on doing when you get out of college, anyhow?"

Tom suddenly acted uncomfortable and changed the subject abruptly. "You know, Barbara, your roommate--she really had quite an operation, didn't she? Is she still out like a light?"

"Honestly, Tom, I didn't even know she was going in for surgery. She sure looks different now, though."

"Think how different she'll look when they remove the *other* tumor, too!"

"The *other* tumor? You mean she has *two* tumors, Tom?"

"Yeah. Her surgeon keeps removing them and they keep growing back. She's really a trooper, though."

Miss Mott made an surprising appearance and interrupted our conversation.

"You two BOTH have procedures tomorrow! See that you're upstairs by 8:00 on the nose. GOT IT?"

"What are they doing to you tomorrow, Tom?" I asked as soon as Miss Mott departed.

"Oh, just another kidney function test, Cheryl." he said.

"Will it be painful?"

"Nope, not at all. And you, kiddo? You're scheduled for a liver scan, if my memory serves me correctly. Right?"

"Yes. I guess there's not much to taking it, either."

"No, there really isn't. You'll have the rest of the day free, then, won't you?"

"Well, so far as I know. But, say--how do you keep track of what all's happening around here anyway, Tom? You seem to know everything about everyone! How come you're so well-informed about this place?"

Tom looked at his watch and decided it was time to return upstairs. "I'm a little tired, Cheryl," he said. He rose slowly, but continued to talk rather nervously, avoiding my personal questions.

"After this one kidney test tomorrow," he went on, "I'll be tied up for several days. Would you like to blow this joint for a couple hours, kiddo? You know, go out and . . . ah . . . paint the town red or puce or something, huh? How would you like to dash out with me for a couple hours after our tests are all finished? What do you say?"

"Well . . . sure, sure! But I hardly think my doctors would allow--"

"You just let me see what I can do, kiddo. We've both got tomorrow afternoon totally free, so I'll see if I can pull some strings. Talk to ya later, now."

Then Tom was gone.

I had no desire to return to my room. Instead, I took the elevator up to the fifth floor and went over to take a look at the newborns.

Gosh! The maternity ward was filled to capacity. Nurses were scrambling here and there--many with infants in their arms, some babies with bottles--how perfectly adorable all the little tykes were!

In one corner of the ward behind glass, however, there was a flurry of activity. Several doctors appeared to be converging on a little fellow who was massively taped and tubed, and there was alarm on the faces of those who were attending him.

A nurse stopped me and asked for identification. I showed her my arm band.

"I've never seen many babies before," I stated. "They're all so precious! What's wrong with that little guy over there in the corner, anyway? Is he pretty sick?"

"He's probably not going to make it through the night," the nurse replied.

"You mean . . . you mean he . . . he might *die*?"

"Yes, unfortunately, but we're doing all we can to save him, hon."

I felt heartsick. It just didn't seem fair for one so young to pass on.

"I should at least pray for him, then, shouldn't I, nurse?"

"Yes. Oh, yes! Nathan needs all the prayers he can get. If you'd like to ask God to take care of him, I think that'd be just wonderful!"

The nurse hurried off to join the others around Nathan's crib.

"Good luck to you in C.R.U.!" she said as she departed. "It was nice meeting you, Cheryl."

I went to the elevator and prayed for Nathan all the way up to my room.

When I got off on my floor, nobody was sitting in the area where Tom and I had talked earlier that day.

Miss Mott saw me and came over to give me a big chewing out. "Where were you this afternoon, Miss Kimes?" she fumed. "Why weren't you up here for Dr. Lobo's visit, anyway?" Whenever you want to get away for a change just come over to our nurses station and we'll see what we can do to help you out! DON'T YOU DARE ever leave again without telling us first! For C.R.U. to operate properly--"

"OKAY! I apologize. It won't happen again."

Miss Mott kept yammering on about this and that, but I successfully tuned her completely out.

I kept staring at the spot where Tom had introduced himself.

It didn't feel right not seeing him there.

It just didn't feel right at *all.*

Chapter Twenty-Nine

Tom and I were both finished with our respective procedures by 10:00 the following morning. He caught up with me as I was being wheeled back to my room from my liver scan.

"How'd it go downstairs, Cheryl?" he asked.

"Oh, fine, just fine. That scan was no biggie for sure. How'd it go for you, Tom?"

"Let's just say it *went* kiddo, like water under a bridge. So . . . so how 'bout we go out and have a bite of lunch somewhere in a couple hours 'round noon?"

"Lunch *out*? Out *where*?"

"Oh, I don't know . . . let me think about it." he said.

"Okay, okay . . . I guess. But how much cash should I bring with me, Tom. I'll have to see if Mom and Dad left me enough 'cause--"

"No way, sister! Lunch is on *me*, today! After all, you bought me a pop yesterday, so today it's *my* treat! And don't trouble the nursing staff with your whereabouts, either. They know we're leaving for a time and we don't have to return till 4:00 or so. I fixed it all up for us."

What? Could he actually do that?

At 12:00, I stood outside my ward door and expected Tom to be there exactly when he had said he would be.

At 12:15, I was still waiting.

At 12:35, Tom finally shuffled towards me, a little paler and a bit more sober than usual.

I should have been upset (after all, my father believed punctuality was a virtue), but how could I be angry with such a nice person as Tom?

"Are you feeling okay, Tom?" I asked. "You look a little rough around the edges. Want to cancel this afternoon? If you do, it's certainly okay with me."

"Make no mistake about it! We're steppin' out together right this minute, and I won't take 'no' for an answer!"

The two of us rode the elevator down to the first floor and headed for the main doors.

"You feel like walkin' a few blocks with me, don't you, Cheryl?"

Boy, how I hated to decline Tom's suggestion, but I was so weak from all the hospital rigmarole that I didn't see how I could summon the necessary strength. Still, if I really tried. . . .

"Well, I suppose we *could* start out and just see how it goes for me, Tom. Sure. I'll make an attempt since you want me to, but--"

"On the other hand, Cheryl, I think you look pretty weak in the knees, so I'll hail a cab instead, and . . . oh, look! Here comes one, now! TAXI! TAXI!" Tom yelled.

Tom took my right hand. "'Onward and upward,' I heard someone say recently, didn't I, Cheryl? Well, come on now, gorgeous! You can't expect that cabbie to hang around all day, can you?"

The taxicab driver dashed around all dignified-like, opened our doors respectfully, and graciously motioned for the two of us renegade patients to take our seats.

"You guys think you can get away with leavin' like this, huh?"

"Drive on, Mack," Tom answered. "I've covered all the bases."

Our driver drove into an area of Columbus that I was entirely unfamiliar with.

"DRIVER! DRIVER!" I questioned. "Where are you taking us, anyway?"

Tom interrupted. "You can trust me, Cheryl. Just relax, hon. We're going to one of the best restaurants in town. It's actually a castle of sorts!"

"A . . . a *castle*? But there are no castles in Ohio, Tom--are there?"

"Yes, believe me, there are *several*!"

All of a sudden, we were in front of a White Castle *restaurant*, while Tom, my benefactor, laughed himself silly--quite without shame!

"SURPRISE, Cheryl! SURPRISE!" he shouted loudly.

The cabbie parked momentarily and dashed around to facilitate our exiting. "Want me to wait, sir?" he asked Tom.

"No, that won't be necessary," Tom replied and told him when to return.

Once again, Tom laughed himself into a veritable tizzy! I was rather embarrassed over his behavior but determined not to spoil Tom's fun, or . . . the incredibly good time *I* was also having!

As we entered the restautant, Tom assured me that White Castle was known as one of the best college hangouts in Columbus. He told me that O.S.U. students frequented the place because they couldn't get their fill of the restaurant's exceptional burgers.

"Won't it be difficult to find a place to sit, then?" I speculated.

"Nope. Not today. They're expecting us, Cheryl!"

We took our places in two reserved seats, and Tom ordered four hamburgers.

"Four?" I asked. "Oh, Tom, I could never--"

"Hey, now! That quartet of burgers is for me *alone,* Cheryl! You can order whatever you want, though. Their fries are phenomenal, too. Go ahead! Get whatever you please, kiddo--just fire away!"

As usual, I felt I could eat out the entire establishment, but I had to be realistic. Maybe, I could handle one cheeseburger if I really pushed it.

After I placed my order, Tom tacked on a chocolate milkshake for me, too.

"You sure do take note of what I like, don't you, Tom?" I said.

Tom nodded affirmatively.

Soon, we ate . . . and ate . . . and ate. Several times, I'd chomp off a big portion of my burger, cover my mouth with my napkin, then discretely spit my mouthful into my napkin when Tom wasn't looking. My friend, I'm quite certain, never once caught on. The important thing to me was that Tom felt he was making me truly happy, and for some reason, he truly was.

When it came to ordering dessert, I had to decline.

Tom, incredibly, decided to have one more hamburger, while I, at the same time, attempted to delve more into my buddy's background.

"So . . . you have an apartment around here, Tom?"

"Right, Cheryl."

"And do you live alone?"

"Yes, I can study better that way. Sometimes my sister comes to visit me a little from our farm, but in order for me to hit the books, I really need my solitude."

Tom's appetite showed no signs of abating, as he ordered a large serving of fries to complement burger number five.

Gosh! His stomach must have been a bottomless pit!

I continued to seek. "Just exactly what *are* they planning on doing to you in C.R.U. anyway, Tom? You've got a kidney problem, you said?"

"Well, yes, that's right--but why do you want to spoil lunch with such prattle as this, Cheryl?"

I waited for Tom to swallow a humongous mouthful, then I tried to see how much more info I could coax out of him. "Because . . . because I thought maybe you'd be willing to share something deeper about yourself with me, and I thought having told you all I did about myself that--"

Tom cleared his throat. "You 'bout finished, Cheryl?"

I sat my ground.

"No, Tom . . . no, I'm *not.* I know almost nothing about what's going on with you. You've been a gentleman and a scholar to me, but I'm interested in hearing about *your* physical problems, too. I just . . . well, I really want to pray for you but I don't know what to pray *about.*"

"Are you gonna start with that Bible talk again, Cheryl?"

"It's what I do, Tom. It's who I am. I'm a Christian, and I focus on others. I want to help *you* . . . if you'll let me. What's so wrong with that idea, anyway?"

I hated silence. Silence was such a waste of precious time. Now, however, Tom insisted on withdrawing.

A waitress moved towards us impatiently and acted like she wanted to clear our table.

Tom stood up. "We should leave now, Cheryl," he said.

"No. Please, not . . . please not just yet, Tom." I protested.

Tom sat back down obligatorily, then ordered a cup of coffee.

"Why won't you talk about what's going on with you, Tom?" I asked.

"Well, it's really pointless, but if you insist, I . . . I have to have a shunt installed."

"A *what*?"

"A shunt. It's a plastic tube that'll fit inside my artery to make it easier for me to have kidney dialysis. I have to have minor surgery tomorrow, and they're going to make the shunt permanent. This was my *last meal*, you might say, for a few days, at least. There, now--are you satisfied, Cheryl?"

I summoned the courage to grab Tom's hand.

I held tightly.

"Thank you so much for telling me, Tom," I said. "I'll pray that your surgery will go beautifully and I'll pray that the Lord will bless you in your future dialyses. You will be fine. You'll see. I just know it! Just be hopeful and trust in Jesus with me!"

Tom and I left before his coffee arrived, but I knew he didn't want it, anyway. The important thing was that he had given me the opportunity to tell him about my faith in Jesus, and for a time, he listened.

Our cab ride back to the hospital seemed like it was over almost before it started. When Tom returned to his room, I felt deeply concerned about my introspective friend. He had suddenly become totally incommunicative, except for indicating that he wanted to be left alone.

I went to my room and took out my Bible. I turned to Jeremiah 17:7-8: "But blessed is the one who trusts in the LORD, whose confidence is in Him. They will be like a tree planted by the water that sends out its roots by the stream. It does not fear when heat comes; its leaves are always green. It has no worries in a year of drought and never fails to bear fruit."

I had always trusted the Lord to help me. Even when I had times of abysmal discouragement, I always believed that my

Savior would be with me and that ultimately, some day, He would answer my numerous prayers and deliver me from the eating problems that had plagued me since I was five.

What hope did Tom--or *anyone*--have without Jesus in his life? How terrible it would be to face surgery of any magnitude if one had to face it without the help of the Lord! I prayed for Jesus to intervene in Tom's surgery and help him with his kidney affliction, however serious it was.

The following day, I had another GI series. Dr. Lobo assured me that the resultant X-rays were normal, which I expected.

Two days later, Tom came into my room to brighten up my spirits. He had a large gauze bandage over his right arm.

"How did your surgery go, Tom?" I was quick to ask.

"Oh, it went okay, Cheryl. It'll help me out a little longer, perhaps. Say. Would you like to see a picture of my dog?"

Tom handed me a picture of his German shepherd, "Shep," his special pal.

"My, what a handsome animal!" I said. "I didn't know you were a dog lover, Tom. My Aunt Sybil has a boxer she's crazy about, too, but I prefer birds. They're way less aggressive and sing so beautifully! I think it's just amazing how they flit about all carefree and happily, don't you? They never have to worry about much of anything . . . and God watches over every one of them."

Tom seemed to study my comments, and when he returned to his room, I noticed he stopped every so often like he was out of breath.

I was concerned about him.

We kept to ourselves for the next few days--Tom occupied with whatever tests he had to have--me, likewise, having one procedure after another . . . after another--testing my stamina, my endurance . . . *and my faith.*

Through it all, I continued to pray for both Tom and myself.

Ultimately, as I had expected, came the inevitable conclusion that an aortogram was indeed called for to confirm Dr. Beman's original suspicions. This was the *one* test when I wanted my parents to be with me; this was the one procedure Dr. Lobo had assured me would tell the doctors if I had a celiac artery construction that should be repaired . . . or *not.*

I was more than ready to find out!

I telephoned my parents on August twenty-fifth, and the two of them promised to drive to O.S.U. to support me. My father and mother arrived in my room the next morning about an hour before I was to be taken downstairs for my conclusive procedure.

"You know you'll be in His hands when you're havin' your big test today, don'tcha, Cheryl?" said my father.

"And you know we'll be praying for you all the time, Cheryl!" added my Mother.

"Of course, you two," I said, appreciatively.

Tom was curiously absent when my parents were visiting me, although I *had* invited him to meet them as soon as they arrived.

Maybe he wasn't feeling so well.

"You seem preoccupied, Cheryl," noted my father.

"I'm doing well enough, Dad. I'm truly okay."

But, was I? I was apprehensive and restless, and I couldn't help wonder why Tom hadn't stopped by to encourage me before I went for my aortogram.

Miss Mott came in to give me a shot to relax me before I was taken downstairs. It was sort of her personal touch.

But . . . no Tom.

Then, within forty-five minutes, I was whisked away by an orderly to have my aortogram.

"You'll get along just great down there!" my mother said.

"And we'll be right here when you get back, Cheryl!" added my father.

I was wheeled to the elevator, then down to third floor. I felt sleepy and lighter than air.

"Your shot is starting to kick in, Cheryl!" I faintly heard my orderly say. "Don't fight it, kiddo. Give in! You don't want to be awake when you have your femoral artery stuck!"

Actually, I DID want to be totally awake and alert!

HELP ME FIGHT THIS, LORD! I prayed. *HELP ME TO STAY AWAKE SO I CAN UNDERSTAND EVERY SINGLE THING THAT'S HAPPENING TO ME, JESUS!*

I pictured Jesus pushing my gurney behind me beside my orderly, like I had pictured Him sitting beside me when I'd played with the Ohio University Orchestra.

My cart seemed to move faster!

Soon, I was parked in a cold waiting area where lots of other patients were stationed in preparation for their respective tests. I tried talking to several of them, but not one responded.

"Hey, you guys!" I protested. "What's the matter with all of you anyway? Don't you know how to make conversation, or what? Brother! You're all so grumpy! You're all so depressing! Man! You guys really take the cake!"

"CHERYL, CHERYL!" a masked attendant spoke up as he forcefully wheeled me away. "Try to keep your voice down, girl! You're upsetting everyone around you!"

When my gurney stopped, I was in what appeared to be an operating room.

"WAIT! WAIT!" I yelled. "I'm not here for any operation, fellas! I'm just here for a simple aortogram!"

"Didn't this patient get something to knock her out before she came down here?" I heard someone closeby exclaim.

"She's a real live wire!" said another. "Must be a reaction to her shot!"

Beside my cart was an IV hooked up and ready to drip whatever it was supposed to drip to keep me hydrated . . . I *guessed.*

I tilted my head backwards and asked, "You still back there, Jesus?"

I saw Him plain as day!

"Yep--she's had her shot, alright!" said another voice.

"Ha! She's so out of it she thinks she can see Jesus!"

I heard lots of derogatory laughter.

"Okay, let's get on with this!" said someone else.

My cart was positioned where my technicians could see an X-ray monitor on my left. So could I!

Good . . . good. . . .

Even better, directly above my head there was a large light with a clear cover that reflected everything the technicians were about to do on my thigh.

How fascinating!

"YOU'RE GOING TO FEEL A GREAT BIG POKE IN YOUR GROIN, CHERYL!" someone stated with authority.

"YOU MEAN IN MY FEMORAL ARTERY, DON'T YOU?"

Keep me awake, Lord! Keep me awake!

"I say we give her some anesthesia--" I overheard, but nobody did.

YOU'RE GOING TO FEEL LOTS OF PRESSURE ON YOUR *FEMORAL* NOW, CHERYL!"

I watched the monitor beside me as a catheter was inserted into the femoral artery in my right leg, and I could clearly see the catheter as it proceeded to travel slowly up . . . up . . . inside my femoral artery . . . almost to my heart! I could even see my spine, too, and it was the most awesome sight I had ever imagined!

People were nervously moving all around getting ready for my big injection.

"ALRIGHT, CHERYL, IF YOU CAN STILL HEAR ME--"

I laughed out loud!

"NOW, HERE COMES THE DYE, CHERYL! YOU'RE GOING TO FEEL A WARM SENSATION AS THE DYE ENTERS YOUR ARTERY--"

Warm? WARM? IT WAS HOT!!!!!

"YEEEEEOOOOOOOOOOWEEEE! I'M ON FIRE!" I yelled. "I'M BURNING UP! GET THAT TUBE OUT OF ME RIGHT AWAY!"

I tried to shift positions and grab the tubing, but many hands took hold of me and many voices declared that if I *didn't* cooperate, I'd have to repeat the whole procedure again the next day!

I paid attention to only one voice, however, the one most important voice coming from behind me which said, "Be still and know that I am God (Psalm 46:10)."

Then, I heard it again.

"Be still and know that I am God."

I concentrated on looking at the overhead light. I could see a large red area fanning out from my femoral like circles radiating from a thrown stone making ripples in water.

THAT WAS MY BLOOD! MY BLOOD WAS SOAKING UP THE SHEET AROUND THE INJECTION SITE! HOW TOTALLY NEATO!

"THANK YOU, JESUS! THANK YOU, LORD!" I said once more.

Moments later, several technicians swarmed to the foot of my cart, the catheter was withdrawn, and much pressure was applied to my femoral artery site.

"You're all finished, Cheryl!" I heard. "You're all done, and you did really well!" another person emphasized.

"Yes, *WE* did, didn't we!" I replied, as I craned my neck to look at the *figure* behind me.

Continuous pressure was applied to my femoral until proper clotting began, then I was taken back upstairs.

"THANK YOU, JESUS!" I reiterated in the elevator." THANK YOU, JESUS, SO MUCH!"

My parents were relieved to see me and were overjoyed when they learned that my aortogram was over.

Miss Mott just missed me, my parents said, and was on her way home for the afternoon.

"You'll have to lay perfectly still for the rest of the day, she told us, Cheryl," Mom relayed. "And Miss Mott also told us that you and Tom should kind of 'lay low' or at least stay on this floor until Dr. Beman comes in to see you--might not be till tomorrow, Cheryl!"

Mother was quizzical. "But, who is this . . . this *Tom* person, anyway, Cheryl? Is he an intern or something?"

"Oh, Tom's just a friend who keeps me company sometimes. He's a real nice person, Mom."

Mother fluffed up the pillow under my head and I drifted into a world where no sickness and no anxiety existed.

When I started to come around, Tom was standing at the foot of my bed and my parents were gone.

"Wake up, Cheryl!" he whispered as he gently shook my bed post.

"Tom? Tom? Is it really you?"

"'Tis me, Cheryl, and do you know what time it is? It's . . . it's almost 10:30, kiddo! Miss Mott would probably shoot me if she knew I was in here, but I just had to see you before I take off tomorrow!"

"Are you leaving, Tom?" I tried to sit up, but my right leg was throbbing, and I knew I was supposed to stay on my back.

"Yes, Cheryl, I'm leaving for a time. They don't need me here for a couple days, so I'm going to my apartment early tomorrow morning. In case you have surgery before I return. . . ."

Boy, did his speculation awaken me!

"What . . . what surgery are you talking about, Tom?"

"You know, Cheryl--your *celiac* surgery! That's about all that's left for them to do to you now, isn't it?"

I blinked my eyes a of couple times to help me awaken, and Tom gave me a glass of ice water with a bent straw so I could suck on it without sitting upright.

"I shouldn't tell you this, maybe, but I heard the doctors talking about you, and they said it's about time to call in Dr. Sam."

"Dr. Sam? Who is Dr. Sam, Tom?"

"Why. . . Samuel Marable! He's just about the most famous thoracic surgeon this side of the Mississippi! He's been here at O.S.U. for many years, and any doctor who *is* any doctor knows Sam Marable by name. You'll be in great hands, Cheryl--if I'm right about your surgery, that is!"

I tried, once more, to rise.

Tom gently pushed me back down.

"Not now, Cheryl. You *know* you shouldn't disobey Miss Mott!"

"But . . . but I wanted to play the piano for you, Tom! I wanted to play something on that old piano downstairs before I returned to Athens and now you say you're getting ready to leave and--"

"I said I'll be back to see you one of these days, didn't I? I promise! You can play for me then, Cheryl. How 'bout that?"

"Do you *promise,* Tom?"

"Absolutely, Cheryl! Hearing you play will give me something special to look forward to . . . a goal to keep me going!"

So many questions plagued my brain.

"But Tom . . . what . . . what if I don't--"

"Don't you *dare* start being negative, now, Cheryl. You are one of the luckiest patients I've ever met here in C.R.U.! People like you are the very reason this clinic exists."

I felt ashamed. Where was my Christian strength all of a sudden? What kind of example was I setting for others--especially Tom?

The night nurse stepped into my room and shined her flashlight directly at the two of us. She gasped when she saw my friend!

"Well, you can just hustle right to your room this instant, young man!" she chastised. "Miss Kimes needs all the rest she can get and you shouldn't be bothering her! You get right out of here, Tom! SHOO, NOW! GO ON!"

Tom winked at me and departed as commanded, but he dashed back to my bedside later that evening when the nurse was away on her rounds.

"That strong faith you've been tellin' me about?" he whispered. "You're not about to lose it now, are you? I mean, if He *is* all you *say* He is . . . now's your chance to prove it to me, kiddo!"

And Tom tiptoed away.

Chapter Thirty

Dr. Beman favored me with a rare visit the next morning. Mother and Dad were in my room at the time, hoping and praying to corral him for any significant test results. It would have taken a team of ten Clydesdales to drag my parents away!

Dr. Beman acknowledged my parents, then addressed me directly. "You're giving us all conniptions around here, do you know that, Cheryl? We never know if we'll find you in pediatrics . . . or at the vending machines . . . or roaming the grounds somewhere . . . or out gallivanting about town--you're leading us all in a merry chase, missy!"

My primary physician was obviously somewhat perturbed with me, but I suspected he was also making light of my behavior to soften an impending blow.

Dr. Beman's mood changed to serious. "I have good news to report about your aortogram--at least, from *my* perspective. I am extremely hopeful, Cheryl," he continued, ". . . *extremely*!"

I took my deepest breath ever and waited for what I had prayed I would one day hear some physician say: "I believe we've found what's wrong with you, Cheryl."

AT LAST--AN ANSWER TO MY PRAYERS!

Mother started to cry. Dad put his arms around Mom and consoled her while Dr. Beman continued to elaborate.

"It appears that you *do* have a celiac artery constriction, Cheryl, and I believe it is possible to repair it surgically."

You would have thought I would have had some intelligent response prepared for this monumental, life-long awaited announcement, but I was too stunned to say one word.

Dr. Beman continued to describe my physical anomaly and tore off a paper towel from the dispenser over the sink. Then he quickly sketched a drawing of my celiac artery on that towel and showed how a little band was choking it off, creating an aneurism--a ballooning out of my constricted artery--on the other side of the compression.

"Quite honestly," he continued, ". . . it's as severe as *any* celiac artery constriction we've ever observed here at Ohio State University, folks."

I thought my mother was going to swoon as she started to sway towards the window.

"CATCH HER THERE, MR. KIMES!" Dr. Beman yelled, simultaneously scooting a chair under Mom as she gracefully cascaded downward.

"You have no idea how I've prayed for this day, doctor!" Mom said.

Dr. Beman smiled. "I'm certain you have, Mrs. Kimes."

"So, then, Dr. Beman," my father interjected, ". . . you're telling us that our daughter would benefit from having surgery. Is that the way it is?"

"Yes, Mr. Kimes, that's precisely what I'm saying. I realize surgery can be a very frightening proposition, but if she were *my* daughter I'd steer her towards the operation. There's no guarantee on the outcome, but truthfully, I believe there's about a ninety percent chance she'd be able to digest her food properly after surgery, and she might even be able to gain . . . oh . . . perhaps thirty or maybe forty pounds."

"THIRTY OR FORTY POUNDS?" I exclaimed. "Gosh! I was only praying for ten or fifteen!"

I could feel a good cry coming on, but as usual, I managed to control any excessive display of emotion.

"There's so much I want to ask you about, Dr. Beman!" I said.

I tried my best to delve into the subject, but Dr. Beman was faster on the draw than I and told me that from this point on, if I were *truly* considering the operation, Dr. Marable would be the one to save my questions for.

"You mean . . . you mean . . . I'd get *Dr. Sam*?"

"Yes, Cheryl, Samuel Marable is the one who'd be doing your surgery, and obviously, you've already heard about Dr. Sam!

"See what I mean?" he grinned at my parents. "See what all that traipsing around did for your daughter?"

Dr. Beman assured me that he would still be my doctor-of-record, and he also reassured my parents that Dr. Marable--like Tom had told me--was one of the most highly regarded thoracic surgeons in the United States.

The United States? Wow! My outcome was looking better and better all the time!

"Well, I know *I'm* ready to have surgery," I uttered "so what's the next step, doctor? Is Dr. Sam going to stop by and talk to me soon?"

"Dr. Marable should be in to see you yet today, Cheryl, right after he's out of O.R."

Dr. Beman made for the door. His visit was over.

"But . . . but WHEN will I have. . . ."

"Talk to Dr. Marable, Cheryl! Dr. Marable's a very congenial surgeon, and I'm certain he'll be more than willing to go over your case in fine detail if that's what you want!"

Dr. Beman fled down the hallway.

"I'll see you periodically, Cheryl. Just bide your time now," he said, as his voice trailed out of hearing range.

My father took hold of mother's and my hands, and we made a circle of prayer to thank the Good Lord for the optimistic news we had just received.

"Thank you, Lord," Dad prayed, "for this blessed opportunity for our daughter. Please give us all, Father, the strength and courage we need to move ahead with whatever Cheryl needs to do next . . . and please give Dr. Marable the guidance he needs to tackle her surgery with total success. Thank you, Lord . . . so very, very much. Amen."

I had never observed obsessive hand-wringing before, but that's exactly what my father did for the next five hours straight. Watching him wring his hands incessantly while pacing back and forth at the foot of my bed nearly drove me berserk! Yet, my father continued to pace repeatedly as if somewhat in a trance. Apparently--although Dad had mountains of faith--he still couldn't quite let completely go and totally trust the Lord at this point in time. I was Dad's "little girl," and he needed to protect me.

Mother, as well, had her own unique way of dealing with her pent-up anxiety. Mother proceeded to purse her lips and whistle, over and over, any melody that popped into her head--hymn tune, classical or operatic melody--*whatever.* It wasn't that I opposed or resented her whistling, it was just that she persisted in consistently whistling way off key!

My parents, whom I loved deeply, were, in short, making me nervous. I didn't need this.

When lunchtime arrived, Mom and Dad decided to eat in the hospital cafeteria. I, of course, remained in my ward awaiting my customary food tray to be delivered. When it came, I ate three bites of Dutch apple pie and returned my tray with the rest of its food to the rack in the hall.

At 2:00, a distinguished-looking doctor strode confidentially through the door into my room. I was taken aback by his impressive appearance as he was wearing green surgeon's attire with a surgical mask dangling from his neck.

He looked like a movie star!

"Are you Cheryl Kimes?" he asked as he extended his right hand to shake mine.

"Indeed, yes," I said.

I never say 'indeed.' I've got to get control of myself here. I need to just relax and be myself. Fancy talk is not necessary.

"I'm Sam Marable. I'm the surgeon who is going to repair your celiac band, if you want, Miss Kimes."

"Yes, yes, you are. I'm . . . I'm happy to meet you, doctor. I- I'm *very* happy."

I had seen a couple old romantic movies on television, and Dr. Sam resembled one of those thirties actors such as Errol Flynn, maybe . . . or was it Ronald Coleman, perhaps, or--

"Miss Kimes? CHERYL?"

"I'm s-sorry, sir. You were saying?"

"I've gone over your case history and reviewed some of your films."

"No . . . no, doctor, . . . I've . . . I've never been in any motion pictures . . . but some people tell me I *do* resemble Audrey Hepburn a little."

Dr. Sam's face twisted into a convoluted shape. He arched his eyebrows questioningly. "Are you feeling well, today, Cheryl?" he asked.

"F-fine . . . I'm just fine, sir. How 'bout yourself?"

My parents entered the doorway.

Dr. Sam turned and greeted them politely. "And you are Cheryl's parents, I presume?"

My father acknowledged that they were.

Mother's mouth dropped open and she had nothing to say. She obviously saw Dr. Sam in the same handsome light *I* did!

"I was just telling your daughter what to expect if she lets me perform surgery. It would take around eight hours, but her prognosis is good for complete recovery."

Mother was mute.

My father, fortunately, had a couple of pertinent questions to ask.

"Have you performed this operation often, doctor?"

How important, Dad!

"Your daughter's disease is quite rare, Mr. Kimes, but I've done this operation on a number of patients here."

"And did those operations turn out . . . okay?"

"Yes--perfectly so, Mr. Kimes."

Mother's mouth was still agape, and I, too, was tongue-tied.

Dr. Sam turned to me.

"Isn't there anything *you'd* like to ask me, Cheryl? After all, you are the person who's considering going under my knife. Aren't there any concerns you'd like me to address?"

Think. Think fast! My surgeon can't help it if he's a hunk!

"Well . . . well, doctor . . . afterwards . . . after t-the operation and all . . . will it take, ahhhhh, will it take long for me to . . . to recuperate?"

I talked like a kindergartner trying to formulate her first sentences!

"I won't kid you about this, Cheryl. Thoracic surgery is a major trauma to one's body. Your incision will be quite long--it will run all the way from your sternum to your navel--and it will be very painful for you to breathe for several days."

"That sounds just awful," my father said.

Mother was still silent.

"She *will* be on strong pain killers for as long as necessary, Mr. Kimes."

"Pain killers? Pain killers like . . . like morphine?"

"Absolutely. Morphine will undoubtedly be indicated for a time, sir. Our nurses will be here to help her use a breathing device, too--to speed her recovery along--and after forty-eight hours or so, she should have much less difficulty taking a breath on her own."

Dr. Marable looked over my chart, and noted that I had been to many other physicians in the past.

"You've really had a challenging existence, haven't you, Cheryl? I'll bet you had just about given up hope that this day would come, in fact. Am I correct?"

"No . . . no, not *really*, doctor. Everybody has some type of a cross to bear, don't they?"

"A 'cross,' did you say?" Dr. Sam looked perplexed.

"Yes, you know--like Jesus did. Metaphorically speaking, at least, Jesus Christ had the whole world on His shoulders, I always thought. In those times when I've become temporarily discouraged, I've tried to look to Jesus' example. I mean, no matter how difficult my life has been from time to time, my emotional and physical pain couldn't possibly compare to the agony my Savior suffered in my behalf."

I didn't know quite how to interpret Dr. Sam's reaction. Actually, his facial expression didn't change a bit.

For a brief time he assessed my words without batting an eyelash.

"You're obviously a Christian, aren't you, Cheryl?" he said, ultimately.

"Why, certainly. I always have been!"

Dr. Sam caught my parents' eyes and uttered something to all of us I'd never before heard any physician say: "In my experience, those patients who have a strong belief in God or a higher power than themselves tend to pull through surgeries much better than those who don't."

He looked back at me. "I see no particular amount of fear in you, Cheryl."

I shook my head.

"Why should I be afraid? Jesus will be there to help me through surgery just as He'll be there to guide your expert hands. If I make it, my life will be far, far healthier than it's ever been up to this point. If I *don't* make it, I'll go on to something way more beautiful than any living human being has ever imagined!" *('What no eye has seen, what no ear has heard, and what no human mind has conceived--the things God has prepared for those who love him--these are the things God has revealed to us by his Spirit.' 1 Corinthians 2:9.)*

My parents nodded agreement.

"Actually, when I verbalize it that way," I went on, "there's really no reason at all I should hesitate to have the operation, is there? So . . . let's do it Dr. Sam! The sooner the better! So far as I'm concerned, I'm ready to go for it!"

At the grown-up age of twenty, I knew my parents had no legal way to deter me from having surgery, and neither of them volunteered any objections to stop me. I had made myself perfectly clear; I wanted a fresh start on life!

For the second time, Dr. Sam took my hand in his.

"I promise I'll do my best not to disappoint you, Cheryl," he said, as he gave my right hand a good squeeze and I started to pump.

"You seem like a thoughtful and courageous young woman to me, and you deserve to enjoy the rest of your life in radiant health," he added.

I continued to shake Dr. Sam's hand . . . vigorously.

"You may let go anytime, now, Cheryl."

I held tight.

"Cheryl . . . Cheryl, kindly unhand me! I'm going to need my right hand to assist my left hand tomorrow if there's any circulation left in it!"

Now *that* announcement aroused my mother to verbosity!

"YOU'RE GOING TO OPERATE ON OUR DAUGHTER TOMORROW, DID YOU SAY--TOMORROW AS IN THE DAY AFTER TODAY--TOMORROW, ON AUGUST THE 28th--DOWNSTAIRS--IN THE MORNING--*THAT* TOMORROW?"

"Yes, Mrs. Kimes. As I recall, there's an opening in O.R. as early as 6:30 a.m. I'll double-check, of course, but I can't see any possible reason to delay this operation. Your daughter has clearly made up her mind. I'll tell the nurses to prepare her for surgery later tonight."

I released my grip.

"No wonder you're such a phenomenal pianist, Miss Kimes. I don't think anyone ever shook my hand with stronger conviction!"

"Well, I'm pretty motivated here. My whole life is going to be in your hands in less than twenty-four hours, and I've got everything to gain by trusting you and Jesus. I intend to do just that!"

Dr. Sam Marable left the room.

Reality set in.

"Are you sure about this, Cheryl?" asked my father.

"You didn't give this very much thought," said Mother.

"You're both kidding me, of course, aren't you? I mean, I've spent practically every waking moment of the last fifteen years hoping and dreaming about what my life would be like if I didn't resemble a walking stick! Don't you understand? There's hardly been a single day when I haven't asked Jesus to please heal me or change my appearance to whatever degree he chose. Just to be able to walk into a room or down the street without hearing strangers or so-called friends point at me and laugh--now *that,* to me, would be worth a million surgeries! At last, for some reason which I'm completely thankful for--Jesus has finally decided to answer my prayers!"

Dad took out his handkerchief and gave two consecutive snorts and blows. "Yes, Cheryl. PRAISE GOD! He's decided to answer *all* our prayers!"

Mother turned away and sniffled repeatedly. "Post-surgery isn't going to be a day at the beach, you know," Mom said, clearing her throat abrasively.

"Of course not, Mom. I *do* understand what you're getting at, but the fact is, I'm skinny as a rail to most people--so skinny that I probably could have a respectable career in a circus side-show!"

"You stop that exaggerating, Cheryl!"

"MOM! MOM! JUST LOOK AT ME! THERE'S HARDLY AN OUNCE OF FAT ON ME *ANYWHERE,* AND MY CLOTHES HANG ON ME LIKE I WAS A CLOTHES HORSE!"

Miss Mott entered the room. She was actually smiling! I'd never, ever seen her smile before.

"Miss Kimes, I just learned that tomorrow is going to be your lucky day!" she said.

"Yes . . . yes, I think it really *will* be, Miss Mott!"

"I'm very happy that Dr. Marable is going to perform your surgery, Miss Kimes. He's the best there is and I know he'll do an outstanding job!"

Miss Mott told me what to anticipate for the rest of the day.

"You shouldn't have any more to eat today, I'm sorry to say, and later on after dinner, you need to bathe thoroughly. Around 7:00, after you've bathed, someone will be in to prep you."

"*Prep*? What do you mean by prep?"

"You'll be thoroughly shaved, Cheryl. Your entire chest and abdomen will be shaved completely to remove any bacteria that might be residing there."

"But there's almost no hair on--"

"We all have fine hair all over our bodies, Miss Kimes. It's all got to go--every last, single, solitary hair where Dr. Marable will be doing your surgery."

"And then?"

"Then, early in the morning, you'll be painted with an iodine solution everywhere you were shaved, and an IV will be inserted in your arm."

Mother went to the hall.

"Is your wife alright, Mr. Kimes?" Miss Mott asked.

"Oh, sure . . . sure, she'll be fine . . . it's just . . . it's just a pretty emotional time for us here. Our daughter doesn't have major surgery every day, you know!"

Miss Mott patted my father on the back. "It's normal to be apprehensive," she said, "but I have every confidence in Dr. Marable. He'll get Cheryl through this with flying colors. He actually performed the very same surgery on his wife a few years ago."

"Is that all there is to it?" I questioned. "I just have to get prepped and painted?"

"Yes, that's it, Cheryl. *Afterwards* comes the difficult stuff, but I think Dr. Marable explained that to you earlier, didn't he?"

"You mean about the breathing device and so forth?"

"Yes. Breathing after your operation will be exquisitely painful for you at times, but you will be given morphine, and we will help you breathe deeply until you can breathe adequately on your own. We will also require you to take a few steps later on tomorrow after surgery, Miss Kimes--even though you will think it impossible--but you *will* succeed!"

"Could she have a radio, Miss Mott . . . I mean, to listen to when she feels up to listenin'," asked my father. "She's a musician, you know, and--"

"Of course, Mr. Kimes! Music would be a great idea when she wants it. By all means, bring her a radio if you like."

Then, Miss Mott left.

"She doesn't seem so stern all of a sudden, does she, Cheryl," Dad noted.

"No, she actually seems rather nice," I added. "This is apparently what she needs to do--take care of us patients."

"That's what Jesus likes to do, too--take care of His own!" added Dad.

Dad and I embraced. "Thanks for raising me in the Word, Dad. Surgery would really be hard for me tomorrow without Jesus!"

"I know, Cheryl, I know. Now I've got to check on your mother. She'll be okay, hon. I'll take her out for a bite to eat somewhere, then we'll see you later on in the morning. Clis just needs to unwind for a spell. You keep the faith and do what your nurses tell you to do. Everyone is on your side, Cheryl. Everything is gonna turn out just swell!"

Mother stepped in once more before she and dad departed.

"I'd trade places with you in a heartbeat if it were possible, Cheryl," Mom said before she left . . . then once again I was alone.

But I was secure in Christ.

Still, I couldn't help wondering why Tom wasn't around. I had so much wanted to see him before my big day in less than twenty-four hours, but . . . for heaven's sake . . . what *had* happened to my friend?

Chapter Thirty-One

I took a shower as directed after my parents left, then my abdomen was shaved thoroughly by some glum, elderly nurse. It would have been nice to have had someone cheerful to talk to before my operation, but no, my barberette was very serious--almost bleak--and extremely preoccupied.

"Do you go to church anywhere?" I asked, trying to soften her up.

"Huh-uh."

"Why not? I really enjoy a good sermon, myself!"

No response.

I tried again. "Do you attend a synagogue or worship in your own way or. . . ."

Not one word.

"To me, life would be pretty scary if I didn't attend church somewhere and have Jesus in my life," I said.

Now *that* statement made my attendant hustle to get away from me, and she never even wished me luck for my surgery the next morning!

Barbara, who'd made pleasant conversation with me since I'd entered Research, tried to compensate for my impersonal nurse.

"If they come in and move you out of here before I have a chance to wish you success tomorrow," she said, "I really hope everything goes well for you, Cheryl!"

"Well, thank you, Barbara. I hope you continue to improve, too. It's been wonderful to have had a roommate who was pleasant and considerate. I'm happy I got to know you, too."

"Well . . . we *could* have gotten to spend much more time together, you know, if you hadn't taken up with that Romeo character down the hall!"

Barbara sounded like I had mildly offended her.

"What?" I replied. "Are you talking about Tom, Barbara? I hardly see him in a romantic light. He's just a nice fellow . . . that's all."

As usual, my other two roommates seemed unconcerned about my existence, but I vowed to keep them both in my daily prayers, anyway. They apparently were not so optimistic about their recoveries.

After I said good-bye to Barbara, Miss Mott stopped in with more instructions for me. She parked a wheelchair just inside our ward and handed me a large, empty bag. "I need to move you to a private room right away, Miss Kimes. Take this bag and transfer all your street clothes and belongings into it. I have to get you resettled before my shift changes."

Miss Mott insisted on taking me to my new abode in a wheelchair, but I would have none of the idea. "Oh, no, Miss Mott!" I begged. "Please let me walk on my own. You'll make me look like a complete invalid!"

"HOSPITAL REGULATIONS, Miss Kimes! Now, you just get your bod into this chair and never mind how it looks. This is my job and it'll go faster if you do as I say and stop fighting me. UNDERSTAND?"

I took my seat like a whipped puppy and counted the door jambs as Miss Mott wheeled me down the hall into new territory.

One . . . two . . . three . . . four . . . we passed Tom's door on the left. It was closed. Miss Mott noted his door, too.

"You two were quite an item there for awhile, weren't you, Miss Kimes?" she asked, almost giggly.

"An *item*? We were friends! Why would you ever think we were more than that?"

I felt somewhat depressed seeing Tom's closed door.

"It's just as well, you know."

"What's just as well?"

"Oh, I mean . . . one has to be realistic. There was no future in your relationship or anything."

What in the world was she talking about?

"Here we are, Miss Kimes!" Miss Mott pushed me into my new residence and let me out of my wheelchair. In no time at all I was situated, but I felt ill at ease.

"Anything I can get for you, Miss Kimes?" she asked.

"No . . . I guess not, but thanks. Please be sure my parents know where to find me, though. Mom would go ballistic if she trotted up here and couldn't locate me later tonight. My parents are just obsessed with my health. You know how parents are."

"I'll be sure they know, Cheryl. Now, you get some rest."

Rest? Was she serious? I was about to have a potentially life-changing operation and the last thing I wanted to do was rest! For heaven's sake. I felt like jumping up and down and springing from wall to wall like a monkey trapped in an experimenter's cage! I wanted to scream, or shout, or dance, or do anything but rest!

Several nurses stopped by to see me over the next couple of hours, just to say hello and welcome me into their unit. All were friendly enough, but all were pushing the same ridiculous lingo: "REST, CHERYL! TRY TO RELAX AND GET SOME

SLEEP! REST IS VERY IMPORTANT BEFORE SURGERY! DO YOU UNDERSTAND?"

Oh, I understood, alright. It wasn't a matter of comprehension, it was a matter of realism. How could anyone who was about to become the fifteenth patient in the whole wide world to undergo celiac band surgery feel cool, calm and collected enough to consider snoozing?

At eight o'clock there was a knock on my door. Mom and Dad strode into my new habitat and tried to act perfectly blasé.

"This is certainly a great view you have here, Cheryl," Dad exclaimed.

"And . . . and just look over there at all that traffic, Cheryl!" said Mom. "Honestly, how *do* people manage to survive in such a big, bustling city as Columbus? I ask you, Cheryl, did you ever see so much activity in your life?"

I didn't answer.

"You know what I think I'll do tomorrow, Cheryl?" said my father. "I think I just might bring my ol' Signet 35 up here and take a time exposure of this view. That direction over there'd be a real good shot to shoot, don't you think?" he said as he pointed towards Levec Tower. "It'd be a daggone shame if I left this place without gettin' a good picture of that awesome skyscraper out there!"

I surely loved my parents, but in trying to make conversation and cheer me up, once again they were making me considerably more anxious than I should have been. I didn't want to be remotely unkind, but I *really* did feel as though I needed solitude.

"How are you feeling, Cheryl?" asked Mom. "Now, tell me the truth--are you doing okay, tonight?"

"Fine . . . fine, Mother . . . I'm doing just fine. I just feel a little bit tense, you know."

"But it'll all be over by this time tomorrow, Cheryl, and you'll be a brand new healthy young woman after you recover from your surgery!"

"I could snap the shutter after dark," Dad interjected--he was in his own little world at the time. "I'd have to figure out just the right exposure, but. . . ."

Was my father evading my impending surgery because he was feeling some apprehension himself?

"Well . . . well don't you think that'd be a great shot over there, Cheryl?" he continued. "Don't you think that'd be an award-winnin' picture if I took it the right way?"

There was another knock on my door and a nurse poked her head into my room. "Visiting hours are enforced tonight, people," she announced. "I realize you're Cheryl's parents, but she really needs some sleep at this time. Please try to leave shortly. You can see her again in the morning if you like--right before her surgery."

My mother took the hint and headed back to the elevator, wiping her eyes.

Dad stayed behind and was bent on being optimistic. "I brought this radio up for you, Cheryl," he said. "Maybe you can find some classical music that would appeal to you. Better yet, maybe there'll be some religious station that'll offer a good message to hear after we take off. Whatever you do, don't stop believin'! I know you're gonna do beautifully tomorrow, daughter. Jesus will be there with you, and Jesus never fails! You know you can count on Him, Cheryl . . . He never, ever fails!"

My father hugged me tightly, then handed me a small pocket Bible that looked ragged, well-used, and worn by the years.

"Oh, thanks, Dad. This ol' book looks like it's taught many a helpful lesson over its lifetime."

"It sure has, Cheryl. I've carried it through thick and thin and figured it was time to pass it on to my daughter tonight. You'll know what to do with it. There's power in the Word, you know!"

For the first time all day, I felt decidedly calm. I thanked God for my incredible, caring parents, and I placed Dad's little Bible right next to me, on my nightstand. I felt certain my heavenly Father would stay with me and comfort me for the duration of the evening when my earthly father left.

He did.

At 10:00 sharp, there was yet a third knock on my door!

"C-Cheryl?" I heard.

Was that my father . . . again?

"CHERYL! CHERYL!" repeated the voice once more, much louder.

Tom? Might that voice belong to Tom?

I got out of bed, slipped my robe on quickly, and hurried to the door.

"Tom? TOM!" I exclaimed. "Do you have any idea what time it is, buddy?"

"Can you come out here, Cheryl . . . please?"

"Tom? Is that really you?" I asked. "I had begun to think I would never see you again! What's been going on with you, anyway, Tom? Where have you been hiding yourself, anyway, and why on earth did you stop by at this time of the night?"

Tom appeared to be in a great mood, and he was smiling broadly.

"Oh . . . I've been around, Cheryl. I've been busy with this, that and the other thing, you know . . . here . . . there . . . everywhere. . . ."

I told Tom to wait in the hall while I put my slippers on, admonishing "You had better keep your voice lower, Tom! Miss Mott would have a cardiac arrest if she knew you sneaked in here tonight!"

"Miss Mott just went home, Cheryl. Hence . . . here I stand!"

Tom and I walked quietly out to the patient waiting room and started to make small talk.

"You really mystify me," I told him. "Honestly, I thought you'd taken off to the Caribbean or something. Where have you been, anyway, Tom?"

"Would it matter, Cheryl? I mean, with your parents being here and all those nurses fussing over you plus the fact that you moved to Timbuktu and everything . . . I thought I'd probably need a special pass to get near you under the circumstances!"

"That'd never be the case. I'd always be happy to see you, Tom."

I felt too focused on myself as I talked to my friend so I decided to discuss my father's photographic bent. "Dad's going to bring his camera up tomorrow and shoot that scene outside my window. Do you think that'll work? Do you think my father will be able to capture that ambience on film . . . that awesome cavalcade of cars and lights and. . . ."

It was obvious to Tom that I was trying to make conversation. He came to the point: "Are you ready for tomorrow, Cheryl?"

I nodded affirmatively. "I'm actually very hopeful, Tom. I sort of come and go in and out of reality a bit, though. Do you ever feel that way when you're here, Tom--you know, like you're not always completely in touch?"

"I feel out of touch *much* of the time, Cheryl--especially when I have to endure another procedure. I've been here so much of my lifetime that my mind tends to play tricks on me, I think. My brain can't quite grasp the fact that C.R.U. is not a permanent place to call home. Sometimes my gray matter likes to pretend this hospital is all just one huge fantasy world. B-but on the other hand, I know I can't survive without this place . . . so C.R.U. has *got* to be real for me. Reality just tends to feel very . . . very *tenuous,* I guess, more often than not."

I felt I should say something encouraging to my friend, but words didn't come easily.

"How are *you* doing, Tom?"

"Didn't I just tell you?" he laughed. "So," he continued, ". . . what time are they coming to take you away tomorrow, Cheryl?"

"You mean to surgery?"

"NO, CHERYL, TO THE LOONEY WARD! YES, of course, to surgery. What time is your operation scheduled?"

My faith in Jesus was very strong, yet I sensed insecurity from Tom as he attempted to soothe what he thought were my fears.

"I'm not sure--early, I guess. Yes. I think they'll be taking me downstairs very early."

"That's a good thing, Cheryl. It's good to get surgery over with early in the day, I think."

"Why? Why is that, Tom?"

Tom was empathetic. "When you have surgery early on, you have the rest of the day to fully awaken, deal with any discomfort, and get up on your feet. If you have to recover at night, it's just harder to be alert and stay reasonably comfortable."

I overheard a nearby patient's radio down the hall that was playing contemporary Christian music. A nurse raced to subdue what she referred to as "noise" and verbally punish the offender. To me, the music brought back many wonderful memories.

"I sure enjoyed old-fashioned hymns like my great grandfather used to sing a lot better than these modern tunes. Do you like today's praise and worship music, Tom?"

"Honestly, Cheryl?" he replied. "To tell you the truth, I can't see the value in any of those hymns, much--old or new. I mean, no matter what I hear those singers sing about or preachers preach about for that matter . . . it just doesn't make much difference to me. I guess I must not understand what it's all about, Cheryl. Religion's just never seemed to . . . to be *necessary* to me, for some reason."

I felt deeply sorry for my friend.

"Where do you go to church, Tom?" I asked, hoping to find out why Tom had apparently rejected the Word.

"Oh, no place in particular, Cheryl. My parents used to drag me with them to a variety of churches on Sundays, but listening to those sermons didn't improve my life or my health any, so I finally refused to go."

I knew I had to talk to Tom about my convictions, but I wasn't sure what to say that wouldn't drive him further away from Christianity.

"My parents always insisted I go to church, too, Tom, from the time I was a little girl," I said. "They had strong feelings about the Lord and the Gospel, so my parents and I went week after week without fail, until attending church became a routine part of life--and it still is."

"Yes, but . . . but do you get anything from it, Cheryl? I mean, do you ever really learn any valuable lessons, or is church just something your family thinks is nice to do on the weekends to fill up time and to keep you . . . out of trouble?"

"Oh, I learn lots of valuable lessons in church, Tom! My mother used to teach Sunday school every Sunday, and I always helped her with a big poster board to teach her little kiddos in class. Helping Mom was actually fun, and I think she was a really good teacher. The children seemed to like her a lot and most of them paid attention to her when she told them about Jesus."

Tom looked at his watch briefly.

I half expected Tom to excuse himself and go back to his apartment at that point, but no, Tom showed no indication of wanting to leave.

I decided to push my luck and stay on the subject of Christianity.

"Say, did you happen to notice my uncle the other day when he was here with his wife, Tom?"

"Yes, I think so, Cheryl. He was a rather large man with a big smile and a great personality. I heard him joking around with the nurses down the hall a lot. Wasn't that he?"

"Yes, that sounds like it was Uncle Frank, for sure. Well, Frank's an organist and the two of us used to play duets together in our adult church service in Athens. You know--he'd play the organ, and I'd play the piano at the same time."

"I know what a duet is, Cheryl, though I can't say I ever heard piano and organ together. Did you enjoy doing that?"

"Oh, yes! I respect my uncle very much, and I found performing in church was a good way to witness to others. It was a whole lot easier for me to express my convictions through music than it was by . . . by talking to someone face to face like we're doing now."

Tom still didn't budge.

I decided to go for it!

"I . . . I was just wondering, Tom. Did you ever have a personal relationship with Jesus, *yourself*?"

"Personal? *Me?* Personal? Are you serious?"

"I sure am, Tom. To me, if I didn't know Jesus was with me tonight, right here, right now, and *especially* tomorrow going into surgery, well . . . I just don't see how I could begin to handle my operation without Him."

Tom grew more ill at ease as he decided to change the subject.

"I guess you never intend to play for me, do you, Cheryl? I mean, several days ago you *did* tell me you wanted to play the piano downstairs before you went back to Athens, but. . . ."

"Want to go downstairs right now, Tom?"

"You mean this very minute, Cheryl?"

"Why not? It'd be risky to maneuver past the nurses station, but it'd be kinda fun to see if the two of us could sneak down the stairs and get away with it, wouldn't it?"

"Say no more!" Tom declared, as he made haste towards the stairwell and motioned for me to follow him.

"The coast is clear, Watson!" he joked.

"Okay, Sherlock. Here I come!"

Tom and I cautiously made our way past my former room and headed down the stairs.

So far, so good!

The two of us zigzagged through staircase after staircase until we ultimately reached the third floor exit.

We did it!

All was dark in the Activity Center, and Tom eagerly turned on the lights. There, pushed into a corner, sat the old upright.

"So . . . take it away, lady!" Tom said.

"You sure nobody can hear us at this time of the night, Tom?"

"We'll never know unless we try! If we *are* kicked out, at least you can manage to get the first few measures of some melody plunked out before we catch 'Hail Columbia.' Come on, Cheryl! I really *do* want to hear you play a little something for me."

I took my seat before the ol' clunker. It reminded me very much of the piano I used to play for opening services at my Sunday school back at the Wesleyan Methodist Church. It was somewhat comforting to remember that period of time. Life seemed so much less complicated when I was younger. . . .

"Cheryl . . . CHERYL?"

"Sorry, I . . . I guess I was daydreaming there for a second. Do you like Chopin?"

"My musical exposure is basically an blank slate, Cheryl. If you want to play Chopin--go right ahead. If *you* like Chopin, *I* probably will, too."

I played one of the first pieces I'd ever performed by Chopin, his *"Raindrop" Prelude,* because it told a story I could describe for Tom, and I had performed it for years without any technical problems whatsoever. For some reason, however, on this particular evening . . . I seemed to make one little mistake after another.

Tom seemed appreciative, anyway--despite my wrong notes.

"You really play fantastic, Cheryl! Gee! I had no idea you could make an obsolete upright like this come to life."

"But my mistakes, Tom, they kind of spoiled. . . ."

"What mistakes are you talkin' about, Cheryl? I sure didn't hear any mistakes. Heck! You don't have to play perfectly for me, you know--I like you just the way you are!"

I tried to swallow my pride. What difference did perfection make, anyway? Why had I wanted to play for Tom, to begin with? What was the real reason I had agreed to come down here and entertain my friend the night before I was to have my torso ripped open?

"Well, Cheryl? Are you going to whang out something else for me, or is that all I'm going to get? Huh? Surely you can come up with just one more piece--we ought to be able to push our luck a little further, Cheryl, don't you think?"

I recalled a beautiful, old, meaningful hymn that my great-grandfather had always received spiritual strength from, and I felt it would do both Tom and me a great deal of good to hear it ourselves. I played "God Will Take Care of You," and as I played I recalled Charley strumming his autoharp while he sang.

"That melody is rather, ah . . . rather comforting, Cheryl. I'll bet it has nice words, too. Well . . . does it have good lyrics?"

I stopped. *Here's my opportunity, Lord. Please help me successfully share my faith through my music, Father!*

"Why, yes, Tom . . . y-yes, it's actually a popular hymn I've known for most of my life--" and I resumed playing it once again, singing the words at the same time:

Be not dismayed whate'er betide,
God will take care of you;
Beneath His wings of love abide,
God will take care of you.

God will take care of you,
Through every day, o'er all the way;
He will take care of you,
God will take care of you.

Tom's eyes were red, so I decided I should probably end my private recital.

"I guess my singing's pretty hard to take, huh, Tom?" I joked.

Just then, a man dressed in a janitorial uniform entered the room, overly alarmed.

"You two young'uns are about to git yourselfs into a heap o' trouble!" he said.

"What are you talkin' about, Mac?" Tom asked our intruder.

"People on the floor above ya are startin' ta complain about the racket down here! If'n I was in your shoes, I'd hightail it outta here before they send the Mob Squad ta gitcha! Git outta here, I tell ya! I'll turn out the lights as soon as you leave and cover for ya if'n I get caught. GO ON, I'M A-TELLIN' YA! MOVE IT, YOU TWO!"

"We were just about to leave, sir," I told the janitor, and Tom and I joined hands and hustled away as fast as we could go. We took the same staircase we had taken before, but by the time we'd raced *up* eight flights--we were both winded!

"Are you okay, Cheryl?" Tom asked as he parked me back in my room.

"Sure, Tom. I feel great!"

"Good for you. I better run off now, but I'll think good thoughts about you and Dr. Sam tomorrow. Thanks for a great evening, Miss concert pianist! You're really a jewel, sis. You really are!" and Tom started for the door.

"Wait! Wait, Tom!" I called to him.

I reached over on my nightstand and picked up the little Bible that my father had presented to me just a few hours earlier.

"Here, Tom, please take this. You might be surprised how much you can learn from God's Word when you have a receptive heart!"

I returned to my bed without undressing and fell fast asleep.

* * *

"Hey, Cheryl! Cheryl! Open your eyes, honey! Come on! Open up!"

Mother was gently shaking me, and my father was there as well, camera dangling around his neck, as he stared into the sunrise.

"Come on, now, Cheryl!" Mom said. "The nurse will be in to give you your shot anytime, hon!"

SURGERY? WAS IT TIME FOR MY SURGERY?

There was hardly a moment to breathe before a nurse entered, injection in hand.

"Have you ever had one of these shots before, Cheryl?" she asked.

"Yes . . . oh, sure . . . probably," I said.

"Well, roll your hind-end over, then. This is a big one!"

OUCH! BY GOLLIES IT REALLY HURT!

Next, I was painted lavishly with iodine--as I'd expected--and sleep beckoned once more.

My parents bowed their heads while I waited for my orderly. I was glad they were praying for me.

In just a few moments, my orderly came to take me away. I was woozy, I was tingly--and I was barely awake.

"She'll be back whenever Dr. Sam's done with her, you two. I think this is going to be a long one. Make yourselves comfy. She'll do just fine!"

Then, I was on my way.

* * *

"WAKE UP, CHERYL! WAKE UP!" I was in a room with many other patients . . . *wasn't I?*

"COME ON CHERYL! IT'S TIME TO MOVE OUT OF HERE!"

"Where am I? Where am I, a-anyway? Am . . . am I in the operating room?"

"IT'S ALL OVER, CHERYL! YOU'RE IN RECOVERY NOW! YOUR SURGERY IS FINISHED AND YOU'RE READY TO GO UPSTAIRS! HERE WE GO, NOW--HOLD ON!"

I was swooped up one hall . . . down another . . . onto an elevator . . . down another hall . . . onto another elevator--

OUCH! My abdomen was covered with gauze and bandages. Much of me was wrapped so tightly . . . I wanted to get off, right then. . . .

"STAY PUT, CHERYL! STAY RIGHT THERE WHERE YOU ARE! YOUR SURGERY IS OVER, AND WE'LL HAVE YOU BACK IN YOUR ROOM IN A SECOND OR TWO! LIE PERFECTLY STILL!"

I was wheeled into my room. No one was there . . . were they?

"HERE WE GO, CHERYL. WE'RE GOING TO MOVE YOU ONTO YOUR BED, NOW! HANG ON, CHERYL! ONE . . . TWO . . . THREE. . . ."

What a jolt! What confusion! Suddenly, nurses were descending on me like vultures on a carcass.

"GET HER IV CLOSER TO HER BEDSIDE! COME ON! HUSTLE!"

"GET HER ARM TAPED DOWN!"

"GET THAT SALINE INTO HER!"

Miss Mott? Was that Miss Mott?

"I'm going to bring you some more blankets, now, Miss Kimes!

It was *Miss Mott! Boy, was I ever happy to hear her!*

"Don't move around, Miss Kimes. Your last shot will wear off in about an hour, then I'll give you another one. Try to lie quietly, so your incision doesn't hurt so much!"

I wanted to say something . . . anything . . . but my brain just couldn't get it all together.

I tried to move my body. *OUCH!*

I attempted to rip my bandages off! *OUCH! OUCH!*

"LIE STILL, I SAID, MISS KIMES! YOU NEED TO PAY ATTENTION TO ME SO YOU'LL RECOVER QUICKLY!"

From my peripheral vision, I could see a slight figure moving around to my bedside.

"Sure, you can hang it over her, Tom, but be quick about it!" said an obviously perturbed Miss Mott. "NO . . . NO . . . you better hang it higher above her head--right up there!"

I felt a soft, gentle kiss on my forehead.

"ENOUGH, I TELL YOU! I LET YOU HANG IT--NOW GET OUT OF CHERYL'S ROOM, TOM! MARCH!"

I tried to focus above my head. Cut-out birds of all descriptions were swinging about in every direction . . . a cardinal . . . a blue jay . . . a robin . . . a canary . . . so many birds . . . dangling from some sort of mobile . . . hanging from wires that appeared to be coat hangers . . . just flying . . . flying about every which way. . . .

"I hope you appreciate what your friend did for you here, Miss Kimes," said Miss Mott. "He's been working on it for days and days. He was afraid he wouldn't get it all finished before you came back from surgery. He put his whole heart and soul into it, Miss Kimes."

So that's why Tom had been keeping to himself. He'd been making me a present!

He wanted to surprise me!

My mother and father were allowed to come into my room at 3:00 in the afternoon--exactly the same time Dr. Sam stopped by to check up on me. My parents squeezed my hands tightly and hung onto my surgeon's every word as though his lips were proclaiming the *Apostle's Creed.*

"YOU'RE CURED, CHERYL!" he announced loudly. "YOUR SURGERY TOOK OVER EIGHT HOURS AND WAS A COMPLETE SUCCESS. YOU'RE CURED!"

Tears of joy flooded my cheeks. Did I hear correctly? Did Dr. Sam say what I thought he said?

"I'll be back to check on your progress again tomorrow, Cheryl." he added. "You do your breathing exercises like you're told, now . . . so you can fly out of here like those beautiful birds above your head and get on with living!"

Thank you, Jesus! I prayed, silently. *Thank you for successfully leading Dr. Sam through my surgery, and Father . . . please help Tom come to accept you personally and trust you completely as I do. Please guide his doctors to help him, too, so he can enjoy the remainder of his life to the fullest and live abundantly under the wings of your love.*

Epilogue

The night before I was released from Ohio State University Hospital, my father took a time-exposure of sleepy Columbus from the top floor. Dad was almost as proud of the resultant photograph as I was of the certificate I was presented from Clinical Research Unit which read:

Be it known that Cheryl Kimes has been an active participant in Medical Research from August 10, 1964, to September 3, 1964. We hereby acknowledge her valuable contributions and award this certificate.

My recognition was merely a single piece of paper, but it was signed by Dr. Beman, Dr. Marable, Miss Mott, and several others committed to improving the lives of courageous patients like Tom and me. If I in any way played a significant part in enabling future patients with celiac band disease to benefit from my tests and surgery, then I am very pleased to have been of service.

Within a year, I gained forty pounds and was able to comfortably eat my fill from every single food group, bar none. Most particularly, I savored, and *still* relish, roast turkey with mother's incredible old fashioned sage stuffing. A tin roof sundae runs a close second for my taste buds--vanilla ice cream smothered with hot fudge sauce, buried in salty Spanish peanuts, topped with a giant pouf of whipped cream, and crowned with a rosy red cherry!

Willowy Cheryl six months after surgery, 1965
Ronald Kimes, Photographer

I graduated cum laude from Ohio University in 1966 where I majored in piano and had every intention of becoming a concert pianist. Instead, God sent me a wonderful Christian man to marry, and the two of us have spent over forty years together teaching and performing music. Happily, we also raised a family and brought them up in the Word.

Although I contracted cancer twice later in life (perhaps partially because of exposure to years of diagnostic radiation), the Lord completely cured me of both malignancies, and I never once regretted my decision to have celiac band surgery.

HEALTHY AT LAST! 1966
Humphrey's Studio

As for my friend, Tom? He and I corresponded for three months following my release from C.R.U. After his letters stopped abruptly, I received a much appreciated, cordial letter from his mother:

Dear Cheryl,

I am sorry to report that Tom lost his battle with kidney disease and he wanted me to let you know. I sincerely value the friendship and support the two of you shared in Clinical Research and wish you continued good health in the years to come.